Endorsements for *It Doesn't Have to Be This Hard: How We Are Transformed by the Holy Spirit* by Mike Nappa:

I absolutely love this book! With the accuracy of a Swiss watch, Mike Nappa teaches us from the Scripture what it means to have God's Spirit work *in* us, and *with* us, to accomplish the Christian life *through* us. *It Doesn't Have to Be This Hard* reminds us that the Christian life was never intended to be a white-knuckle ride, but rather a life given over to the One who has the power to live in and through you on a daily basis. This book is not based on opinion or mindless musings; it's grounded in biblical truth that transcends personal opinion or conjecture. I was enthralled by it.

—*Dr. Michael Anthony*
Professor of Educational Ministries & Leadership, Dallas Theological Seminary

Mike Nappa's writing is inviting, clever, and makes you want to keep reading—and learning. Each page is a beautiful reminder of the love, joy, peace, patience, kindness, goodness, gentleness, faithfulness, and self-control the Spirit grows within us. Filled with entertaining and informative stories, alongside well-researched Biblical truths, *It Doesn't Have to Be This Hard* is a great read for anyone curious about a better understanding of the Holy Spirit, or who is exhausted in their attempts to be a "good Christian."

—*Laura L. Smith*
Best-selling author, *How Sweet the Sound* and *Restore My Soul*

The title says it all—the Christian life as we've framed it in the church doesn't have to be so hard. Here, Mike Nappa is exploring the most important (and sorely overlooked) practice for walking in the way of Jesus—our commitment to Spirit-dependence. And Mike, with his rare combination of theological depth and relatable invitation, introduces us to a Spirit-dependent journey that is both broad and deep. Jesus tells us, repeatedly, we must become like children if we hope to live like He does—to live in the Kingdom of God. And here Mike invites us to play with the Spirit on God's playground. Ingest the message of this book and you'll find freedom."

—*Rick Lawrence*
Executive Director, Vibrant Faith
General editor, the best-selling *Jesus-Centered Bible*
Author, *Editing Jesus, Spiritual Grit,* and the *Jesus-Centered Daily*

Thank you, Mike Nappa, for writing this practical and biblically grounded book! The role of the Holy Spirit in our lives has been too often overlooked—but this book steps in with clarity and insight right when it's needed most. Mike is not only a fine writer and storyteller—he's a gifted teacher of biblical truth. Reading this book feels like sitting down over coffee with a wise and trusted friend. In these pages, you'll discover how to live your faith with power, authenticity, and confidence. I'm grateful I got to read *It Doesn't Have to Be This Hard*. Read it—you'll be grateful, too.

—*Jim Denney*
Author, *Answers to Satisfy the Soul*
Co-author, *The Magic of Teamwork*

MIKE NAPPA

IT DOESN'T HAVE TO BE THIS HARD

HOW WE ARE TRANSFORMED BY THE HOLY SPIRIT

WHITAKER
HOUSE

It Doesn't Have to Be This Hard is published in association with Nappaland Literary Agency, an independent agency dedicated to creating books that are Authentic. Relevant. Eternal. Find us online at NappalandLiterary.com

It Doesn't Have to Be This Hard
How We Are Transformed by the Holy Spirit

Nappaland Communications Inc.
Nappaland.com
Bible-Smart.com

ISBN: 979-8-88769-449-8 | eBook ISBN: 979-8-88769-450-4
Printed in the United States of America
© 2025 Nappaland Communications Inc.

Whitaker House | 1030 Hunt Valley Circle | New Kensington, PA 15068
www.whitakerhouse.com

Library of Congress Control Number: 2025903826

1 2 3 4 5 6 7 8 9 10 11   WH   32 31 30 29 28 27 26 25

DEDICATION

For John Sokolowski,
a friend to sinners (like me).

"You know what Jesus is like, and the Holy Spirit is exactly like Jesus, for Jesus was God and the Spirit is God."[1]

—A. W. Tozer, in *How to be Filled with the Holy Spirit*

"As we cooperate with the Spirit, he can flow from us freely, impacting every room we enter, every situation we give our attention to. This is the character of the life of someone filled with the Holy Spirit."[2]

—Bill Johnson, in *The Holy Spirit*

"The terrible thing, the almost impossible thing, is to hand over your whole self—all your wishes and precautions—to Christ. But it is far easier than what we are all trying to do instead."[3]

—C. S. Lewis, in *Mere Christianity*

"My only job today is to stop trying to do the Holy Spirit's job for him."

—Anonymous

CONTENTS

Introduction: A Rock and a Hard Place... 9

PART 1: WHAT THE HOLY SPIRIT DOES *IN* YOU

1. The Holy Spirit Creates Life in You 18
2. The Holy Spirit Makes You His Family 33
3. The Holy Spirit Prizes You.. 52
4. The Holy Spirit Fills and Baptizes You....................................... 70

PART 2: WHAT THE HOLY SPIRIT DOES *WITH* YOU

5. The Holy Spirit Lives Your Daily Faith 88
6. The Holy Spirit Energizes Your Passion in Worship,
   Song, and Prayer 105
7. The Holy Spirit Empowers Your Ability to Live for Christ 119
8. The Holy Spirit Walks Beside You.. 134

PART 3: WHAT THE HOLY SPIRIT DOES *THROUGH* YOU

9. The Holy Spirit Communicates Christ Through You............... 148
10. The Holy Spirit Flaunts Christ Through You............................ 162
11. The Holy Spirit Incarnates His Church Through You 186

Afterword: How to Make Your Christian Life Harder
Than It Really Is 201

Appendix 1: 246 Direct References to the Holy Spirit in the New Testament..209

Appendix 2: Common Greek Terms for the Holy Spirit in the New Testament..212

Acknowledgements 214

About the Author..216

End Notes..217

INTRODUCTION

A ROCK AND A HARD PLACE

The way my grandmother used to tell it, her wedding ceremony lasted seven days, included a fair amount of alcohol—and featured a very large boulder stuck in the middle of the road.

The year was 1930, and on this particular day, they were all gathered on the road that led into my grandmother's hometown of Barouk, in Lebanon, which was then under Syrian governance. To one side was Mike Hassen, her groom-to-be and the man who would one day become my *Jidee* (that is, "grandfather"). On the other side was the jewel of Lebanon: Wahidee Mahmoud herself, a dark-eyed beauty only sixteen years old. She was surrounded by several strapping, protective older brothers who, perhaps, had been influenced by the past few days of strong drink and revelry.

My *Jidee* had traveled—literally—across the world to meet his bride. His father, Farris, had earned American citizenship by fighting for the US during World War I. After the "war to end all wars," he brought his family to the United States. Now, some ten years later, it was time to find a wife for his oldest son. That meant, of course, returning to Lebanon.

It was an era of arranged marriages and ethnic loyalties, and Mike and Farris were given a hero's welcome back in "the old country." They embarked on a journey to meet with families of several acceptable young women, and as it turned out, my grandmother's name was first on the list.

Suffice it to say, the kids hit it off.

When it was time for Mike to leave for the next name on his father's agenda, Wahidee put a fist on her hip and said, "You can search all over Lebanon, but you'll never find anyone better than me." And, well, she was right. Young Mike couldn't get that girl out of his mind. The proper conversations were held, the appropriate approvals given, and before long, they were engaged.

Joy ensued for both families....

Until that fateful day on the road, just before the wedding was to be finalized.

Wahidee's older brothers, it seemed, had had a change of heart. No man was good enough for their only sister, they reasoned, especially not this tiny fellow from somewhere in far-flung America. So they blocked the way to Barouk, interrupting the wedding procession just as it was heading into their village. They found a large boulder, rolled it into the middle of the road, and issued a challenge.

Wahidee would need a strong man out there in the vast United States, they said. So, unless Mike Hassen could move that stone, they wouldn't allow their sweet baby sister to marry him. Then they stood aside and waited.

My grandmother, bless her heart, used to laugh and say her brothers were just kidding, it was only a tradition, and they wouldn't have really stopped her wedding. My *Jidee?* Well, let's just say he told this part of the story to me differently, whispered discreetly into my ear. Regardless....

Mike Hassen was never a large man. I remember towering over him when I was grown, kissing the top of his bald head and wondering how a man so small had accomplished all he had in his life. Still, he threw himself into the task that day, grunting and straining to roll that rock off the road.

It didn't budge.

Wahidee's brothers laughed and, maybe, said a few unflattering words.

Young Mike tried anew, sweating and pushing and kicking. The stone, however, was unmoved by his efforts. It remained resolutely in place.

Finally, the tearful bride intervened. Please, she begged her brothers, at least let his family help him!

How could they say no to their dear baby sister? And so the wish was granted. Several Hassen men quickly rolled up their sleeves and leapt to

Mike's aid. With them lending their strength, he tossed that rock aside like it weighed nothing at all.

The wedding procession continued jubilantly into town. The rest, as they say, is history.

THE CHRISTIAN LIFE IS NOT AS HARD AS WE'RE MAKING IT (IT DOESN'T HAVE TO BE THIS HARD)

When I picture my future-grandfather as that young man, straining alone to lift an immovable stone, I see more than just an entertaining story from my family's history. I see in that image a picture—an unflattering one—of the Christian life before I understood the Holy Spirit's part in it.

Despite all the evidence to the contrary, I assumed that Christian faith was like that immovable stone, an obstacle weighted down with endless regulations and obligations for which I was responsible. It was up to me alone to move that stone—to resist every temptation, to live better than others, to make myself into a hero of faith. I mean, who else was going to do that for me? God? Pfft—everybody knows He just watches over us so He can be sure to punish us when we fail…right?[4]

Perhaps you're something like me. Maybe you've heard it said—well, had it pulpit-pounded into you—that you'd better "act like a Christian" at all times because "You may be the *only* Jesus someone sees today!" I heard that so often I thought it was actually true. So every morning I'd get up and steel myself for the day. I'd look at Christ's commands like *"Be perfect, therefore, as your heavenly Father is perfect"* (Matthew 5:48) and say to myself the mantra my church leaders had taught me: "If it is to be, then it is up to me."

And every day I'd fail to move that massive boulder of Christian living because, not only is that guilt-ridden, legalistic attitude unbiblical—it's just an exhausting, impossible way to live.

You see, the Christian life isn't meant to be experienced from the outside-in, with strict behavior modification as the hallmark of faith, or as something that's dependent on whether or not others are watching. That type of "righteousness" was, for me, like a huge boulder blocking the road, and something Jesus dismissed as disturbingly fatal, akin to *"whitewashed tombs"* (Matthew 23:27). Isaiah described it as having the same value as contemptible *"filthy rags"* (Isaiah 64:6).

It probably won't surprise you to hear, then, that one night I'd had enough.

Like my grandmother on her wedding day, I was sixteen years old. I was alone in my bedroom, arguing with God about His unfair challenge of a so-called Christian life. Nothing I did, it seemed, was good enough for Him. That whole Christian thing was not just hard, it was *impossible*—not only for me, but for any human being. Jesus said so Himself on more than one occasion. (See Matthew 19:25–26; John 15:4–5).

Finally, I said to God: "Look, if I'm not good enough for You, then You know what? I don't need You."

As soon as I said that, I felt a weight lift off my shoulders. *Relief.* It felt pretty good to abandon God, actually. No longer would I force myself to adhere to His outdated, overbearing standard of living, which, realistically, no one could meet. Instead of moving His stone, I'd decided simply to walk the other way and forget about Him completely.

I laid myself down in bed and relaxed. "Tomorrow will be a bright new day," I thought. One unencumbered by Jesus, the Bible, or any of that disappointing Christian stuff.

I was happily asleep in seconds.

I woke up around two o'clock in the morning. In silence.

But it was more than just quiet.

I don't know how to explain it exactly, except to say that, for the first time in my life, I felt totally alone. I listened to myself breathing, confused as to what had changed, trying to figure out why isolation now surrounded me as if it were a living thing. And suddenly it dawned on me.

"Oh, I get it now. There's absolutely nothing I can do to be good enough to earn God's favor. So He has to do all of that for me. My job is simply to let Him."

I slid out from under the covers and knelt beside my bed. Jesus and I had a few words and then—again, I can't explain it correctly—it felt almost as if a wind swept through my dingy apartment bedroom and into my soul, erasing the darkness and isolation I'd felt only moments before.

Christianity for me, up to that point, had been a legalistic boulder I couldn't budge—an empty, self-righteous failure I experienced daily. Then, suddenly, God's Holy Spirit rolled up His sleeves and came to my aid, opening the way for me to live each moment in His power instead of my own. *The Christian life was never supposed to be as hard as I was making it.*

Years later, my pastor Chuck Swindoll explained that more clearly for me, this way: "First and foremost," he said, "we must realize that the authentic Christian life is impossible and unexplainable without the Holy Spirit. God's Spirit is the power behind authenticity...that's what makes it so phenomenal."[5]

It is an understatement, but that realization, on the night when God woke me up at two o'clock in the morning, changed everything.

IN, WITH, AND THROUGH

An anonymous philosopher once said, "My only job today is to stop trying to do the Holy Spirit's job for Him."

When I tell people that, they almost always chuckle and say, "Well, yeah, but Jesus can't do *everything*. We've got to do our part to be righteous and follow all the rules and make ourselves pure and earn God's favor and keep other people in line and vote correctly and make sure Christian baked goods aren't eaten at sinful wedding receptions and blah blah blah (insert your favorite Pharisaical rule here and you'll get the idea.)" Christian history is littered with casualties of that kind of destructive, self-important thinking—sometimes we even call those people "saints." But I digress...[6]

Not long ago a well-meaning pastor friend told me (again) that "God can't do everything for you, Mike." That frustrated me so much that I decided to figure out once and for all what the Holy Spirit's responsibility really is, and what's mine. So I took on a new project of study.

First, I researched the New Testament to identify all the direct references to the Holy Spirit. I cross-checked Greek terms (the language of the original texts) and multiple English translations of the Bible. I pulled a few theology books off my shelves and spent time with them, too. When

I was done, I had a list of 246 direct references to the Holy Spirit in the New Testament. (You can find that full list on page 209, near the end of this book.)

I was tempted to make a second list of indirect references to the Holy Spirit, too (for instance, when Christ said in Matthew 28:20, "*I am with you always,*" that was an indirect Holy Spirit reference)—but I decided to stick with direct mentions this time. That meant only Scriptures that specifically stated "Holy Spirit" or capital-S "Spirit," or one of the synonyms for Him like "power from on high" or "Advocate."

I copied down the text of all 246 passages in my list, and asked myself, "What does the Holy Spirit actually *do*?"

To find an answer, I went through all those Scriptures, verse by verse, and underlined verbs associated with the Holy Spirit in them. Yeah, it felt like an overwhelming task at first, but I'm a word nerd, so it had to be done. Verbs tell us what the subject is *doing*—so when the Spirit is the subject, underlining the verb reveals what He is doing in that Scripture. (That was a fascinating exercise, by the way, and it only took about a week. You should try it.)

Next, I printed out all 246 Scriptures and glued them to 3 × 5 cards—one Scripture per card. Then came the fun stuff. I went to the library and spread out those hundreds of cards on a very large table, sorting and reading them, and thinking and re-sorting and, well, pretty much making a mess. After a few days of organizing, I was done, and I'd stacked my cards into eleven categories of what the Holy Spirit actually does in our lives. I took those stacked cards and transformed them into the main chapters of this book, which you now hold in your hands.

Then I asked: If this is *what* the Holy Spirit does, can I learn anything about *how* He does what He does? I came to the conclusion that He uses three primary methods to accomplish His constant work in our lives:

God's Spirit works *in*, *with*, and *through* us.

What was shocking to me was not that the Holy Spirit is active in each of our lives, but that *He's so extensively involved* in every little detail of our Christian experience—even more so than I'd been teaching for decades. I mean, wow. (But we'll talk more about that later.)

A REDNECK PASTOR AND A GRAND OLD MAN

All right, I think that catches us up to where we are at present, but before we dive into the rest of this book, let me tell you one more story about my *Jidee*. This one took place in the early 2000s, some seventy-five years after his fateful wedding encounter with the giant rock.

By that time, my grandfather was well into his nineties. At some point in his life, he'd turned from Islam to become a Christian and started attending a little church about two blocks from his home in a small town in Oklahoma. And then when he was ninety-four years old, he had a stroke, something that left him bedridden for the remainder of his life. When he passed away at age ninety-five, I traveled back to my grandmother's house for the funeral and was introduced to the man who had been my *Jidee's* pastor.

I'm going to be honest; I wasn't impressed.

He was a big fella; a country boy I was more likely to call a redneck than anything else. Because I am Arab-American, people like that usually are...oh, let's say "nonplussed," by people like me. I didn't even bother to learn his name. But after a bit, I noticed that my family absolutely adored that oversized white guy—and he appeared to have genuine affection for them as well. I wasn't sure what to think about that.

After he left, I sat in my grandmother's living room and she started talking. "That man," she told me, "loved your *Jidee*."

"That's nice," I said politely. She put a hand on my knee. "Every Sunday since the stroke," she said, "he came and took your *Jidee* to church." I nodded amiably.

My aunt broke in at this point because, obviously, I didn't understand. "Mikey," my aunt said to me, "he *carried Jidee*."

"What do you mean?" I asked.

"Every Sunday," she said, "he'd walk down from the church to the house. He'd go into *Jidee's* room, pick him up in his arms, and walk back to the church. Carrying your grandfather all the way. Then he'd set *Jidee* down in the front row and they'd have church. And afterward, he'd carry him home and lay *Jidee* gently back into his bed. Every single Sunday, rain or shine."

My grandmother patted my knee and said again, "He loved your *Jidee.*"

And now I understood—and felt ashamed for underestimating a "redneck." I had not seen who he really was because of my own presumptive bias.

It's now a few decades later, and when I picture my grandfather as that old man, resting in the big guy's arms—trusting him to accomplish that which my *Jidee* could not, I see more than just a heartwarming story from my family history. I see myself in the arms of God's Holy Spirit—*who loves me.* And every day, rain or shine, I see Him faithfully carrying me into righteousness, into hope, into joy and service and kindness and so much more. My job, I understand now, is the same as *Jidee's* was then: to cooperate, to go along and let Him do the heavy lifting for me.

And that brings us to this moment, which also brings you a choice.

Tomorrow when you wake up to your Christian life, you might see (figuratively) a huge, immovable stone in your path. You might see infirmity of sin that keeps you from doing things that should be easy, like walking or even standing. You might see any of a hundred other reasons why your Christian life is simply too hard, or too discouraging.

But it's my prayer that, by the time you and I are done with this book, when you contemplate your daily Christian life, you'll choose to see, instead, that *the Holy Spirit is carrying you through to glory like a redneck pastor and my grand old man.*

All right, that's enough for now. When you're ready, turn the page and we'll get started.

PART 1

WHAT THE HOLY SPIRIT DOES *IN* YOU

EXPLORING THE INVISIBLE THINGS THE HOLY SPIRIT DOES IN YOU,
ALL BY HIMSELF.

ONE

THE HOLY SPIRIT CREATES LIFE IN YOU

Life was invented by God's Holy Spirit, and He persistently
creates it in you in multifaceted ways. That includes:
your physical life, your spiritual regeneration, and His indwelling
presence within you.

Inhale deeply right now, in through your nose, and hold your breath while you read the following paragraph.

Take this moment, quickly, to measure the tightness caused by your inflated lungs pressing against the inside of your chest. See if you can feel the beating of your heart within you, or even hear it thrumming in your ears. Check for tingling in your fingers and toes. Is pressure building behind your eyes? What else do you notice going on in your body?

OK, exhale.

If you're like most of us, you involuntarily let out a long breath, followed immediately by another deep inhale of oxygen before your body instinctively settled back into a steady breathing rhythm. That's good. It's normal. It's the way you are designed.

What you've just experienced is what's known as "signs of life." Heart beating, skin tingling, oxygen cravings within you—these are just a few of the simplest, most rudimentary proofs that you're a living being. This stunning miracle of life goes beyond just your body, though, involving your spirit and soul as well. And then when your *daily life* becomes a *Christian life*, well, that's when it gets really exciting.

Let me show you what I mean.

YOUR PHYSICAL LIFE

(See John 6:63; Romans 8:10–11; 2 Corinthians 3:6; 1 Peter 3:18; Revelation 11:11.)

John 6:63 reports that Jesus taught His disciples this truth: *"The Spirit gives life."* He was, of course, speaking about the animation of the physical human body.

The apostle Paul echoed that truth when he wrote to the church in Rome, saying, *"Even though your body is subject to death because of sin, the Spirit gives life because of righteousness"* (Romans 8:10). Simon Peter understood this "Spirit equals Life" equation as well, because he saw it happen—dramatically—with his own eyes, in the physical resurrection of Jesus. *"He was put to death in the body,"* Simon wrote, *"but made alive in the Spirit"* (1 Peter 3:18).

Theologians such as Greg Allison and Andreas Köstenberger are quick to point out that this concept of life by the Spirit was not a new idea. It was, after all, the Spirit of God *"hovering over the waters"* (Genesis 1:2) that began the seven days of the first creation, when all living things were made. As such, they say, "Life is divinely sourced, a gift from God as the opening chapters of Scripture make clear...The Spirit of Genesis 1:2 has an active part in the creation of the world and its living inhabitants."[7] And what about human life after the original creation, including ours? For that question, Allison and Köstenberger turn our attention to Job 33:4, which records Elihu's testimony and a "reference to the creation of his life in the womb." That verse reads, *"The Spirit of God has made me; the breath of the Almighty gives me life."* That, it seems, applies to us too.

The point I'm making here is the same one that Jesus did: *The Holy Spirit alone is what makes all living things physically alive—and that includes you.*

This can seem a little counterintuitive because it happens so seamlessly, for everyone, and with such meticulous, miraculous regularity that we've become very good at taking it for granted. I mean, have you noticed that the only thing really surprising about death is that we're always surprised when it happens? That's because, instinctively, we wholly and mindlessly trust the Holy Spirit to do exactly what Jesus said: *"The Spirit gives life."*

Biologists tell us that seven factors must be present in order for something to be classified as "living." They are (in no particular order)[8]:

+ Respiration

+ Growth

+ Sensitivity

+ Movement

+ Nutrition

+ Excretion

+ Reproduction

Right now, without any intentional effort on your part, you're demonstrating at least five of those seven factors (unless you're reading this chapter on the toilet, then you're probably demonstrating six!). Assuming there's not a physiological or psychological limitation, you also have the innate potential to accomplish the remaining factor as well.

You are alive, by all definitions—even though you are *not trying* to be alive.

Despite that, the truth remains that humans alone can never actually *create life* like that which we define as "living" and which we assume to possess in ourselves. Sure, we can reproduce the life that already exists within us through sexual union and children, and we can nurture or destroy life, both in ourselves and others. But to create life from scratch? Or to make a dead thing live? Simply not possible. No human has that ability.

In fact, life itself contradicts a proven scientific principle. Brian Cox taught me that, in his book, *Wonders of Life*. Dr. Cox is a particle physicist, a working scientist, a popular broadcaster, and an international speaker on scientific matters. He is *not* Christian in his thinking, nor even vaguely theistic. Because of that, I find his observations on the Second Law of Thermodynamics particularly interesting. He says:

A pile of atoms will never assemble themselves into a teacup if left alone or even gently agitated for a billion years, and a tremendous amount of work would have to be done to build such a well-ordered thing as a teacup. In contrast, it is relatively easy to turn a teacup into, if not a pile of atoms, then a highly disordered mess on the floor. This is a universal law of physics—things tend to get more disordered because it is overwhelmingly more likely for them to do so.

Life is a notable exception. At first sight, it appears to be second-law defying...It actively assembles itself into extremely complex structures. No wonder it is tempting to attribute the properties of living things to a designer or supernatural action.[9]

Stanley Miller tried to create life once, back in 1953.[10] No, he wasn't some Dr. Frankenstein mad-scientist type. Stan was just an inquisitive university student at the time, studying science and the origin of life. He created a lab designed to simulate the chemical conditions that scientists theorized had made the first living thing. Using a complex arrangement of glass tubes, bottles, gases, water, and electric sparks, he flipped a switch and then waited to see what might appear.

On the positive side, he managed to transform his existing materials into some of the amino acids found in living organisms. But he was completely unable to create anything remotely resembling life. Why?

For starters, the few amino acids that formed in his lab were also present in dead things, so they by themselves were not indicators of life. Second, only some, not all, of the amino acids required for life were able to form. Third, and probably most important, the conditions required to create the amino acids that did form were *inherently harmful* to other amino acids needed for life. In other words, it's impossible to create one kind of amino acid without destroying another kind—yet both are necessary for life to exist.

In the decades since 1953, and benefiting from enormous advances in science and study, researchers have repeatedly attempted to improve Miller's experiment and create life in a laboratory. Every attempt has failed. This is frustrating for those who work in scientific knowledge as a career, but it also emphasizes the truth that God's Spirit alone is the source of life. And here's what I find most interesting about this "Holy Spirit equals Life" idea:

In order to create life, God's Spirit must also sustain life.

The absurdity of the human body in full function is, by itself, a testament to that. Ask an expert why the heart beats, and chances are good that person will go through the mechanisms of *what happens* without being able to explain *why it happens*. For instance, in an article titled, "Why Does Your Heart Beat?" the Franklin Institute offers this tepid explanation: "The heart pumps oxygen-rich blood to the rest of the body through one main artery called the aorta. The muscular walls of the aorta and the other arteries help the heart pump blood. When the heart beats, arteries expand as they fill with blood. When the heart relaxes, the arteries contract."[11]

Interesting—but not an explanation *why*.

The most honest answer I've ever heard from a medical professional about why the heart beats is this: *"Because it does."* That response makes me laugh, but it's true. The heart beats because it does—because God's Holy Spirit, the Giver and Maintainer of life, arbitrarily makes it so.

Beyond that microcosm of life, I'm also fascinated by the macrocosmic, intensely interrelated web of conditions that must constantly be at work in order to make life even possible on Earth. For instance, if our planet didn't spin, we wouldn't experience day and night, which would functionally make half our Earth uninhabitable. If our planet were not tilted at a twenty-three-degree angle, we wouldn't have our four seasons, which are crucial to plant life and growth—something that manufactures oxygen for us and provides the food we consume each day. If our Earth were a wee bit smaller, the gravitational force would be too weak to keep our oxygenated atmosphere from dissipating into space (like the atmosphere of the moon).[12] How long do you think any of us would survive without oxygen?

Here's the one that amazes me: Did you know that our oceans hide fast-moving rivers that run *within them?* These are called gyres (pronounced "Jires"). In the Atlantic Ocean, the gyre is roughly 13,000 miles! It circles the entire ocean and is distinctly recognizable as something separate from the ocean water that surrounds it. The Gulf Stream is part of the gyre in the Atlantic. This famous river's water is warm, bluer than ocean water, and in constant motion. That rushing, warm, river-within-an-ocean actually mitigates the effects of extreme winter in Great Britain—thus enabling that geographical land mass to support life.[13]

Why are gyres necessary in general? Because without them running inexorably through our oceans, those great bodies of water would be stagnant, causing death and decay to accumulate in the seas until, as oceanographer Tjeerd van Andel described it, "The unstable ocean would eventually turn over and vent the whole mess to the surface, with catastrophic effects."[14]

These are just a few of the everyday miracles that cooperate to sustain your life on Earth. I mentioned Dr. Brian Cox earlier. This esteemed scientist holds a view about the Bible shared by many (but not all) in his scientific community: "The Genesis story is a myth." Yet even he, who dismisses God as a nonexistent fable, can't help but wonder at the improbability that your kind of life thrives in our little corner of our galaxy—*and nowhere else.*

"Why is the Earth," Cox muses, "a living oasis amid, as far as anyone can tell, a forbidding expanse of nothing? What is special about our pale blue anomaly of a world that makes it home to life?"[15]

Hmm.

Your physical life right now is utterly dependent on an intricate cosmological balance with so many interconnected, global, and galactic factors that it'd be impossible to number them all. At the same time, your individual body must also have so many unconscious, unreasonable, flawless functions (like a heart that just keeps beating!) that even if you could number them, it'd be an exercise in futility for you to attempt to manage them all. And yet this morning you woke up, stretched your muscles, and got out of bed as if that action in itself were no miracle at all.

Amazing.

All right, before we move on to the next section, I want you to try this again: Inhale deeply right now, in through your nose, and hold your breath while you read the next paragraph.

The Holy Spirit is currently giving life to your mortal body. He goes to cosmic lengths to sustain your life—even now—and this is evident with every breath you take. So...what are you going to do about that?

THE HOLY SPIRIT RENEWS YOUR SPIRIT

(See John 3:6; Romans 8:2; 1 Corinthians 6:11; Titus 3:5.)

When we speak of the Holy Spirit creating life, we must also acknowledge that, for the Christian, that life which He invests in us is more than simply a physical one. Your human spirit is also miraculously made alive by the Spirit of God. By way of example, let's consider the experience of C. S. Lewis.

Today, most people think of C. S. Lewis as one of the great Christian minds of history. His astonishing intellect and imagination brought us both the fantastic allegorical fiction of Narnia and the foundational academic work, *Mere Christianity*—a book still widely used for its insightful, logical arguments in defense of our faith. What we sometimes forget is that Jack (as Lewis's friends called him) was a late convert to Christ. His initial thoughts were decidedly antagonistic toward Jesus.

In his autobiographical work, *Surprised by Joy*, Lewis explains that, from his teen years well into the scholarly adulthood of his thirties, he was an atheist, firmly anti-God in general, and anti-Christian specifically. His great interests were philosophy and mythology—not religion. While he was teaching at Magdalen College (part of Oxford University), he began to struggle with his disbelief until…well, I'll let him tell the rest:

> You must picture me alone in that room at Magdalen, night after night, feeling, whenever my mind lifted even for a second from my work, the steady, unrelenting approach of Him whom I so earnestly desired not to meet. That which I greatly feared had at last come upon me. In the Trinity Term of 1929 I gave in, and admitted that God was God, and knelt and prayed: perhaps, that night, the most dejected and reluctant convert in all England.[16]

What Jack describes as the transformative, "steady, unrelenting approach of Him" is what theologians call *spiritual regeneration*. Here's the stuffy, academic definition for that: "That act of God by which the principle of the new life is implanted in [a human], and the governing disposition of the soul is made holy."[17] For our purposes, however, it suffices to say that spiritual regeneration is best understood *as the moment when God enables us to know Him.*

The Calvinist scholar will tell you this happens before a person chooses to follow Christ, thus empowering that person to subsequently believe in Christ with authentic faith. The non-Calvinist theologian will say that regeneration occurs after that choice to follow Jesus, or simultaneously with it. Yet, by fixating on the "when" rather than the "what," both these academic groups tend to gloss over this stunning truth:

Christ's Holy Spirit takes that sin-cancered, corpse-like human spirit within you and miraculously breathes relentless new life into your soul.

The apostle John quotes Jesus explaining it this way to the Pharisee, Nicodemus: *"Flesh gives birth to flesh, but the Spirit gives birth to spirit"* (John 3:6). My friend, Pastor Dustin Scott, is a Greek language scholar. Although I know my way around a Greek-English Dictionary, I can't read the original language as Pastor Dustin can, nor can I assemble the nuances of tense, inflection, and inference like he can. So one day I put John 3:6 in front of him and asked him to translate from the New Testament Greek text.

According to Dustin, if we translated John 3:6 more literally, that capital-S, Holy "Spirit" and lowercase-s, human "spirit" could read like this: "The Breath gives birth to breathing."[18] This calls to mind the moment of creation when God *"breathed"* life into Adam (see Genesis 2:7) and foreshadowed what Christ would do after His resurrection: *"And with that he breathed on them and said, 'Receive the Holy Spirit'"* (John 20:22).

Now pay attention: This kind of *Breath-to-breathing* regeneration of spirit is what the Holy Spirit did *within you* to bring your soul from death in sin to life in Christ.

The apostle Paul preached it this way: *"He saved us through the washing of rebirth and renewal by the Holy Spirit, whom he poured out on us generously through Jesus Christ our Savior"* (Titus 3:5–6). And because one breath requires another to maintain life, this is what Christ continues to do in you today—and what He will faithfully perform in you tomorrow. As Paul wrote to the church in Corinth, *"Outwardly we are wasting away, yet inwardly we are being renewed day by day"* (2 Corinthians 4:16).

This continuous "making alive" of the human spirit is astonishing; it's a daily miracle happening deep within the core of our very being—yet we're barely even aware of it.

Notice how this played itself out in the subsequent months of C. S. Lewis's life. After that night of conversion at Magdalen College, Jack set about exploring world religions to see if his nascent belief in God could be substantiated in an organized religion. For him, that came down to two possibilities: Hinduism and Christianity. Before long, his intellect forced him to dismiss Hinduism, but he wasn't yet ready to turn his newfound faith toward Jesus.[19] Then, he later reported:

> I know very well when, but hardly how, the final step was taken. I was driven to Whipsnade [zoo] one sunny morning. When we set out I did not believe that Jesus Christ is the Son of God, and when we reached the zoo I did. Yet I had not exactly spent the journey in thought ... It was more like when a man, after a long sleep, still lying motionless in bed, becomes aware that he is now awake.[20]

As we've seen from Scripture, this kind of spiritual movement and growth is only made possible by the renewing presence of the Holy Spirit in a person's life. Now, I'm a curious person by nature, so some years ago, while I was working as an entertainment journalist, I decided to find out how God accomplished this work described in Titus 3:5–6 and 2 Corinthians 4:16 in the lives of people who were not named C. S. Lewis.

My job at that time was to report on pop culture trends, particularly (though not exclusively) within the Christian industry. This involved conducting frequent interviews with random celebrities, which, let's face it, can get a little boring at times. At one point, I began asking every Christian I interviewed the same question: "How did you meet God?"[21]

Did God come with a bang, exploding into the consciousness and demanding a surrender? Did He arrive quietly, unnoticed until that moment of realization when it became clear He'd been nearby all along? Did He call loudly from a distance? Whisper in our ears? Show Himself with startling clarity or with muddy impressions? Amaze us with His power? Tickle the longing within? How?

The answer to all those questions, I found, was "Yes."

For instance, gospel music legend and twelve-time Grammy Award winner Shirley Caesar had been "playing church" in the backyard with her siblings one Tuesday afternoon when God came for her. "I was out there jumping and dancing," Reverend Caesar told me, "and anointing came on my life, and the presence of the Lord just took over. Before I knew it, I'd gone from 'playing' church to really having church! A sense of repentance fell on me that I can hardly express it." That night at a revival service, she says, "I didn't even give them time to make the altar call. I made my own altar call [and] that night I gave my life to the Lord."

Television actor Chris Castile was just a boy sitting in a car with his mom, watching clouds in the sky as they drove to their destination. The beauty of that view suddenly sparked something in his little heart. "Mom," he asked, "who's God?" By the time the car was parked, the kid in the back-seat had also become a child of God.

Eddie "El Gato" Elguera had once been one of the most famous names in professional skateboarding. He won national championships, invented tricks that became standards in the skateboard community, and was even ranked as the number one pro skater in the world. Then, seemingly over-night, the abuse of drugs and alcohol took away the fame and fortune he'd grown accustomed to. Still in his early twenties, he found himself a has-been, dejectedly serving burritos at his brother's fast-food restaurant. That was when sixty-eight-year-old May Hubolt, hankering for a burrito, stepped up to the counter and into Eddie's life.

"Man, she was a fireball!" Eddie told me. She started talking about Jesus, and for the first time, El Gato felt a deep longing to know the Person she so obviously knew. "So I received the Lord that day," Eddie told me. (And so did his mother and brother!)

Then there's Amy. She was four years old when the Holy Spirit got her attention. My future wife was sitting at the breakfast table on Easter Sunday. That particular morning, her father told her why they celebrated that holi-day. She told me later, "I remember very clearly sitting there, eating a bowl of cereal, and suddenly it dawned on me. If Jesus had been willing to do such a wonderful thing for me, then I wanted to follow Him. I prayed right then and there, over my Cheerios, and that was how my Christian faith began."

Forty-eight years later, as Amy lay dying, that preschooler's renewed spirit was still thriving and very much alive within her. Because of that ongoing spiritual regeneration, God's Holy Spirit brought to her an unshakable peace, despite the months and days of difficult passing.[22]

One more story—just because I like it—and then we'll move on. This one was told to me by Sharon Ketcham in her book *Reciprocal Church*.

Anthony's parents subscribed to the belief that kids shouldn't be taught about religion, that they should be allowed to make that kind of choice in a vacuum, without "pressure" from anyone else. So they studiously avoided the subject with their son. Meanwhile, Anthony and his family lived just down the street from a church. They didn't know anyone who attended there, nor did they bother to go in themselves, yet nearly every time his family drove by the church, the young man would find himself quietly praying: "God, are You in there?"

According to Anthony, one day, when he was a teenager, God answered "yes," and told him to go inside. So he did.

He went into a worship service alone, arriving late. He sat in the back and waited. A youth pastor (Sharon Ketcham, of course) noticed him and went to strike up a polite conversation. But Anthony couldn't wait for the niceties of society to be established. "God told me to come here," he told her bluntly, interrupting. So Sharon did what any good youth pastor would do—she told him about Jesus. She later reported, "For the next three years, Anthony responds to God's invitation, which brings him right to Jesus... Twenty years later, Anthony continues to respond to God's invitation as a social worker caring for foster kids."[23]

Like Anthony and the rest of these individuals, every story of spiritual regeneration is as unique as the person who experiences it. I suspect that simply reading about these others brought to mind your own, one-of-a-kind answer to the question, "How did you meet God?" Still, all of us have one thing in common: *God's Holy Spirit intervenes in the lives of people,* drawing us to Him in unmistakable ways, renewing us day by day with His strength and ability—regardless of our weakness and infirmity of sin.

The point here is this:

He saved us through the washing of rebirth and renewal by the Holy Spirit, whom he poured out on us generously through Jesus Christ our Savior. (Titus 3:5–6)

Amen!

THE HOLY SPIRIT RESIDES WITHIN YOUR SOUL

(See John 14:17; Romans 5:5; 2 Corinthians 1:22; Galatians 4:6; 1 John 3:24, 4:13.)

Now, realistically, God's Holy Spirit could've stopped at creating your life and regenerating your spirit. I mean, seriously, those two things by themselves are over and above what you or I should expect from anyone, right? But God is generous, both with His creation and with Himself, so He freely gives us even more:

The Holy Spirit chooses to live His own eternal life within your temporary being, placing Himself alongside, inside, and everywhere throughout all aspects of you.

This is what Christ Himself promised (see Luke 11:13; Acts 1:4), and what the first Christians considered an astonishing, priceless "gift." (See Acts 2:38, 8:20; 10:45.) The theological term for this amazing gift in action is "indwelling," a concept based on Scriptures like Ephesians 2:22, *"You too are being built together to become a dwelling in which God lives by his Spirit,"* and 1 John 3:24, *"This is how we know that he lives in us: We know it by the Spirit he gave us."*

Scholars explain that indwelling as a "spiritual union," meaning "the life of Christ is the life of the believer."[24] Or as Dr. Lawrence Richards puts it, "In brief, the Holy Spirit is the active agent in every Christian's life, the Person through whom the Godhead presently works out the divine will in the world."[25]

Yawn.

Those are both nuanced understandings of the concept of "indwelling." They're accurate and academically defensible in any seminary classroom or pastoral study. But if you're like me, you don't live your Christian life in a seminary classroom or pastoral study. Instead, your day-to-day experience is out in the real world, encountering frustration and temptation, joy and awe, and all the multivariate, mundane moments of human existence. So I'll tell you the way I think of the Holy Spirit's indwelling, out here in the real world:

God is always near.

When I was a child, we would sing the old hymn, "He Lives," in church as a way of celebrating Christ and His constant, living nearness to us. Perhaps our music leader was a bit melodramatic, but the high point of that song was always when he gesticulated fiercely and the congregation roared, "You ask me how I know He lives? He lives within my heart!"[26]

That's a beautiful sentiment, and true, but also so generically vague that I never understood why my worship leader got so excited about it. I'm older and mildly wiser now and, although I still don't have a full grasp of the profound secret of spiritual union with Christ (who does, really?), I am at least more comfortable with the idea.

Christ's life within my heart is one of those "intangibly tangible" mysteries, explaining the unseen reality of the Holy Spirit through simplified symbolism. Biblically speaking, the "heart" has only slightly to do with that aortic pumping mechanism in your chest. Instead, it encompasses all of your human existence, including your physical life, your personality, intellect, memory, emotions, desires, hopes, dreams, thoughts, personal history, will, and anything else you can throw into that kitchen sink of humanity.[27]

So, when the Apostle Paul declared to the Galatians: *"God sent the Spirit of his Son into our hearts,"* (Galatians 4:6) and when Christ promised, *"Surely I am with you always, to the very end of the age"* (Matthew 28:20), they were both saying the same thing: Your finite soul has mystically, irrevocably merged with the infinite Spirit of Jesus. And now, as John recorded, *"He lives with you and will be in you"* (John 14:17).

It's impossible to overstate the enormity of this supernatural residency.

The Holy Spirit is no passive, neutral "guest" within your soul. The obvious assumption in all the Scriptures listed above (and more) is that Christ's ever-present Spirit is dramatically active, constantly nurturing new life within you, communicating His never-ending love for you, and guaranteeing the promises He made to you. Perhaps best of all, the Holy Spirit living in you is proof that you are always welcome in God's presence. *Always.*

We'll discuss this more in-depth in the next chapter, when we delve into what it means that the Holy Spirit makes us part of God's family. For now, though, let me share with you the way Charlie Brown once (unintentionally) illustrated this theological concept for me. I found this in an old *Peanuts* comic strip some years ago and have never let it go since.

Standing outside his father's workplace, Charlie Brown explains the way things are to his snobby friend, Violet. "See this?" he says to her, pointing toward a plate glass window:

> This is my dad's barber shop. He works in there all day long. He has to deal with all sorts of people. Some of them get kind of crabby… but you know what? I can go in there anytime and no matter how busy he is, he'll always stop and give me a big smile.[28]

This, to me, is a perfect picture of the always-welcome aspect of Christ's indwelling Holy Spirit—and the kind of intimacy we continue to experience from Christ with every prayer we pray, each day of our lives. "No matter how busy he is, he'll always stop…" Why? It's simple, really: *God is always near.* And so when you call out, the indwelling Holy Spirit is always willing to stop…to listen…to help. This is your benefit as recipient of the gift of God—the Person and presence of the Holy Spirit in every moment of your life.

Do you understand what this means for you and me?

+   It means that your Christian life is not as hard as you're making it.

+   It means Christ is always near to you.

+   It means His greatest gift to you is not mere power, but His very own Person, unified with your spirit in ways that are deeper and stronger than any soul mate.

+   It means that the life of faith is not your responsibility—it's God's. Your job, then, is simply to cooperate with what the Holy Spirit is already doing in, with, and through you.

+   It means God is not simply available to you, but willing to help you in ways you may not even be able to acknowledge or understand.

+   It means you are priceless, precious, loved, and secured by One who will never feel differently about you.

There's more, but I think my time in this chapter is running out, so I'll skip to the end and let Paul tell you the last thing on my list. The Person and presence of the Holy Spirit in every moment of your life means:

> *We know how dearly God loves us, because he has given us the Holy Spirit to fill our hearts with his love.* (Romans 5:5 NLT)

FOR FURTHER REFLECTION AND SMALL GROUP DISCUSSION:

1. What discoveries would you most like to remember from this chapter? Write a letter to yourself, to be read one year from now, recounting those things and telling why you chose them.

2. If you could ask the author any question about this chapter, what would it be? How do you think he'd answer?

3. According to the author, the indwelling of the Holy Spirit means "God is always near." What are five words that describe your feelings about that? Explain.

TWO

THE HOLY SPIRIT MAKES YOU HIS FAMILY

You are not a guest in the kingdom of God; the Holy Spirit
makes you one who belongs. By Him you are: Adopted into
God's family; recipient of the gift of God's Person; grafted into
Abraham's legacy; and sealed, reserved, and guaranteed for glory.

Have you ever wondered why we in the US and Canada don't live in *North
Bjarnica?*

Or thought that the "United States of Herjulfson" had a certain appeal
to it?

If so, you know your world history better than most! For the rest of us,
maybe a little explanation is in order.

We've all heard that "In fourteen hundred ninety-two, Columbus
sailed the ocean blue," and landed in North America. Most of us have also
learned that our continent—and the United States of America itself—are
named after the intrepid Italian explorer Amerigo Vespucci, who traveled
this way in 1497, five years after Columbus visited the continent.

Some even know that Viking explorer Leif Erikson (aka, "Leif the
Lucky") was the first European to set foot on North America, nearly five
hundred years *before* either Columbus or Vespucci glimpsed our shining
seas. But the name that most of us have never heard belongs to the man
who beat all those other Europeans to this shore:

Bjarni Herjulfson.

It seems that the good captain Bjarni came to North America way back in AD 986—more than a decade before Leif Erikson, and centuries ahead of the others. It was an accident, of course. Bjarni and his Viking crew had been in Iceland and were now heading over to Greenland to reunite with his father and family. Then [insert ominous music here!] a mighty storm blew up over the ocean. For four days straight, the men in the boat couldn't see the sky through the fog and rain. Since the Vikings navigated by using the sun and the stars above, they traveled aimlessly for nearly a week. The storm-soaked sailors had no idea where they were or where they were going; they were focused on simply staying alive.

Finally, the weather broke and the sun reappeared. The Viking seamen were overjoyed to find that not only had they survived—they were within sight of land! Bjarni and his crew had unknowingly crossed the Atlantic Ocean and arrived at the Eastern coast of what is now Canada. His men shouted for joy and begged their captain to let them go ashore to rest and replenish their supplies. But the good Mr. Herjulfson refused. Why?

He wanted to see his family.

That's all. After days and days of fighting to survive, the only thing on his mind was rejoining his father and loved ones in faraway Greenland. He could've made history and been the first European to set foot in North America—and if he had, we might be calling ourselves *Bjarnicans* today. But, as one historian put it, "Bjarni was intent on going home, not going down in history."[29]

So the homesick sailor and his Viking crew stayed in their boat, turned its prow toward open water, and sailed back to Greenland—to *family*. A few years later, Bjarni told his seafaring tale to his friend, Leif. That guy was so impressed, he literally bought the boat. (Ancient Vikings believed that ships knew where they'd been and could find their way back to those places.) You guessed it: Leif Erikson took Bjarni's ship back along the same naval route and became the second European explorer to discover North America—but the *first* European to actually step out onto dry land.[30]

I enjoy this story because it reminds me that even the bravest, strongest, most adventurous people in the world—past, present, and future—still desperately long for something that God gives to us freely:

Family.

What's more, the family our heavenly Father gives to us is eternal, immeasurable, and overflowing with blessings of love. To be honest, this strikes me as an unnecessary extravagance. God could have simply called us His servants, or His followers, or His *DLFs* (that's "Dear Little Friends" for those of you who haven't read *The Chronicles of Narnia*). But instead, He calls us His children. In fact, God's *Holy Spirit deliberately, proactively, and definitively makes us His family.* That seems impractical to me, but you know, I'm not complaining.

THE HOLY SPIRIT ADOPTS YOU INTO GOD'S FAMILY

(See Romans 8:15–17; Galatians 4:6; Ephesians 2:18–19.)

So, how does God make you (and me) His family?

He does something that you cannot do for yourself: *He adopts you.* The apostle Paul put it this way: *"The Spirit you received brought about your adoption to sonship. And by him we cry, 'Abba, Father'"* (Romans 8:15).

Notice that Paul doesn't say, "God thought you were such a good person that He adopted you into His family." Nor does he say, "God heard you begging and felt sorry for you," or "God saw you had a lot of talent and resources, and He wanted you on His team," or "the Holy Spirit tallied up the pros and cons and decided, aw shucks, why not?"

The straightforward truth is you had nothing to do with it. "The Spirit…brought forth your adoption." It is God's Holy Spirit *alone* that accomplishes this fantastic act. And realistically, the Holy Spirit could've saved you without adopting you. He could've made you a guest in His kingdom, or a close friend, or a kitchen scullery maid, or a hair sweep-up boy in the halls of glory, or whatever He wanted. So it says something about Him that *He wanted* to make *you* His child.

There are a few things that strike me as important in this whole "Holy Spirit makes us His family" thing.

First, the idea of family was paramount within ancient Jewish culture. A family in ancient Israel was almost its own little nation; it could be as small as a few people, or as large as a few hundred, including father, mother, unmarried children, in-laws, cousins, grandparents, servants and slaves, concubines, and sometimes even long-term visitors or others who had some kind of clan association. It was within this structure that people could thrive—and for whom family members would sacrifice all. To be named as one in this kind of household meant "a communal responsibility for assistance, protection, the sharing of work, loyalty, and cooperation for the general well-being of the family."[31] These people would *literally go to war* for their family members (see Genesis 14:11–16, 31:1–31, and others).

This kind of deeply ingrained dedication meant being in a family was not simply a nice thing; it was almost a necessity for survival. That also meant that if you were someone without a family connection—for instance, a widow, or an orphan—you lived in constant hardship and were exposed as a target for slavery or victimization.

At the same time, Jewish society throughout history, up to the time of the Apostles, *didn't* have a custom of legal adoption. It simply wasn't part of their vocabulary or practice, and there was no such thing as adoption legislation. In fact, in the entire Hebrew text of the Old Testament, the word "adopt" (or any variant of it) never appears.[32] [33]

Now, that doesn't mean the Jewish people never practiced what we'd call adoption, because they did. For instance, Scripture indicates that Mordecai took responsibility as guardian and caregiver for his younger cousin, Esther, who'd been orphaned as a child. (See Esther 2:7.) We'd call that "adoption" today, even if they never did. Still, for the Jews, this kind of thing was a family/tribe responsibility; people were expected to take care of their own people, and that included both children and the elderly. (See, for example, how Jesus bound His mother, Mary, and disciple, John, in an adoptive-style relationship in John 19:26–27). Generally speaking, though, there was no formal Jewish law regarding adoption in ancient Israeli society.

Second, when Paul wrote about the Holy Spirit's adoptive work, it wasn't a nod to Jewish customs but a reference to Roman laws regarding adoption. This makes historical sense, I suppose, because this letter was sent to Christians living in Rome, and that was something they'd find familiar. But to say that God adopts in a way similar to the legal standards of Rome carries some important implications for you and me. Consider:

+ According to Roman law, adoption marked a complete change in status for the person who was adopted.

+ There was no age limit for adoption, nor race barrier, nor gender obstacle, nor social prerequisite. A person could be adopted as a child, a young adult, a man, a woman, a Greek, a Jew, or even an elderly man or woman.

+ Roman law dictated that when a person was adopted, *all* of their debts were cancelled.

+ The adopted person took the name of his or her new family and was thereafter to be known everywhere as a full member, as if born to that family by blood.

+ The adopted person was entitled to all privileges enjoyed by that family, including property, social status, and Roman citizenship (if not already a citizen).

+ The adopted person was granted full rights to share in any inheritance of assets within the family.

+ The adopted person was thereafter to live under the authority of the adopter, which could include surrendering choice of career, living location, daily activities, and so on.

+ The adopter took full responsibility to provide safety, well-being, and family support for the rest of the adopted person's life.[34]

Are you beginning to glimpse the incredible, excessive, absolutely unnecessary generosity of this work that God has done in you? Does it yet begin to take your breath away? Adoption into God's family, brought forth by the Holy Spirit on your behalf, is no inconsequential thing.

Because God chooses to make you His family...

...you can now be completely changed for the better (see 2 Corinthians 5:17);

...your age, race, gender, and so on cannot prevent you from joining God's family (see Galatians 3:28);

...your grievous debt over sin has been cancelled (see Colossians 2:13–14);

...you can now be fully known in heaven and on Earth as a member of God's household (see Ephesians 2:18–19);

...you now have access to all the privileges of being family with God (see 2 Peter 1:3–4);

...you've been granted full rights to share in Christ's eternal inheritance (see Galatians 4:7);

...you can trust in God's loving direction and oversight of your daily life (see Psalm 32:8);

...and God has taken full responsibility for your well-being—from now and through eternity (see Philippians 4:19).

Whew. Somebody say Amen!

And guess what? There's even more.

It's significant, from a legal perspective, that Paul described the Holy Spirit's inward work in us as an "adoption to sonship." Now, since we look back at history and see the heavily patriarchal way the ancients viewed women and society, our first instinct is to do what some of our modern translations do. We mitigate that "sonship" statement with culturally justifiable language editing. We understand that Paul obviously meant to include women in this statement; after all, he addressed his letter of Romans *"To all in Rome who are loved by God..."* (see Romans 1:7). It'd be pretty hard to exclude women from *all* who are loved by God!

So, from a gendered perspective, it's certainly appropriate to translate the Greek term *huiothesia* ("adoption to sonship") in Romans 8:15 as the NASB does: *"adoption as sons and daughters;"* or as the NLT does, *"adopted you as his own children." However,* my old pastor Chuck Swindoll suggests that Paul—while clearly including women in this miracle of heavenly adoption—was making a deliberate claim of higher legal status under the standards of Roman law for those women. In that view, "adopted to sonship" (the more literal translation of the Greek term) becomes very important.

You see, daughters in that time had different, *lesser* rights than legal sons did. Historians tell us that in Rome, adoption was typically about transferring *paterfamilias* power. Because of that, "females were rarely adopted, and women could not adopt by law."[35] Yet Paul, in Romans 8:15, seems to be claiming full "sonship" rights for Christian women rather than his culture's diminished understanding of a daughter's rights. In other words, he made a heady statement of legal status, not so much one of gender difference.

Listen to how Pastor Chuck explains it:

> By the way, we shouldn't replace the word "son" with "child" [in Romans 8:15], even for women. Paul could have chosen the neutral Greek term for child, but he deliberately chose "son" to indicate that believers stand to inherit something. Women are "sons of God" because they, no less than men, are a part of God's estate.[36]

All right. At this point, we should all be feeling really good about ourselves as recipients of this great gift of the Holy Spirit's adopting work. And, indeed, that's justified. But...there's one more—less popular—thing we need to discover about God's spiritual adoption process. I can't promise you'll like it, but I do promise it's important.

Here it is:

When Paul wrote, *"The Spirit you received does not make you slaves, so that you live in fear again; rather, the Spirit you received brought about your adoption to sonship..."* (Romans 8:15), that word-picture about slaves and fear wasn't just empty sentiment. It was a harsh, daily reality of life for his readers living in the capital city of Rome. And it was important enough that he also repeated that message in Galatians 4:7, saying, *"You are no longer a slave, but God's child; and since you are his child, God has made you also an heir."*

Why did he do that? The answer was tragically littered outside the gates of Rome.

Remember earlier when I told you that being without family in those ancient times made a person a target for slavery or victimization? There was no place this was truer than with unwanted children—often girls— in the Roman Empire. These were known as the *res vacantes*, or "vacant things," which the owner has abandoned as worthless.

The brutal fact was that in this time and place, helpless infants and children were routinely left to die along the roadsides and in garbage dumps. One historian reflects, "Abandoned children [could] be found anywhere in

Rome, but particularly at the Columna Lactaria in the vegetable market (Forum Holitorium)."[37]

If a girl was born to a family with too many children, if a child had a deformity or was of uncertain paternity, or if a father simply didn't want to—or couldn't—deal with another mouth to feed, the child was abandoned to the elements, and everyone else went on with their lives.

Many of these children simply died of exposure. Others became prey for unscrupulous predators. Most often, those "rescued" were raised as slaves and prostitutes. Many a gladiator was pulled from a garbage dump and trained as a slave to fight and die in the arena as entertainment for others. We know from historical records that some were taken and raised as human pets for wealthy families. There are even ancient reports of professional beggars taking abandoned infants, mutilating them in some way, and then displaying the tortured infant publicly in the hope that their cries would increase profits from almsgivers.[38] [39]

I don't tell you of these horrors because I want to frighten or offend. I just want you to understand that when Paul said in Romans 8:15, "*The Spirit you received does not make you slaves, so that you live in fear again,*" *this* was the picture that would've come to mind for his readers in Rome. They'd seen firsthand the fear and helplessness of the *res vacantes.* They'd likely interacted with older children or adult slaves who'd been dragged from the side of the road and raised in lives of abuse and hardship. They *knew* what Paul was talking about. And we must know it too.

"*You are no longer a slave, but God's child,*" Paul tells us in Galatians 4:7. "*The Spirit you received brought about your adoption,*" he reminds us in Romans 8:15. From our modern perspective, the Apostle seems out of touch when he says those things. He's not suggesting that God found us living in a crowded foster home, or under state-mandated childcare, or even with distant relatives who made us sleep in a cupboard under the stairs. When the Holy Spirit brought about your adoption, He went out of His way to *rescue* you, to *redeem* you, and to *provide* your permanent escape from the evil consequences of spiritual slavery as a *res vacante.*

In the gravest spiritual sense, you, dear one, were like an ancient infant left in garbage, wailing fecklessly to deaf ears, terribly afraid, and doomed to either slow death or a lifetime of abusive slavery to sin. Then God did the unthinkable. He waded right into the heaping dung and rotting sludge. By His Holy Spirit, He reached out His strong arms and lifted you out of your appalling fate. "I love you," He said. "I want you. To Me, you are precious."

And then…

He made you His family.

Are you starting to get it now? Are you beginning to see?

If God did absolutely nothing else for you or me, if He never answered another prayer nor turned His ear to another sputtering cry, that would still be enough. *That alone* would still be all we could ever hope to ask for, or imagine.[40]

Take a moment now to let that sink in.

All right, let's move on.

THE HOLY SPIRIT GIVES HIMSELF TO YOU

(See Luke 11:13; Acts 1:4; 2:38; 8:20; 10:45; 11:17; 15:8; Romans 5:5; 8:15–16; 1 John 3:24; 1 Thessalonians 4:8; 1 John 4:13.)

God, despite what seems fair, is not limited in His generosity—and this is also true in the Holy Spirit's work as adoptive Father to you and me. Paul showed us this millennia ago when he wrote his letter to the Romans.

When he begins his pronouncement in Romans 8:15, the Apostle leans heavily into Roman family law. Having established civilly our *"adoption to sonship,"* he then draws his readers' attention dramatically away, into something much deeper, more visceral, and profoundly personal: the intimacy of a Jewish family. God's Holy Spirit has made you His sons, Paul tells us, and that's not all:

"…by him we cry, 'Abba, Father.'"

In a Roman family home, the father was most often called by his first name, although we might assume that a child of that age might've also called him *pater*, the most common Latin word for "father." In that kind of formal structure where the father exercised total control over his children as property,[41] it would've been nearly unthinkable for a child to call the father some endearing pet name like "Daddy" or "Pops" or…*Abba*. Yet, by virtue of our intimacy with God's Holy Spirit, we can cry *Abba*, Father, anytime we want to speak to the heavens.

It's hard to overestimate that kind of relational license, because it means that when we're adopted, God gives not only His benefits (like heavenly inheritance and forgiveness of sin's debt)—the Holy Spirit also gives to us *the gift of Himself*. The intimacy of *Abba* means our God is no absentee father or deadbeat dad; He is always near, always ready to give and receive affection, always involved in our lives, even when we feel like He's far away.

I want us to dig into the history and meaning of that fantastic name, *Abba*, just a little bit at least—but first I need to tell you about a guy named Kevin.

See, when I first heard that God was my *Abba*, that didn't mean much to me. I had no experience with which to compare it. My parents split when I was three, and divorced when I was four. My first earthly memory is watching my dad drive away because, as my mother said matter-of-factly, "Your father won't be living here anymore."

My father moved to a small studio apartment about forty-five minutes from where I lived, but my memories of him over the subsequent years are few and far between. He was never unkind or abusive toward me; he just wasn't interested in me. And after a while, I felt the same way about him. So when someone told me what a great thing it was that God had become my *Abba*, my internal reaction was something along the lines of: *meh* [insert shrug here].

Then I met Kevin. Over the last forty-plus years, Kev has been my best friend, my closest confidante (besides my wife), my strong supporter, the one guy in my life who is always near (even though he lives far away), always ready to listen, always honest with me (even when I don't want to hear it), always up for a new adventure, and always ready to help, even in the worst of times. Kevin is my age, so he's certainly not a father figure to me—but he's still the closest thing to an *Abba* that I know. He's the one person who makes me understand what a wonderful thing it is to receive the gift of God's intimate Spirit in my life.

I'll tell you one story about that, and then we'll get back to the meaning and history of *Abba*.

Decades ago, when I stood at the wedding altar to marry my favorite person in the whole world (Amy!), Kevin stood next to me. He held the rings and made me proud as my best man. Thirty years later, the absolute worst had happened. Amy lay in a hospital bed, dying from a ruthless cancer that simply would not go away. I was drowning in grief, knowing it was time to plan a funeral, unable to answer all the questions people were asking me about that.

When I look back on it, I realize that what I did was too much to ask, even unfair to ask, but at the time, it never occurred to me. I just knew I needed him, and that he'd never shrink away from me. So I turned to my closest friend.

"Kev," I said. "I can't do it. I need you to plan Amy's funeral. I don't want to even think about it. I just want to spend myself loving my wife for every moment she has left alive. OK?" Kevin didn't hesitate, didn't object, didn't ask questions. He just said, "OK, I'll take care of it."

And he did.

Honestly, I don't even know everything he did or how much it all cost. I just know he flew out to sit with Amy, they talked through what she wanted, and he made it happen. At one point, I asked the Funeral Home Guy (I never learned his name—ask Kevin, he knows it) when I was supposed to pay for everything. Did he need my credit card before or after Amy died? FHG just looked at me across the table and said, "It's taken care of." I started to ask again, and Kev put a hand on my knee. "Mike," he said, "it's taken care of." And it was.

So when it came time for Amy's beautiful funeral, all I had to do was show up, cry, accept hugs and kind words from friends, cry some more, and then go home.

Interestingly, sometime in the months after the funeral, Kevin decided I should never have to be alone on the anniversary of Amy's death. So every September, he makes plans to see me, or for me to see him. He doesn't even ask for my permission, check the dates with me, or wait to hear if I want him to come. He just sends me a note that says, "My plane arrives on this date. I'll rent a car and should be at your house by this time."

It is now nine years since Amy died, and Kevin still won't let me be alone on the date of her passing. At this point, he's turned Amy's death anniversary into something I both dread (reliving the pain) and look forward to (I get to see Kevin!). How strange is that?

What I'm saying is this: Kevin is my friend, yes, but I have lots of friends. This guy, though, has also given me something no one else has: himself.

And that's why now, today, in this moment, I can find such joy in telling you that *God has given us Himself* through adoption. It's because Kevin has taught me something my earthly father couldn't: All the privileges of family are great, but what really matters most is simply the opportunity to know the Father, a precious gift of a Person provided by the Holy Spirit Himself. So let's reread it:

"God's love has been poured out into our hearts through the Holy Spirit, who has been given to us,…and by him we cry, "Abba, Father" Paul wrote in Romans 5:5 and 8:15

All right then.

History tells us that the word "Abba" was a uniquely Jewish term. It was a joyfully childlike, Aramaic distortion of the Hebrew word "Ab," which meant more formally, "Father."[42] The closest comparison we have to it in the English language today is "Daddy." *Abba* evokes in today's imagination both the jubilant screech of a toddler who happily greets her father coming home from work, and the quiet affection of a preschooler curled up in his daddy's lap while they read a story together before bedtime.

Surprisingly, although *Abba* was commonly used inside the Jewish home, it was *not* used in the Jewish Temple or synagogue for worship— or even found anywhere in the Old Testament text. Jesus was the one who broke that barrier of formality with our Father. In the garden of Gethsemane, He cried out in agony, *"Abba, Father,…everything is possible for you. Take this cup from me. Yet not what I will, but what you will"* (Mark 14:36).

Following Christ's example, the earliest Christians made the intensely personal *Abba* an everyday call in their worship and prayers. "They adopted it for themselves," renowned pastor Stuart Briscoe said, "because they were adopted into a position of intimacy with Him. To pray 'Abba' is, therefore, to express unashamedly and joyfully an endearment born of love."[43]

What this means for you and me is that when the Holy Spirit adopts us into God's family, He also gives us the unimaginable best thing possible: *Himself.*

THE HOLY SPIRIT GRAFTS YOU INTO ABRAHAM'S LEGACY OF BLESSING

(See Romans 2:29; Galatians 3:14.)

The first time I saw a "fruit cocktail tree," I was visiting my wife's family in Phoenix.

Maybe that kind of tree is a familiar thing to you, especially if you live in the American Southwest, but for me, it was like staring at an unearthly, alien thing. There, in front of my eyes, on branches that spread out from top to bottom and side to side *on the same tree*, were both oranges and lemons, mixed in nature—like that was a totally normal thing. It was all I could do not to quote Bill Murray's classic exclamation of disbelief in the first *Ghostbusters* movie, "Dogs and cats living together...Mass Hysteria!"[44]

That was also my first, in-person view of a common horticultural practice called "grafting." Of course, *you* know that's a technique where the gardener inserts an orphaned shoot from one plant into the healthy trunk of another (but I didn't know that!). The two plants merge so that the "adopted" shoot can take nourishment from the other's mature root system and grow.[45] The result, as I saw with my own eyes, can be a tree that grows oranges and lemons, or peaches and plums, or different varieties of apples, and more.

The apostle Paul knew quite a bit more about grafting than I did, and he used that gardening practice as an allegory for your adoption by the Holy Spirit. *"Some of the branches* [representing Jewish people] *have been broken off,"* he wrote in Romans 11:17, *"and you* [non-Jews], *though a wild olive shoot, **have been grafted in** among the others and now share in the nourishing sap from the olive root* [representing God and His promises to the Jews]." This spiritual grafting happens by virtue of the Holy Spirit's adoptive work, which allows Gentiles (non-Jews) to be miraculously joined into the blessing and promise that God gave to the ancient forefather of the Jews, Abraham.

"*He redeemed us,*" Paul wrote to a first-century Gentile congregation,[46] "*in order that the blessing given to Abraham might come to the Gentiles through Christ Jesus, so that by faith we might receive the promise of the Spirit*" (Galatians 3:14).

That "*promise of the Spirit*" was signified physically in the Jewish man's body through circumcision. So, to be circumcised was (and still is) literally understood as being one marked as belonging to the family of Abraham and his God. (See Genesis 17). When God makes us His family today, though, He no longer requires that physical mark. Why not? Because at the moment the Holy Spirit brings forth your adoption to sonship, He also accomplishes for you spiritually what had previously been a physical ritual for newborns. Or, as Paul said in Romans 2:29:

Circumcision is **circumcision of the heart, by the Spirit,** *not by the written code.*

This concept of "*circumcision of the heart*" wasn't new for Paul or his Jewish readers. It was God's idea, first given by God to, then through, the prophet Jeremiah. Here's how God put it: "'*The days are coming,*' declares the LORD, '*when I will punish all who are circumcised* **only** *in the flesh—Egypt, Judah, Edom, Ammon, Moab and all who live in the wilderness in distant places. For all these nations are really uncircumcised, and even the whole house of Israel is uncircumcised in heart*'" (Jeremiah 9:25–26). In other words, circumcision in the flesh is certainly important, but it's only a physical symbol, meant to represent a change of heart in the people of Abraham's tribe.

Now, if you're like me when I first heard this, your reaction to this whole circumcised-into-Abraham's-tribe thing might be something like: *Big whoop. I'm heart-circumcised. Snore.* OK, since you're smarter and prettier and more grateful by nature than I am, you probably didn't say that. *Ahem.* Regardless, let me take a moment to help us discover what I later learned about why that whole heart-circumcision thing is actually a Brobdingnagian-sized whoop.[47]

The defining element in the history of all Israeli people is bound up in the life of their famous forefather, Abraham, and his history-changing relationship with God. Originally named Abram, he was a pagan man living in the pagan city of Ur, in what is now believed to be southern Iraq.[48] Most likely, he was first a worshipper of the supposed "moon god," Nannar, who was the recognized local deity in Ur.[49]

One day, without apparent warning, God himself intruded into Abraham's life and gave this command and promise, *"Go from your country, your people and your father's household to the land I will show you. I will make you into a great nation, and I will bless you; I will make your name great, and you will be a blessing. I will bless those who bless you, and whoever curses you I will curse; and all peoples on earth will be blessed through you"* (Genesis 12:1–3). Scripture succinctly records Abraham's response: *"So Abram went"* (Genesis 12:4).

The specifics of God's promise to this man are:

+ land;
+ establishment of a national identity;
+ great reputation;
+ blessing on friends and a curse on enemies;
+ the ability to funnel God's blessing to all people.

Those are all superb things, but notice what happens when you add them all together and recognize that in the short three sentences of this text, God uses a variant of the Hebrew word *barak* ("to bless") five times. God, in making these individual promises to Abraham, is guaranteeing this man and his family a *legacy of blessing*.

The Old Testament understanding of blessing was exclusively a positive thing. It was an outpouring of good that included (but wasn't limited to) power, success, abundant provisions, family growth, long life, and more.[50] The New Testament Greek (*eulogia* and *makarios*) continued these same themes, but carried a much heavier emphasis on the "spiritual inheritance reserved in heaven for the believer."[51] In both testaments, blessing is understood as something for which God alone is the ultimate provider. In other words, blessing is impossible without God—and He promised it unreservedly to Abraham.

By far, the most important *legacy of blessing* left to us by God's covenant with Abraham was this, found in Genesis 15:6, *"Abram believed the* Lord, *and he credited it to him as righteousness."* For the people of Israel—Abraham's descendants—this was the defining instance of God's free grace for salvation. Remember, Abraham came out of a pagan past that worshipped false gods—yet in this moment, God erased all of the man's idol worship and sins and, in a transformative act of redemption, established him in a fully righteous state.

For the apostle Paul, this was the basis for our salvation in Jesus's death and resurrection. Here's how he explained it:

> *The words "it was credited to him" were written not for him alone, but also for us, to whom God will credit righteousness—for us who believe in him who raised Jesus our Lord from the dead.* (Romans 4:23–24)

So you see, not only are the history and promises of the Jewish tribe now wrapped up in our own daily experience as children of God, but the very salvation of our souls is borne out of the *legacy of blessing* that comes from being grafted into the family of Abraham. That's what it means to be granted *"circumcision of the heart, by the Spirit"* (Romans 2:29), and to be redeemed by the promise of the Holy Spirit *"in order that the blessing given to Abraham might come"* (Galatians 3:14).

That, my friend, is most definitely a big deal.

THE HOLY SPIRIT SEALS, RESERVES, AND GUARANTEES YOU WILL SHARE IN HIS ETERNAL HOME

(See 2 Corinthians 1:22; 5:5; Ephesians 1:13–14; 4:30.)

All right, you've let me wander a bit into the fascinating world of ancient Hebrew and Roman history in this chapter, and I appreciate it. Believe it or not, I actually left out several things I wanted to include! But I figured this would be enough. So for this last section, I'll try not to bloviate as much and just tell you this:

When the Holy Spirit makes you His family, it's not an empty promise or an absentee declaration. In view of all of creation, both physical and spiritual, on Earth and in heaven, He *seals, reserves,* and *guarantees* your status and future in His adoptive care.

Listen:

Now it is God who makes both us and you stand firm in Christ. He anointed us, **set his seal** *of ownership on us, and* **put his Spirit in our hearts as a deposit, guaranteeing** *what is to come.*
(2 Corinthians 1:21–22)

Now the one who has fashioned us for this very purpose is God, who has **given us the Spirit as a deposit, guaranteeing** *what is to come. Therefore we are always confident and know that as long as we are at home in the body we are away from the Lord.* (2 Corinthians 5:5–6)

And you also were included in Christ when you heard the message of truth, the gospel of your salvation. When you believed, you were **marked in him with a seal,** *the promised Holy Spirit, who is* **a deposit guaranteeing our inheritance** *until the redemption of those who are God's possession—to the praise of his glory.* (Ephesians 1:13–14)

Let's look at this from a different perspective. History records that Julius Caesar was already a cadaver when he adopted his son, Gaius Octavius (or simply, Octavian). The adoption took place under the terms of the dictator's last will.[52] It was a posthumous political maneuver intended to promote succession to power for the future Caesar Augustus (as Octavian would later be called). As the dead Caesar's adopted son, he'd have a familial weapon to use against his rivals, Mark Antony, and the illegitimate prince, Caesarion, whom Julius had fathered with Cleopatra, queen of Egypt.[53]

What a tragedy that adoption was! Octavian was Caesar's son in name only, with no guarantee of inheritance or even existence. It was a legal adoption, sure, but not a full one—not even a real one in terms of his family relationship. What kind of father is a corpse? Also, Augustus couldn't claim his so-called inheritance as supreme leader of Rome until after he waged a bloody civil war against Mark Antony, conquered Cleopatra (who committed suicide in defeat), and ordered the gruesome murder of his adoptive younger brother, Caesarion. What a waste.

The Holy Spirit, on the other hand, has adopted you *in full*, into the family of His eternal life. He cannot die, and so will never abandon you to fight and die alone; He instead has given you *Himself* for your intimate, always *Abba* and friend. He's even grafted you into the legacy of blessing found in belonging to Abraham's tribe.

And, having done all that, He's made Himself your unbreakable seal of adoption, a deposit (or down payment/pledge) of eternity in your soul, and an inviolable guarantee of your heavenly inheritance as one who now bears His name. I love the way that Reverend Billy Graham once described this, so I'm going to let his be the last words in this chapter. Read along, and I'll just whisper, "Amen!" at the end:

> It seems to me that Paul had two main thoughts in his mind concerning our sealing by the Holy Spirit. One concerns security, and the other, ownership. Sealing in the sense of security is illustrated in the Old Testament when the king sealed Daniel into the lion's den so that he could not get out. Also, in ancient times, as when Esther was queen (Esth. 8:8), the king often used his own ring to affix his mark or seal to letters and documents written in his name. Once he had done this, no one could reverse or countermand what he had written....
>
> As we trust in Christ, God gives us the Spirit not only as a seal, however. He is also our pledge...In the apostle Paul's day, businessmen considered a pledge to do three things: it was a down payment that sealed a bargain, it represented an obligation to buy, and it was a sample of what was to come.
>
> The Holy Spirit likewise seals God's purchase of us. And His presence shows God's sense of obligation to redeem us completely. Perhaps best of all, the presence of the Holy Spirit, living in fellowship with us, provides us with a foretaste, a sample, of our coming life and inheritance in God's presence.[54]

FOR FURTHER REFLECTION AND SMALL GROUP DISCUSSION:

1. What's one insight from this chapter that makes a difference in the way you see yourself as a child of God? Why?

2. The author states early on: "The straightforward truth is you had nothing to do with it. 'The Spirit...brought forth your adoption.' It is God's Holy Spirit *alone* that accomplishes this fantastic act." How do you feel about that?

3. Now that you've read this today, what happens with you tomorrow?

THREE

THE HOLY SPIRIT PRIZES YOU

You matter—because you matter to the Holy Spirit. He prizes you so much so that He: brings you freedom; sets you apart for spiritual purpose; anoints and rests on you; and continually sanctifies you in preparation for eternity.

"Hi Genevieve!"

The woman in the video is beautiful, of course, but not because she's trying to be. She sits in a cluttered family room, wearing no makeup and sporting my plain, gray sweatshirt.

"I heard you came to my house today and I was not here. But I miss you!"

I used to tease her about making these kinds of silly, short videos on her cell to send to our preschool granddaughter. "Genevieve doesn't even have a phone," I'd grumble. "And you're going to see her when she comes over tomorrow anyway. What's the point?" But Amy, being much smarter than her husband, just ignored me and kept recording anyway.

"So I'm looking forward to seeing you very soon. Hopefully, in maybe one or two days, I'll get to see you."

She'd save those video messages and text them out to our son for him to share with his daughter.

"Hope you have a good night. Sleep well. Mwah! [*She blows a kiss to the screen*]."

OK, quiet now. This is the part I don't want to miss:

"I love you."

My wife made that particular video a little more than a year before she died, and a few months before we even knew she was sick. I found it on her iPhone after the funeral and—despite my earlier protestations while she was living—kept it for myself. If you were to ask me today what my most prized possession is, I'd tell you it's that 19-second clip of Amy happily chatting into the camera…and saying, "I love you."

Because I think we're becoming friends, you and I, I'm going to tell you one of my secrets. There are times—when I'm feeling lonely, or can't sleep, or am just overwhelmed by the sorrows of this world—when I pull out that video made for my three-year-old granddaughter and play it for myself. Sometimes, when I need it, I'll sit in the darkness, close my eyes, and just listen to Amy's voice saying those last three words over and over and over again.

"I love you. I love you. I love you…"

If this is my most prized possession, what would you guess I've done with it? Yes, that's right. I've kept the original on my own cell phone. I've also made a copy as a backup on my laptop. And another backup copy on an external hard drive. In fact, I think I currently have five backup copies of that single 19-second video in five different locations. I'd be devastated if I ever lost the sound of Amy's voice saying, "I love you." It's precious to me, so I guard it with passion.

We do that with things we treasure, don't we? Care for them in sometimes extreme ways. For instance, I know a guy who bought an old comic at a used bookstore: *Batman* #121, published in 1959. Turns out it's valued at around $12,000—and increasing every year. So he spent another hundred dollars or so just to have it professionally graded and encased in an oxygen-sealed container. He's never going to sell *Batman* #121; he just prizes it, so he wants to keep it safe and sparkling.

I knew another man who, for decades, kept an ink-stained baseball wrapped in tissues, in a box, in a drawer in his bedroom. Sometimes he'd bring it out and show it off to friends or family, but mostly he kept it safe and pristine, untouched in the drawer. Why? Because that ink stain on it was the signature of New York Yankees legend, Mickey Mantle. When my friend's widow finally sold her late husband's prized baseball, she got more than $1,000 for it.

People like you and me, we go to great lengths to care for what we prize—it's human nature, really, deeply ingrained in everyone who's ever lived. In that respect, we reflect something of the image of God, except that when He prizes something, He doesn't waste time making multiple backup recordings or encasing it in an oxygen-sealed container. He does much, much more.

Ask God what He prizes most in the universe, and His answer will be *you* (and me, and us). And so each day His Holy Spirit goes to great lengths on your behalf: He brings you freedom; He sets you apart for a spiritual purpose; He anoints you with power to serve; and He continually sanctifies you in preparation for eternity with Him.

I think it's just His way of saying, "I love you. I love you. *I love you…*"

THE HOLY SPIRIT BRINGS YOU FREEDOM

(See Romans 8:2; 2 Corinthians 3:17.)

"Where the Spirit of the Lord is, there is freedom," the apostle Paul declared to the church at Corinth, in 2 Corinthians 3:17.

Taken in the context of his thoughts from 2 Corinthians 3:12–18, that statement comes across as almost an intrusion. Up to that point, he'd been talking about Israeli history in the time of Moses, recorded in Exodus 34:29–35. It seems that when Moses would go speak privately with God, his face would start, well, *shining*, I guess. I don't know exactly how that looked, but I do know that afterward, Moses would cover his face with a veil because it was scaring people to see him *"radiant"* like that.

So Paul was talking about that in 2 Corinthians 3, and then, abruptly, he interrupted himself to say this: *"Now the Lord is the Spirit, and where the Spirit of the Lord is, there is freedom."*

The ramblings of an old man, maybe? Or misfiring synapses in the Apostle's brain? I don't think so. I suspect that Paul was remembering to whom he was talking—people who lived in Corinth—and he wanted to refocus their attention with a reference to their personal lives.

History tells us that ancient Corinth in Paul's time was a gem in the Roman Empire. A port city situated on an isthmus at the Eastern coast of Greece, it had been completely demolished by the Roman army in a battle of conquest in 146 BC. It lay in ruins for one hundred years, and then in 46 BC, Julius Caesar ordered the city to be rebuilt as a Roman colony. By the middle of the first century AD, it was actually a capital city, the headquarters of the Roman governor of that region.[55]

It shouldn't go without notice that history also records Caesar's new colony in Corinth was founded by former slaves ("freedmen").[56] We also know that the economic engine of the Roman Empire was slave labor, with roughly half of Rome's population being made up of slaves. Corinth, by virtue of its location as a major trade center of the empire, "was a clearing house for the slave trade, and the wealthy in Corinth were able to buy the best slaves available in its slave market."[57]

In other words, chattel slavery was an ingrained, extremely commonplace experience in that city, and it showed up in every aspect of its inhabitants' lives, including agriculture, private homes, government agencies, mining, public works, mercantilism, and so on. What's more, slaves weren't the only "unfree" people in Corinth. There were also "poorly paid free labor, to some extent undistinguishable from slaves…[and] debt bondsmen and peasants who were tied to the land."[58] These people were not specifically called slaves, but they were trapped in human bondage nonetheless.

Acts 18:11 reveals that *"Paul stayed in Corinth for a year and a half,"* on one of his missionary journeys. There was no way he missed seeing firsthand this citywide plague of slavery. And 1 Corinthians 7:21 makes it clear that the Apostle knew his letters to Corinth would speak directly to some who were slaves in that place. That, I believe, is why he inserted this message of hope for freedom in 2 Corinthians 3:17—because *many, if not most, of the people to whom he was writing were not free.*

What I find so dramatic about this message is that Paul declared, *"Where the Spirit of the Lord is, there is freedom"*—but he *didn't* promise Corinthian Christian slaves that they'd be emancipated from their current bondage. That raises a significant question for me:

If these people were still slaves, how could Paul tell them the Spirit had given them freedom?

Romans 8:2 expands on Paul's meaning somewhat, pointing to the spiritual aspect of freedom in the Spirit, saying, *"Through Christ Jesus the law of the Spirit who gives life has set you free from the law of sin and death."* This is important, and transformative....

But is that all there is to it?

That question of biblically understood freedom burned in me for some time, long enough that I finally spent several weeks in study over it. (Yes, there may have been 3 x 5 cards involved.) The result was something I've taken to calling "The Five Freedoms." Here's what I mean by that.

As I see it, the concept of freedom in Scripture encompasses five distinct forms. They are: (1) Freedom *From*; (2) Freedom *To*; (3) Freedom *In*; (4) Freedom *For*; and (5) Freedom *Because*.

1. FREEDOM *FROM*

Freedom *From* is the idea of *liberation or emancipation.* This is our most common understanding of the word "freedom," and it takes the meaning of a release from some kind of captivity or oppressive circumstance. In Scripture, we see it physically in the emancipation of the Hebrew slaves from their rulers in Egypt. (See Exodus 1–15.) We also see this kind of freedom in the spiritual sense (that is, law versus grace), in the way Paul talks about it in Romans 8:2, and in the moral and emotional sense in Romans 6.

So when the Holy Spirit brings *freedom from*, He may bring physical release from captivity (or He may not). He does bring release from the impossible standards of the law of Moses and replaces that with His grace and forgiveness. And He imbues us with a growing moral and emotional freedom from the constraints of sin, such as freedom from the captivity of bitterness, anger, fear, need for retaliation, and punishment. (See also John 4:1–42; 8:36.)

2. FREEDOM *TO*

Freedom *to* is the next step after freedom from: *Opportunity.* The history of America's Jim Crow laws shows how important this kind of freedom is. Black enslaved people had been emancipated by the outcome of the Civil War—but rampant racism and oppressive, discriminatory social practices actually prevented Black people from living as free men and women. It was another one hundred years before the civil rights movement of the 1960s began to add the opportunities of "freedom to" upon the basic rights of "freedom from" for the descendants of formerly enslaved people. Even today, lack of access to "freedom to" is still an obstacle, to some extent, for most non-white minority groups in the US. As an Arab-American, this is something I've learned firsthand.

When Scripture speaks to the idea of "freedom to" bestowed by the power of the Holy Spirit, it addresses complexities such as the opportunity to: succeed, avoid exclusion, take risks, love better, speak out, live righteously, hope confidently, reconcile with others, fail, trust, and so much more. There are too many Bible verses dealing with this kind of freedom to list them all here, but two sweet examples of this are found in Jesus's healing of blind Bartimaeus (see Mark 10:46–52) and the woman with an issue of blood (see Luke 8:43–48). When you have time, read through those passages and ask yourself, "In what ways do I see Jesus giving 'freedom to' simply by restoring sight and health?"

3. FREEDOM *IN*

Freedom *in* is that beautiful gift the Spirit gives us when emancipation is not an option. This, I think, is at least part of what Paul was talking about in 2 Corinthians 3:17 when he told the slaves reading (or hearing) his letter in Corinth, "*Where the Spirit of the Lord is, there is freedom.*" This is the Holy Spirit-empowered, supernatural ability to maintain dignity and self-worth even in the most oppressive of situations. We see this in the history of Joseph and his unjust imprisonment (see Genesis 39), in the life of Jesus during His trial and execution (see John 18–19), and even when Paul and Silas sang hymns after being tortured and chained in a prison cell (see Acts 16:16–40).

What I find most interesting about this kind of freedom, though, is that it's not limited to external impositions only. Scripture teaches us that "freedom in" can also be found in physical weakness, illness, sorrow, and more. By God's Holy Spirit, we can somehow mysteriously find strength to rise above, maintain dignity, and even experience joy. Paul is our example here, with his declaration in 2 Corinthians 12:7–10. Here's my favorite part of that: *"For Christ's sake, I delight in weaknesses, in insults, in hardships, in persecutions, in difficulties. For when I am weak, then I am strong."*

4. FREEDOM *FOR*

Freedom *for* is the gift of purpose, the opportunity to live a life of meaning. This is such an important part of the Holy Spirit's freedom-giving kindness that we're actually going to talk about it in detail in the next section of this chapter. But for the moment, let me say that "freedom for" encompasses the removal of any obstacles that would prevent you from giving yourself completely to new spiritual purpose, to a right-minded perspective, to passionate living, to service, impact, and significance. Matthew 14:12–21 (recounting the time when Jesus forced His disciples to unexpectedly feed five thousand people) is a fun example of this kind of freedom.

5. FREEDOM *BECAUSE*

Freedom *because* is the overarching kind of freedom that makes all the others possible. It's the understanding that you haven't earned any of the freedoms Christ has given you; they are yours simply *because* He chooses it to be so. It's God's grace alone that set you free; you do not earn it or deserve it—yet all these freedoms are your right and entitlement, regardless of the circumstance. Yes, you're receiving what you didn't merit, but it's irrevocably yours nonetheless.

Galatians 5:1 speaks to this kind of *freedom because*, saying: *"It is for freedom that Christ has set us free,"* and we see a beautiful example of this happening in real life, in Luke 7:36–50 (the time when a sinful woman poured perfume on Jesus's feet). We also see a declaration of it in Ephesians 2:8–9 (*"by grace you have been saved…"*), an all-encompassing promise of it in John 8:34–36 (*"if the Son sets you free, you will be free indeed"*), and…well, I should probably stop there for now.

Let's move on.

THE HOLY SPIRIT SETS YOU APART FOR SPIRITUAL PURPOSE

(See Romans 8:9; 1 Corinthians 3:16; 6:19; Ephesians 2:22.)

When God's Spirit set your soul free, He didn't leave you to wander aimlessly thereafter. He didn't pat you on the head, say, "Go, be free!" and then turn His back on you to struggle through the rest of life on your own. No, when He set you free, He also set you apart—*He elevated you to a life of eternal purpose.*

As I said before, this is your *Freedom For,* given to you by the Holy Spirit Himself, creating the opportunity for your life to mean something beyond just the days in which you live in it. What a gift! If you're like me, you've known a few who—for whatever reason—just haven't figured out what to do with their lives. They spend days, weeks, months, and years longing for true purpose beyond just earning money and acquiring things, but they struggle to find that by themselves.

You and I, though, we don't have to be like that. The Holy Spirit—by His own will and kindness—gives us purpose for existing that can guide each day we live and breathe. Because of God's Spirit, we are now physical containers of heavenly intent and ability—little "temples" where Christ forcefully brings His realm of the Spirit to interact with our daily circumstances. We've been set apart as a sacred tool that God's Spirit both inhabits and holds, in order to improve the world He's created. Here's where I learned that truth:

*You, however, are not in the realm of the flesh but **are in the realm of the Spirit**, if indeed the Spirit of God lives in you.*　(Romans 8:9)

*Don't you know that **you yourselves are God's temple** and that God's Spirit dwells in your midst?…God's temple is sacred, and you together are that temple.*　(1 Corinthians 3:16–17)

*Do you not know that your **bodies are temples of the Holy Spirit, who is in you**, whom you have received from God? You are not your own.*　(1 Corinthians 6:19)

*In him the whole building is joined together and rises to become a holy temple in the Lord. And **in him you too are being built together to become a dwelling in which God lives** by his Spirit.*
(Ephesians 2:21–22)

This, then, is our great calling and purpose: To be people who are *set apart to live as human temples for God*, who host His Holy Spirit's presence and influence in our world. This is God's doing, accomplished naturally, inexorably, by His intimate association with your soul, mind, body, and spirit. This is who you are, and who you were always meant to be.

The architectural reference for this purpose-defining aspect of the Holy Spirit's work in you was the Hebrew Temple in ancient Jerusalem. There was a specific, geographical spot that had been set apart as the divine location for this Temple. By the time of Jesus, it had been built, destroyed, and rebuilt three times—always on the same ground.

When the New Testament was being written, this temple (then known as "Herod's Temple," named after the king who renovated it) loomed large in every aspect of Jewish life. It was a center for religious, social, economic, and even legal and judicial activity. Additionally, in the minds of the generations for over 1,000 years, this place "continued to symbolize, in prophecy and tradition, God's relationship with his people."[59]

In that respect, the Jerusalem Temple was where people went to "do business with God," so to speak. If you wanted to pray, you went to the Temple. If you needed forgiveness for sin, you went to the Temple. If you wanted to learn more about the Scriptures, or announce a birth, or give to the poor, or pay taxes, or celebrate holidays, you went to the Temple. You get the idea.

Herod's Temple included a courtyard specifically for Gentiles, where non-Jews could make sacrifices and prayers to God. Beyond that was another area known as the Court of Women—a place of greeting and meeting. Families and friends would gather here, preachers and teachers would deliver sermons in this place, while scribes and scholars would debate finer points of theology and their hopes for a Messiah. The Temple also held a large treasury made up of thirteen chambers that held gold, silver, and other valuables—part of which were routinely distributed to the poor. There were rooms for storage, for oil and wine, and even a room for lepers to testify that they'd been healed. Finally, there was a Court of the Israelites, reserved only for men, and a Court of Priests where a high altar was built. This is where animal sacrifices occurred, rituals meant to reconcile people to God.[60][61]

So, among other things, what we see in the image of the Temple is this:

+ a place where people from all nations and ethnicities could interact;

+ a place of social relevance and supportive community;

+ a place of learning about God and the Scriptures;

+ a place of discussion and civil debate about theology;

+ a place filled with treasures;

+ a place that provided help for the poor;

+ a place for celebrating God's healing; and

+ a place for reconciliation with God.

You see where I'm going with this, don't you?

You see why it's important that Scripture calls you "God's Temple," proclaims that you're living *"in the realm of the Spirit,"* and *"a dwelling in which God lives by his Spirit,"* right? That's because by naming you His movable Temple-on-two-legs (again, so to speak), God has set you apart for a dramatic spiritual purpose in your world. Because of the Holy Spirit's presence within, you will be:

+ a person with whom people from all nations and ethnicities can interact;

+ a person of social relevance who contributes to a supportive community;

+ a person with authority to learn—and share—about God and the Scriptures;

+ a person capable of discussing and civilly debating life-changing theology;

+ a person filled with treasures of God's grace;

+ a person capable of providing help for the poor;

+ a person who can celebrate God's healing—physical, emotional, and spiritual; and

+ a person who can lead others into reconciliation with God.

This is you, right now. Not because you're so great and powerful, but because He is—and He's chosen to imbue your life with His eternal purpose—to make you into His human Temple with access to His spiritual realm.

THE HOLY SPIRIT ANOINTS AND RESTS ON YOU

(See Matthew 3:16; Mark 1:10; Luke 2:25; 3:22; John 1:32; Acts 10:44; 11:15; 1 Peter 4:14; 1 John 2:20; 2:27.)

Not only does God's Holy Spirit set you apart for a spiritual purpose, but He takes it one step further and *anoints* you with His limitless power to serve. This is also seen in the New Testament as the Spirit *"resting on"* or otherwise descending and staying on someone—first on Jesus, then on others.

Anointing (or resting on), in Scripture, carries with it some of the same ideas that we just talked about, as in setting you apart for a spiritual purpose. But there's more to it than just that, so I wanted to bring it up with you separately here.

Where should I begin? How about if we try a few modern parables…

To what shall I compare the anointing of the Holy Spirit?

It's like a man who invited his entire family to enjoy s'mores at a campfire—but forgot to bring a lighter. He threaded the first marshmallow onto a skewer, set out chocolate and graham crackers, and began waving the skewer over the unlit coals. Everyone waited, but nothing happened. Despite his best efforts, all he had was an uncooked marshmallow. Finally, his wife lit a match and dropped it into the grill. Minutes later, everyone had warm, toasty s'mores, with plenty to spare.

What else can I compare to the Holy Spirit's anointing?

It's like a woman who was trying to use a hand pump to draw water from a well, but came up empty instead. Then a friend poured out a bottle to prime the pump, and suddenly fresh, clean water came gushing out of the spout.

And the last thing to which I can compare the Holy Spirit's anointing?

It's like an unmoving windmill hooked up to an electrical grid. While the blades of the windmill sit motionless, no power can run through the grid. Then God sends a current of air to blow through the plain, causing the windmill to crank and turn. As the blades begin to rotate, electricity courses out from them, sending much-needed power to the homes nearby.

So what is the Holy Spirit's anointing (or resting) to you? It's *holy fire* that ignites your soul with the power of God's truth. It's *holy water* that primes the pump of your spiritual experience. And it's *holy wind* that teaches you to access heaven's power in your everyday life. Listen to the way the apostle John talked about it:

*   *"You have an **anointing from the Holy One**, and all of you know the truth"* (1 John 2:20).

*   *"The anointing you received from him remains in you, and you do not need anyone to teach you. But as **his anointing teaches you about all things** and as that anointing is real, not counterfeit—just as it has taught you, remain in him"* (1 John 2:27).

I also like the way the *New Living Translation* phrases those verses:

The Holy One has given you his Spirit, and all of you know the truth… You have received the Holy Spirit, and he lives within you, so you don't need anyone to teach you what is true. For the Spirit teaches you every-thing you need to know, and what he teaches is true—it is not a lie. So just as he has taught you, remain in fellowship with Christ.

(1 John 2:20, 27, NLT)

Today, we don't use anointing as a ritual in the same way the ancient Israelites did, so it may be unfamiliar to your ears to hear that the Holy Spirit has unilaterally anointed you with power to serve. In our day, it's mostly just a dab of olive oil on a forehead along with a request for God to heal our sick. Historically, though, it was much more than just an empty gesture and intoning prayer.

Scripture reveals that three kinds of people were typically anointed in the Old Testament era: kings, priests, and prophets. For instance, David was anointed as God's choice to be Israel's king long before he actually became king—but God's anointing made his kingship inevitable. (See 1

Samuel 16:1–13.) Priests were anointed as a confirmation of their office, and that anointing was considered to be a perpetual appointment. (See Exodus 28:40–41; Leviticus 7:35–36.) And God commanded Elijah to anoint Elisha as his prophetic successor. (See 1 Kings 19:16.)

Christ Himself filled all three of these roles of king, priest, and prophet. It's no surprise, then, that by New Testament times, the Messiah (or "promised deliverer") came to be synonymous with Jesus and with the term "Anointed One."[62]

In every instance of anointing (or *"resting on"*) in the Bible, the understanding was that a person anointed in the name of God:

+ received holiness from God;

+ gained imputed righteousness from God;

+ received a "special endowment of the Spirit" that included a "transfer for divine powers and authority";

+ had been singled out for God's favor;

+ had been designated by God to "a particular place or office in God's plan"; and

+ was being prepared for service through the ongoing gift of God's Spirit.[63]

We see all these things summed up succinctly in the moment when the prophet Samuel anointed David to be the future king of Israel: *"So Samuel took the horn of oil and anointed him in the presence of his brothers, and **from that day on the Spirit of the LORD came powerfully upon David"*** (1 Samuel 16:13).

In this, we begin to understand what it means when Scripture tells us, "You have an anointing from the Holy One," and "The anointing you received from him remains in you." God hasn't only set you apart for a spiritual purpose (though that by itself is pretty cool), He's also shared with you a part of Jesus's legacy as the Anointed One. Here's how Paul put it:

"The Spirit of him who raised Jesus from the dead dwells in you" (Romans 8:11 ESV).

So what I'm saying to you right now is this: You may not feel worthy, or particularly strong in a spiritual sense. You may think of yourself as mostly a failure, or maybe just mediocre in the kingdom of God. But it's time for you to own the truth.

The Holy Spirit *prizes* you, so much so that He's *anointed* you with His own holiness, divine favor, power, authority, and more.

That doesn't mean your life is going to be all sunshine and cotton candy (just ask King David or Jesus about that), but it does mean you can't escape your exciting destiny as an integral part of God's great plan. This anointing you possess is something bigger than you, that depends on Him, not you (after all, you can't anoint yourself with the Holy Spirit!). And, if history is any indication, He intends it to be a perpetual thing, growing stronger with time, as you also grow in your understanding and maturity of faith.

God's choice, not yours. So you might as well get used to it.

THE HOLY SPIRIT CONTINUALLY SANCTIFIES YOU IN PREPARATION FOR ETERNITY

(See Romans 15:16; 1 Corinthians 6:11; 2 Corinthians 3:18; 2 Thessalonians 2:13; 1 Peter 1:2.)

I'm told this is a true story, so I present it to you now as something that actually happened. In the Scottish Highlands in the mid-1800s or so, a number of fishermen were sitting around a table at a local pub, laughing and drinking and telling tall tales of their seafaring adventures. At one point, one of the more boisterous anglers stretched out his hands to demonstrate just how large the fish was that got away.

Right at that moment, however, a barmaid with a platter of drinks was arriving at the table. You guessed it. The fisherman accidentally smacked into the tray and sent all the ale-filled glasses smashing against a newly painted, white wall. A deep brown stain quickly spread; the wall was ruined.

The rest of the pub patrons went silent at the sound of the crash, turning to stare at the new mess of beer and glass and tarnished paint. Then, without warning, a man who'd been drinking alone in a corner stood and gave a careful look at the stain. While everyone watched, he produced a piece of charcoal from his pocket and began to meticulously sketch around that big, yellow-black stain.

First, a line here. Then a shadow. Then a curve and curl. Is that a hoof? Antlers, wind, and even a gray-scaled meadow for a background. When the artist was done, that ugly beer stain had been transformed into a breathtaking scene: A mural of a glorious stag sprinting across a highland field.

The quiet man took a step back, nodded, then signed his name on the wall. He pocketed the charcoal and went back to finish his drink.

The rest of the patrons of this particular pub applauded. They'd just witnessed Sir Edwin Landseer—Britain's most celebrated wildlife artist at the time—create a masterpiece out of misery. What was first only a dreadful blemish on an otherwise pristine wall had been transformed into a priceless work of art right before their very eyes.[64]

Now, when I say to you that the Holy Spirit continually sanctifies you in preparation for eternity, this is the image I want you to keep in your mind's eye: A master artist taking stock of the ugly stains of sin that discolor your life, and then transforming it all into something more beautiful than you can even imagine right now.

The Greek word root that the New Testament uses for sanctification is *hagiazó*, and it means something along the lines of "to make holy," or "purify" or even "to hallow." It's the same word Jesus used in Matthew 6:9 when He prayed, *"Our Father in heaven, hallowed be your name."* This is the idea at play when Paul says that gentiles can be *"sanctified by the Holy Spirit,"* (Romans 15:16), or when the apostle Peter talks about *"the sanctifying work of the Spirit"* (1 Peter 1:2) going on in the lives of believers scattered across the world.

Still, *hallowing*, or *making holy* feels somewhat abstract to my way of thinking, so let's make it easier, shall we? Here's how the venerated writers of the *Westminster Confession of Faith* (1643–1646) explained sanctification for us common folk:

By his Word and Spirit dwelling in them: the dominion of the whole body of sin is destroyed, and the several lusts thereof are more and more weakened and mortified; and they more and more quickened and strengthened in all saving graces, to the practice of true holiness, without which no man shall see the Lord. This sanctification is throughout, in the whole man; yet imperfect in this life, there abiding still some remnants of corruption in every part; whence ariseth a continual and irreconcilable war, the flesh lusting against the Spirit, and the Spirit against the flesh. In which war, although the remaining corruption, for a time, may much prevail; yet, through the continual supply of strength from the sanctifying Spirit of Christ, the regenerate part doth overcome.[65]

There, that's solved it all for you, hasn't it? No?

Of course not! This is the kind of dense, convoluted thinking that they make us study in seminaries, and which serves mostly just to make biblical understanding off-limits to everyday pew-sitters like you and me. So, even though I want you to have confidence that I *did* go to seminary, and I *have* studied the Westminster Confession, *you don't* have to do that in order to understand what sanctification means in your daily life.

Paul said plainly for us:

"We all…are being transformed into his image…" (2 Corinthians 3:18).

That's what Scriptures like Romans 15:16, 1 Corinthians 6:11, 2 Thessalonians 2:13, and 1 Peter 1:2 mean when they talk about sanctification. The Holy Spirit is engaged in an ongoing work within your soul to gradually *transform* you into a thing of beauty, into someone who looks, thinks, and acts like Jesus—even while you live in a sin-stained world. Pastor Bill Johnson explains it this way, "The Holy Spirit makes it possible for us to behold God's glory as though we were looking in a mirror, seeing what he has done in our lives. And this overwhelming miracle of grace happens because we always become like the one we worship. We become like the one we behold."[66]

Now, if you're like me, you'll hear many preachers and teachers and Christian leaders tell you it's your responsibility to work your transformation from day to day. You must obey all the right rules. You must force yourself to think only holy thoughts. You must refrain from laughing at crude jokes or voting for godless heathens or saying scatological words and, of course, put on a good example for all the millions of sinners who are apparently keeping you under constant surveillance. You must do all the external things to make sure people know you are sanctified—or as a pastor friend told me once, "You have to fake it 'til you make it, Mike."

The problem with that point of view is, it's just not a true understanding of the Bible's teaching on sanctification. Look at these Scriptures below and, based on what you see there, answer this question: Who sanctifies?

> *But we ought always to thank God for you, brothers and sisters loved by the Lord, because God chose you as firstfruits to be saved **through the sanctifying work of the Spirit** and through belief in the truth.*
> (2 Thessalonians 2:13)

> *You were washed, **you were sanctified**, you were justified in the name of the Lord Jesus Christ and **by the Spirit of our God**.*
> (1 Corinthians 6:11)

> *To God's elect, exiles scattered throughout the provinces of Pontus, Galatia, Cappadocia, Asia and Bithynia, who have been chosen according to the foreknowledge of God the Father, **through the sanctifying work of the Spirit**...*
> (1 Peter 1:1–2)

> *He gave me the priestly duty of proclaiming the gospel of God, so that the Gentiles might become an offering acceptable to God, **sanctified by the Holy Spirit**.*
> (Romans 15:16)

All right, here's your pop quiz: *Who sanctifies?*

That's right: The Holy Spirit Himself, by Himself, accomplishes your sanctification.

Noted Dutch theologian Abraham Kuyper once advised, "Cut off at once every representation which makes 'sanctification' to consist of the human effort to make oneself holy or holier"[67]—and that seems like good advice. You have no right to try to steal God's glory in sanctification, nor do you have even the slightest ability to successfully take that responsibility from Him. You're being sanctified because *He's* doing that work in you, by His grace, not because some feeble good works of your own are somehow making you holy. Why is that so hard for many of us to accept?

So what's your job in the process of sanctification? Cooperate. Don't fight the growth happening in you. Be alert so you can see where the Holy Spirit is working in your soul, and follow along. Don't try to create your own self-sanctification, but depend on His leading for that. And rejoice in the Holy Spirit's transformative work when you become aware that it's happening.

Really, just don't make this harder than it is, because here's what we know:

God's Holy Spirit *prizes* you.

He prizes you so much that: He's accomplished your five-fold freedom; He's set you apart for spiritual purpose; He's anointed you with His power to serve; and He's constantly nurturing a transformation inside you that makes you into someone holy, someone more beautiful each day—someone who looks, thinks, and acts like Jesus.

Hey, *He's got this.* Let Him keep doing His thing, and you just concentrate on doing this:

"Being confident of this, that he who began a good work in you will carry it on to completion until the day of Christ Jesus" (Philippians 1:6).

FOR FURTHER REFLECTION AND SMALL GROUP DISCUSSION:

1. What do you find hard to believe in this chapter? Why?

2. How do you see "The Five Freedoms" at work in your life right now? What would you like to pray about in that regard?

3. Which Scripture from this chapter is most meaningful for you? Write it on a 3 x 5 card or a slip of paper, and carry it with you as a reminder for the next twenty-one days.

FOUR

THE HOLY SPIRIT FILLS AND BAPTIZES YOU

God is not passive about you, nor is He some disinterested, disengaged deity. The Holy Spirit fills you with awareness of His active presence; and immerses you in His power and love.

Now's a good time for a Juha story, don't you think?

In case you've never heard of him, Juha is a character of legend in ancient Middle Eastern folklore—an "Everyman" type who has adventures and teaches life lessons. He's been called the "Aesop of the Arab World," and his fables have been told for thousands of years. So for today's Storytime, children, pull up a carpet square and let's remember together the tale of *Juha and the Donkey*...[68]

It was a fine summer day when Juha and his son took their donkey and set off for the market. Juha rode proudly upon the beast, and the son followed on foot. Along the road another family passed by.

"Would you look at that," they said scornfully. "That man rides comfortably on the donkey and forces his son to trudge along behind. Tsk, tsk, how sad this world is today."

Juha was humbled by their words, so he switched places, letting his son ride while he walked along behind. Just then a group of religious leaders happened by.

"Harumph," they said loudly, so Juha could hear. "Look at that ungrateful boy, riding like a king on the donkey while his aged father straggles along after. Kids today have no respect for their elders!"

So Juha and the boy stopped to think about that. Since it wasn't right for either of them to walk, they decided they both would ride instead. Father and son climbed up on the donkey and went on their way. Before long, a group of social activists came by.

"How heartless!" they said. "Both those people forcing that donkey to carry their heavy weight. Have they no pity for their animal?"

Juha and his son felt immediately ashamed. So they dismounted and instead picked up the donkey between them, carrying the beast in their arms toward the market. That was when a group of teenagers happened along.

"Ha ha ha," the teenagers sneered. "Look at those idiots! They're carrying the donkey that should be carrying them!"

So Juha and his son dropped the donkey, embarrassed. Finally, all three of them marched ahead on foot: man, boy, and donkey. And when they reached the market, they all plopped down in the dirt, exhausted.

Moral of the story: *If you try to please everyone, you'll end up pleasing no one.*

This tale seems appropriate to me because today we'll be talking about the Holy Spirit's work in filling and baptizing the believer. I know from experience that anything I say on that subject will make somebody angry, or argumentative, or surprisingly insulting. I can't please everyone so—fair warning—I'm not going to try.

Here's all I'm going to do:

I'm just going to tell you what I see in the relevant Scriptures, and what I think that means for us. If you disagree, it's OK (no need to send me angry letters arguing your points—believe me, I've heard it all already). I make no claim of denominational authority or superiority, and I give you full permission to ignore anything in here you find unhelpful.

Fair enough? All right, then. Let's go!

THE HOLY SPIRIT FILLS YOUR SOUL WITH HIS ACTIVE PRESENCE

(See Luke 1:15; John 7:38–39; 14:17; Acts 7:55; 9:17; Ephesians 5:18; Jude 1:19. Also, John 20:22; Acts 8:15; 8:17–19; 10:47: 19:2; Galatians 3:2. And, John 4:23–24; 1 Corinthians 14:16; Ephesians 6:18; Colossians 1:8; 1:9; Revelation 1:10; 4:2; 17:3; 21:10.)

Some Bible teachers tend to view being "filled with the Spirit" and being "baptized in the Spirit" as pretty much the same thing. I understand that viewpoint, and could even defend it if I needed to. However, after studying it for some time, I've come to believe that "filled" and "baptized" with the Spirit are two distinct things. One describes the *invisible presence* of God's Holy Spirit. The other describes what theologians call the *manifest presence* of God's Spirit—that is, the observable activity of God by humans.

Yes, they're related, and yes there is some overlap, but biblically speaking, each of them also demonstrates unique elements that the other does not. In other words, they may be two sides of the same coin, but there are definitely *two* sides. So for this book, I've decided to discuss them separately instead of lumping them into one category. (I figured you wouldn't mind.)

Also, most books I read on this subject that do discuss them separately present first the baptism of the Holy Spirit, followed much later by the idea of being filled by the Spirit. I'm going to invert that order for us here, and I'll tell you why: A quick study of the Gospels reveals that Jesus's disciples had already received God's Holy Spirit, on at least three different occasions, weeks, months and years before the great outpouring and baptism by the Spirit that's described in Acts 2. Here, I'll show you.

First, Jesus declared in Matthew 12:28 that His ability to drive out demons was empowered *"by the Spirit of God"* present in Him. Then, Mark reveals that Jesus gave that same Spirit-vested power to His twelve disciples, which they used to great effect for both exorcism and healing of the sick (Mark 6:7, 12–13). The disciples performed these miraculous acts while separated from Jesus, and that could only have been possible by the Spirit of God in them. This was the first time the Gospels indicate those men had received some kind of filling of the Holy Spirit.

The second time they received the infilling of the Holy Spirit was similar to the first, but with more people. This time, seventy-two of Jesus's disciples were appointed with Spirit-vested power, which would (we assume) include the twelve disciples closest to Him. (See Luke 10:1.) So again, these men were separated from Jesus, yet filled with the Spirit's presence and power. Then Luke 10:17 adds, *"The seventy-two returned with joy and said, 'Lord, even the demons submit to us in your name.'"* If Jesus was telling the truth in Matthew 12:28, then authentic exorcism of demons is only possible *"by the Spirit of God,"* so those seventy-two followers had to have received God's Spirit to accomplish the miracle of making *"demons submit"* to them.

The third time the disciples were filled with the Holy Spirit was shortly after Jesus's resurrection, when Christ visited them behind locked doors to prove He'd returned from the dead. At that time, *"He breathed on them and said, 'Receive the Holy Spirit'"* (John 20:22). Again, this filling by the Spirit was weeks before the first baptismal outpouring at Pentecost recorded in Acts chapter 2.

This historical progression indicates two things to me. One: *"baptism"* by the Holy Spirit (as in Acts 2) is something different than *"filling"* of the Spirit. (See John 20:22 and so on.) Two: a less dramatic, but no less important, filling of the Holy Spirit seems to precede the event of baptism by the Holy Spirit. So, before we dig into Holy Spirit baptism, I think we need to talk about the work God's Spirit does in filling us.

OK! Here goes…

Our New Testament uses three related terms to describe the filling of God's Holy Spirit in us. They are (in no particular order): Filled with the Spirit (*Pneumatos plēsthēsetai*); Receive the Spirit (*labete Pneuma*); and In the Spirit (*en Pneumati*). All three of these phrases seem to indicate the same thing, which is the continual indwelling of God's Holy Spirit within an individual person in a way that:

+ is an ongoing process that's experienced on a regular basis. (See Ephesians 5:18.)

+ includes heightened awareness of the nearness of God and the invisible spiritual realm (for example, Acts 7:55, and Revelation 1:10);

+ empowers heightened spiritual authority (see John 20:22–23, and others);

+ infuses fresh desire and ability to pursue authentic, daily Christian living under God's direction, such as loving well (see Colossians 1:8), prayer (see Ephesians 6:18), praise/worship (see John 4:23; 1 Corinthians 14:16), and spiritual wisdom/understanding. (See Colossians 1:9.)

"It is interesting," the Reverend Billy Graham comments, "that the Bible nowhere gives us a neat, concise formula for being filled with the Spirit. I believe that may be because most believers in the first century did not need to be told how to be filled. *They knew that the Spirit-filled life was the normal Christian life.*"[69] Amen, brother Billy!

A. W. Tozer adds: "The Spirit-filled life is not a special, deluxe edition of Christianity. It is part and parcel of the total plan of God for his people."[70] That just makes sense, and we see it in Paul's command to *"be filled with the Spirit"* in Ephesians 5:18. The Greek term for *"be filled"* here is *plērousthe*, and it's in the present tense (or as one of my favorite professors clarifies it, "present active indicative,") which indicates Paul was referring to "ongoing action," or something that keeps on happening over and over.[71] I have a friend who likes to say it means "be being filled," although the more proper way to word it would be, "keep being filled."

So this is what it means when we say the Holy Spirit fills your soul with His active presence: You are in a state of being that's fully given-over, daily, to God's leadership, guidance, power, and kindness for the ongoing function of your Christian life. In other words, you're daily giving up control for your righteousness and letting God be God, in charge of your moment-by-moment existence. Here's how Dr. Mark Roberts insightfully describes this state in his commentary on Ephesians 5:18:

> The imperative "be filled with the Spirit" is in a passive form both in Greek and English. Filling with the Spirit is not something we can do by our own power. Rather, the passive reveals God to be the agent who fills us with his Spirit…
>
> But if God does the filling, then how might we respond to the imperative "be filled with the Spirit"? Since we cannot fill ourselves

with the Spirit through some magical formula, Paul is telling us to make ourselves available to God as vessels ready to be filled. We can worship him with openness to the Spirit. We can step out and minister in his name. The more we make ourselves available to God, the more we will be ready to be filled with his Spirit.[72]

Now, with that in mind, I need to deal with two mistaken perceptions about the filling of the Spirit in your life.

First, some will tell you that God is a fickle, passive Holy Spirit, and that He's really looking for ways to renege on His promise of presence in your life. OK, they won't say that *exactly*, but they will tell you that you alone are responsible for making God's Spirit fill your soul, that He will refuse to act unless you beg Him to act, and you back it up by being especially holy before He gets there.

For instance, I read recently a prominent Christian leader who said "The Holy Spirit…is a gentleman. He will never impose His will on us. If we refuse to engage with Him, He will be silent."[73] With all due respect to this person, whom I actually admire in many ways, that kind of thinking is a cartload of legalistic manure. It's not consistent with the biblical record, and it also places an unfair burden on the believer to accomplish the Holy Spirit's work for Him.

So let's clear things up a bit. Yes we can "quench the Holy Spirit" to some extent (which we'll talk about later in this book), but God needs no permission to act in your life. A few obvious biblical examples:

Abram was a pagan man living in a pagan land when, apparently out of nowhere, God abruptly interrupted his life and said (basically) leave everyone and everything you know, Abram, and follow Me to someplace far, far away. (See Genesis 11:27–12:6.)

Moses was an old shepherd, married to the daughter of a pagan priest, when the Holy Spirit lit up a bush with unburnt fire to get his attention. Then, without asking permission or allowing excuses, He straight-up commanded Moses to set the Israelites free—something that was actively against Moses's free will. As I recall, Moses's exact words were, *"Please send someone else!"* God didn't. (See Exodus 3:1–4:17.)

Jonah wasn't simply unconcerned about God; he was in *vigorous rebel-lion* against Him. Ignoring God's command, the prophet ran away and jumped on a ship headed to Tarshish. God's Spirit was not "a gentleman" to Jonah. He didn't respect the prophet's free will, nor did He even say, "Please reconsider, Jonah." You know what happened next: God Himself coerced the prophet into obedience by having a big fish swallow him whole and then vomit him out days later on the appropriate shore. (See Jonah 1–3.)

Similarly, the apostle Paul in the New Testament had made himself a sworn enemy of Jesus Christ. He was actively persecuting Christians, and heading to Damascus where he planned to happily arrest and torture any Jew who claimed to be friend of Christ. The Spirit of Jesus was no gentle-man to Paul either. Instead, He literally blinded the guy and made him grovel in the dust in order to impose His will on the now-famous Apostle. (See Acts 9:1–9; 22:1–22.)

John the Baptist didn't even have a fully formed brain or nervous system when God demanded his lifetime of service. He was, in fact, still an embryo in his mother's womb when he was filled with the Holy Spirit. (See Luke 1:15.) Likewise, the prophet Jeremiah was forced into service to God *before he was born*; the unformed fetus of Jeremiah had zero choice in that decision. (See Jeremiah 1:4–5.)

There are more examples, sure, but I think you get the point. So if you've been laboring under the opinion that the Holy Spirit is a gentleman who'll never impose His will in your life, go ahead and get over yourself. "The Holy Spirit does not hesitate," Madeleine L'Engle once wisely observed, "to use any method at hand to make a point to us reluctant creatures."[74] The reality is that God will do what He wants to do whether you want Him to do it or not. Better to sail with the wind than against it, my friend.

The second thing people tell me is that you must adhere to some con-stantly changing, human-prescribed list of abstentions or else God's Holy Spirit will flee from you like a demon that just heard you say "Jesus" out loud.

When I was in high school, the big thing on that list was Christian music. My friends and I had more than one album stolen from us by well-meaning youth leaders who told us that listening to Petra sing "Praise

Ye the Lord" or Farrell and Farrell's pop music retelling of Acts 16 meant that we were taking a highway to hell—and they were going to save us from it. When I was older, in Bible college, I had to sign a pledge vowing not to dance (even in my own dorm room) and not to play with cards. If I refused to sign, they said they'd revoke my admission to the school.

This kind of intoxicating Pharisaism has been popular for a while. I read recently a book praising the virtues of nineteenth century evangelist Dwight L. Moody, who supposedly proved that he was filled with the Spirit because he "[did] not need to run after the theater and the opera and the dance and the cards and the other pleasures...He gives these things up."[75] (The opera? Seriously?) In Moody's home state, the General Court of the Massachusetts Bay Colony once passed a law banning Christmas completely. The Christian Puritans there decided that celebrating Christ's birth was "a Sacrilege" and "Satanical," so for more than two decades they made it a criminal offense to exchange gifts, or even merry greetings, on December 25.[76] And, in our Legalism Hall of Fame, we mustn't forget the Christian Emperor of Rome, Theodosius I, who ended the peaceful, 1,000-year tradition of the Olympics in 394 AD because, in his view, the athletic contests were too sinful for Christians to watch.[77]

Judging from what Christians preach at me today, in addition to opera and the Olympics, Dr. Moody and Emperor Theodosius would probably want to outlaw things like all social media, cell phones, workplace diversity, school libraries, comic books, children's cartoons and toys, streaming TV services, and the internet in general as well.

I fear sometimes that our historically ingrained emphasis on self-created righteousness would lead us today to conclude that Jesus Himself was not worthy of the Holy Spirit. After all, Christ was a man who shared meals with sinners, showed compassion to prostitutes and tax collectors, attended joyful celebrations, and even drove out corruption from the Temple with righteous anger. He did *not* live up to the righteous expectations of the religious leaders of His time, nor would He pass muster among many Christians today. And yet, He alone in all of history, lived a life without sin.

Go figure.

We must be careful not to substitute our own cultural pet peeves for God's eternal values—or to assume that His Holy Spirit values our vain attempts at righteous works. Instead, we must embrace the continual filling of His Spirit within us—something that He graciously does in spite of our sin and not because of our supposed holiness—and let that ever-growing nearness to Him draw us joyfully closer to His vision for us each day.

The infilling of God's Spirit in your soul is an extraordinary, everyday-ordinary gift. It's time we began to enjoy that.

THE HOLY SPIRIT IMMERSES YOU IN HIS POWER AND LOVE

(See Matthew 3:11; 28:19; Mark 1:8; Luke 3:16; John 1:33; Acts 1:5, 7; 2:1–13; 11:16; Romans 5:5.)

"I hate waiting."

I always crack up when Inigo Montoya says that line in *The Princess Bride* movie—mostly because that's how I constantly feel!

In the film, Inigo (portrayed by Mandy Patinkin) is a master swordsman, working as a henchman for a Medieval-style crime boss. He and his cohorts have just kidnapped the princess, and are being chased by a mysterious, "Man in Black." They use a rope and a very strong giant to climb The Cliffs of Insanity(!). At the top, they cut the rope, only to discover the Man in Black is still miraculously climbing up—by hand. So Inigo is left behind to finish off the pursuer, in case he makes it to the top.

Inigo stands at the peak while the Man in Black slowly, precariously rock-climbs his way up the sheer cliff face. The swordsman grows impatient. He shouts down, "I do not suppose you could speed things up?" The Man in Black declines. Inigo paces. "I promise I will not kill you until you reach the top," Inigo says, hoping to hurry things along. "That's very comforting," the Man in Black says, "but I'm afraid you'll just have to wait." Inigo Montoya is disgusted, and he spews that now-famous, perfect line:

"I hate waiting."[78]

Reading Acts 1–2 today makes me wonder if Jesus's disciples were like Inigo and me, filled with pent-up frustration, waiting impatiently as hours, days, and weeks passed by, not even knowing exactly what was to come—only knowing that Jesus had told them to *wait*. I suspect they were more like you, though: patient, serene, calm, and not the least bit annoyed that it was taking so lonnng for anything to happen! Ahem.

Acts 1:4-5 tells us that, after His resurrection, Jesus gathered with His disciples and gave this instruction, *"Do not leave Jerusalem, but wait for the gift my Father promised, which you have heard me speak about. For John baptized with water, but in a few days you will be baptized with the Holy Spirit."* That baptism with the Holy Spirit happened dramatically on the Jewish day of Pentecost (*Shavuot*), which seems to have been at least ten full days after He commanded them to wait.[79]

There were 120 disciples in Jerusalem anticipating that baptism, including Peter and the inner circle of Jesus's followers, as well as many other unnamed disciples, and a number of women who followed Jesus, including His mother, Mary. Scripture tells us they spent their time praying, organizing, choosing someone to replace Judas (the betrayer), and… waiting. (See Acts 1:21–26.) And then, finally, history's first baptism with the Holy Spirit occurred. The ancient gospel writer, Luke, describes that event much better than I can, so I'll let his words from Acts 2:1–13 fill you in on what happened:

When the day of Pentecost came, they were all together in one place. Suddenly a sound like the blowing of a violent wind came from heaven and filled the whole house where they were sitting. They saw what seemed to be tongues of fire that separated and came to rest on each of them. All of them were filled with the Holy Spirit and began to speak in other tongues as the Spirit enabled them.

Now there were staying in Jerusalem God-fearing Jews from every nation under heaven. When they heard this sound, a crowd came together in bewilderment, because each one heard their own language being spoken. Utterly amazed, they asked: "Aren't all these who are speaking Galileans? Then how is it that each of us hears them in our native language? Parthians, Medes and Elamites; residents of Mesopotamia, Judea and Cappadocia, Pontus and Asia, Phrygia and Pamphylia, Egypt and the parts of Libya near Cyrene; visitors from Rome (both Jews and converts to Judaism); Cretans and Arabs—we hear them declaring the wonders of God in our own tongues!" Amazed and perplexed, they asked one another, "What does this mean?"

Some, however, made fun of them and said, "They have had too much wine."

I mean, that's pretty cool, right?

I think it's fascinating that Christ's promise in Acts 1:8, *"You will receive power when the Holy Spirit comes on you; and you will be my witnesses in Jerusalem, and in all Judea and Samaria, and to the ends of the earth,"* was actually fulfilled in Act 2:1–13. People from Jerusalem, Judea, Samaria, and the ends of the earth were already gathered nearby when this event occurred! And once the crowd was there, Peter gave his first great sermon, empowered by the Holy Spirit baptism. Thousands responded, turned to Jesus and became the first church—our forefathers and mothers, the beginning of our legacy.

With Acts 2 as our starting point, then, we can begin exploring more deeply this whole "baptism with the Spirit" thing—but how?

My experience has been that many people have many questions, and, most often, I have only a few answers. Still, let's try this: How about if we approach this section as an FAQ session with you and me? I'll share some "frequently asked questions" that people pose to me, and then my thoughts in answer. After that, you can decide what you think is worthwhile.

Here goes:

FAQ: WHAT DID "BAPTISM" MEAN TO THE FIRST CHRISTIANS?

In the ancient Jewish experience, baptism was most often understood as a *mikveh*—that is, a ritual bath (by immersion in water) intended as a means for religious purification.[80] This type of ceremonial washing was practiced by the high priest on certain high holidays, and by men and women according to the guidelines of everyday living in the law of Moses. Baptism was also required of Gentiles who wanted to convert to Judaism.[81] Although John's baptism wasn't exactly the same as a *mikveh*, it was derived from this custom.

In the New Testament, the Greek root word used for baptism was *baptizó*, which literally means "dip under," or more naturally, to immerse or submerge. So when we speak of any kind of baptism for the first Christians, their understanding would've been that the one baptized was fully engulfed (or overwhelmed) by the thing used for baptism. This is important to grasp because the New Testament indicates three types of baptism: (1) water, (2) the Holy Spirit, (3) fire. In every case, the idea is that the one baptized is immersed, or submerged by those things.

Baptism by water (sometimes called, "John's Baptism") is an expression of repentance and the start of a new life dedicated to God. It also came to represent (figuratively) Jesus's death, burial, and resurrection. Baptism with fire is an image of future judgment to come at the return of Christ. Baptism with the Holy Spirit (who is also associated with "wind") is an act of empowerment and endowment of prophetic ability.[82]

So when the New Testament talks about *"baptism with the Holy Spirit,"* it refers to an immersive experience in the Spirit that's observable by others, and which brings supernatural spiritual power and ability to testify about Jesus.

Two things I find interesting about this:

First, the three baptisms discussed in the New Testament represent the beginning, middle, and end of the Christian life. The first baptism (water) signifies the beginning of a new relationship with Jesus. The second baptism (Spirit) is part of the ongoing Christian experience. The third baptism (fire) is the moment of final judgment, when Christ's righteousness in us will shine as refined gold.

Second, it struck me that the images Scripture uses for baptism are correlated to three of the four elements of creation: water, wind, and fire. I was talking about this with my father-in-law (a former seminary professor) and wondered out loud why earth wasn't represented? He said, "We people were made from the earth, so earth is present at every baptism." *Hmm*. It may mean nothing that creation's four elements are represented in this way in baptism, but I thought it was at least interesting enough to mention to you here.

FAQ: HOW IS BAPTISM WITH THE SPIRIT DIFFERENT FROM RECEIVING THE SPIRIT AT THE MOMENT OF BECOMING CHRISTIAN?

Baptism with the Holy Spirit is about *power* and *testimony* of Jesus.

*"You will receive **power**,"* Jesus explained in Acts 1:8, *"when the Holy Spirit comes on you; and you will **be my witnesses**."* Some variation of this purpose plays out every time the Holy Spirit baptizes people. In this respect, baptism with the Holy Spirit is always *an event,* an elevated moment in time with a beginning, middle, and end. Because it demonstrates *observable activity of God* in a particular time and place, it falls into the category of "God's manifest presence" on display among us.

Being filled with the Spirit is similar, in that it provides God's power for daily Christian living and enables us to speak confidently about Christ to those in our circle of influence. Yet it's also a noticeably different experience, because it's a *continuous, sanctifying, invisible presence* of the Holy Spirit rather than a single definable event of God's manifest presence. This filling has a beginning (at the moment of becoming Christian), but no end; it is the steady and faithful presence of God with us to the end of our days. This is no less powerful than baptism with the Holy Spirit; it's just a different expression of that power.

FAQ: WHAT DO YOU SEE AS CHARACTERISTICS OF HOLY SPIRIT BAPTISM?

Other than supernatural empowerment and testimony of Jesus, the Bible doesn't seem to define one universally prescribed experience for baptism in the Holy Spirit. In light of that, we must be careful not to say, "It's *always* like this" or "It's *never* like that." However, here's what happened when the Holy Spirit baptized in the book of Acts:

Acts 2:1–14

+ Rushing wind (v. 2)

+ Fire (that doesn't burn) rests on people's heads (v. 3)

+ Speaking about Jesus in foreign languages (v. 4)

+ Gathering of a crowd (vv. 5–6)

+ Similarities to drunkenness (undefined) (v. 13)

+ Bold testimony about Jesus (v. 14)

Acts 4:31

+ Earthquake-style shaking

+ Bold testimony about Jesus

Acts 6:15, 7:55–56

(This *appears* to be a moment of Spirit baptism, but it's not expressly identified as that.)

+ Physical appearance changed: *"his face was like the face of an angel"* (Acts 6:15)

+ Heightened perception of the spiritual realm: *"I see heaven open…"* (Acts 7:56)

+ Bold testimony about Jesus (Acts 7:55–56)

Acts 8:14–25

+ Bold testimony about Jesus (a rebuke and call to repentance) (vv. 20–23)

+ No indication of anything else besides "they received the Holy Spirit" (v. 17)

+ This Spirit baptism did, however, have some kind of noticeable feature, because Simon the Sorcerer wanted to be able to duplicate it later (vv. 18–19)

Acts 10:44–48

+ Speaking about Jesus in foreign languages (v. 46)

+ Fervent praise to God (v. 46)

+ Water baptism (vv. 47–48)

Acts 19:1–7

+ Water baptism (v. 5)

+ Speaking about Jesus in foreign languages (v. 6)

+ Prophesying (this could also be considered "bold testimony about Jesus") (v. 6)

FAQ: IS SPEAKING IN TONGUES *THE* EVIDENCE OF HOLY SPIRIT BAPTISM?

No, of course not. The only way to believe that authentically would be to believe that Scripture is untrue. That doesn't mean I'm trying to diminish the wonderful gift of speaking in tongues, nor to suggest that I think speaking in tongues doesn't sometimes accompany baptism in the Spirit. It's just a statement of the fact that this ecstatic expression isn't something that *always* happens with baptism in the Holy Spirit. (For example, see and compare the Scriptures from Acts mentioned in the previous FAQ.)

We know that the apostle Paul spoke frequently in tongues. (See 1 Corinthians 14:18.) At the same time, he never indicated that this was a universal gift for all Christians—that doesn't seem to have ever crossed his mind. Instead he said, *"All do not speak with tongues, do they?"* (1 Corinthians 12:30 NASB). And he told the Corinthians, *"Now I wish that you all spoke in tongues…"* (1 Corinthians 14:5 NASB). There's no reason for him to wish that all spoke in tongues unless some didn't speak in tongues.

So, no, speaking in tongues is not *the* evidence for baptism in the Holy Spirit, though it can certainly be something that does accompany that experience. As they say, peanut butter and jelly definitely go together, but the absence of jelly doesn't dictate that peanut butter can't be on your sandwich.

FAQ: HAVE YOU EXPERIENCED HOLY SPIRIT BAPTISM? AND IF SO, WHAT'S IT LIKE FOR YOU?

Yes, many times. I'll tell you what typically happens with me, but please remember this has been *my* experience—not a description of a universal experience. I've found that the Holy Spirit baptizes people in somewhat different ways, unique between each person and God, as is appropriate.

Anyway, my experience is usually something like this. First, I have zero control over when and where baptism with the Spirit happens. It's always sudden and unexpected, sometimes when I'm hoping for it, other times when I wasn't even thinking about it. It typically begins with what feels like a gentle wind swirling inside my soul (not a physical wind, but something I can feel nonetheless). Pretty quickly that wind works through me until it feels like I can't contain it inside me; adrenaline begins to flow, and my body must react in some way. Usually my hands go up, sometimes I clap or just move side to side. Occasionally I'll dance, but I should tell you I'm not a great dancer, so I've had to get over the idea that anybody besides God might be watching!

My intellectual focus becomes absorbed by Jesus, so much so that other worries and concerns seem to fade away, at least for the moment. I think in that way it's like what business folks call "flow," where all distractions seem to disappear. Time becomes irrelevant, and my soul feels a certain amount of peace and joy. I almost always weep, not because I'm sad, but I think because it's such a relief to feel the nearness of God so clearly to me in those moments. As you know, this life is a hard thing. It's comforting to me when He draws noticeably near.

At some point, my mouth opens, not because it's being forced to do so but because it feels like if I don't, then the rocks are going to have to cry out in praise of Jesus. And really, why would I let a rock steal that opportunity from me? Often I sing; sometimes I shout, sometimes I whisper. Sometimes I can only say the name "Jesus" repeatedly and revel in the warmth and security that name brings. In this moment I usually feel heightened awareness of spiritual activity and circumstance, and often find I have a message to share. That can be a word of encouragement for someone near to me, specific prayers to pray for others, or words to scribble down and share in a book or article. I can't count how many times I've felt compelled to sit down to write after experiencing a baptism in the Holy Spirit—it's *a lot.*

Interestingly enough, I've never been given the gift of speaking in tongues, though I'm convinced of the validity and use of that gift among Christians today. I used to complain to God about that sometimes, until one day I seemed to hear Him speak into my soul, saying, "Have I not given you enough of Me already?" After that, I stopped worrying about whether I spoke in tongues. God has definitely been generous with His Spirit in me.

All right, again, that's generally been my experience. Remember it doesn't have to describe yours exactly. Your baptism with the Holy Spirit will be something God does uniquely in you, and it will be a moment of *His power and testimony* being elevated in your life.

FAQ: HOW CAN I RECEIVE HOLY SPIRIT BAPTISM?

Stop worrying about it. All four gospel writers taught that Jesus *exclusively* is the one who baptizes with the Holy Spirit (see Matthew 3:11, Mark 1:8, Luke 3:16, John 1:33); it's not something you can control. In fact, when

Simon the Sorcerer tried to buy the power to baptize with the Spirit, it was a disaster. (See Acts 8:14–23). So my advice is this: Pursue Jesus with all your heart, soul, and mind; and love your neighbor as yourself. Then let Him worry about when, where, and how often He chooses to baptize you with His Spirit.

All right, I know there are more questions than these, but this will have to do for today. Now, I'd like to ask you to take a little time to think about, and pray about, what we've talked about in this chapter, before we launch into part 2 of this book.

I promise to do the same.

FOR FURTHER REFLECTION AND SMALL GROUP DISCUSSION:

1. Do you agree with the idea that Holy Spirit baptism is "an event" while being filled with the Holy Spirit is a "continual indwelling"? Why or why not?

2. What did you find most helpful in this chapter? How will that influence what you do tomorrow?

3. Who would you like to tell about what you've discovered so far? How will you do that?

PART 2

WHAT THE HOLY SPIRIT DOES *WITH* YOU

EXPLORING THE INVISIBLE THINGS THE HOLY SPIRIT DOES IN YOU,
BUT WITH YOUR COOPERATION.

FIVE

THE HOLY SPIRIT LIVES YOUR DAILY FAITH

Christianity is not a solo sport—you are not alone in faith. The
Holy Spirit actively cooperates to help you: Think rightly; act
rightly; and serve rightly—all by the Spirit.

Have you ever noticed that Jesus didn't *actually* feed the 5,000?

This event was recorded for history in the Gospels (Matthew 14:13–
21; Mark 6:30–44; Luke 9:10–17; John 6:1–14), and here's what happened: John the Baptist had been cruelly murdered by the wicked King
Herod. When Jesus heard about that, He took His disciples by boat to
a *"solitary place,"* presumably so they could mourn privately. Crowds of
people followed them anyway, and when they landed there were thousands
waiting. Jesus had compassion on them, healed their sick, and taught about
the kingdom of heaven all day long.

Late in the day, everyone was hungry—but there was no food. The
crowd contained at least 5,000 men, plus women and children. Modern
estimates say about 20,000 people were there.[83] Then Jesus looked out over
all the people (imagine a rock concert or sporting event packed with fans)
and gave His disciples this *impossible* command:

"You give them something to eat" (Matthew 14:16).

God-in-bones was asking too much.

How were the disciples supposed to give away something they didn't
have? Philip, at least, had the guts to tell Christ that He was being

unreasonable. *"It would take more than half a year's wages,"* he said, *"to buy enough bread for each one to have a bite!"* (John 6:7). Yet Jesus was undeterred.

"How many loaves do you have?" He asked. *"Go and see"* (Mark 6:38).

So they checked around, and pretty soon Andrew dragged over a little kid. *"Here is a boy with five small barley loaves and two small fish,"* he reported, *"but how far will they go among so many?"* (John 6:9).

Now, watch what happened next.

Jesus said a short prayer and broke the loaves in half. Then He completely checked out. He did nothing more but give the bread and fish to His disciples. They in turn trudged it out into the massive crowd, walking literal miles back and forth to give everyone something to eat.

So, here's what we've got:

A boy gives away his lunch. The disciples do the actual, sweaty, tiring task of logistically feeding 20,000 people. And what does Jesus do? Not much, really. Says a prayer, and then He sits around and watches while everybody else does the work. At least that's the empirical perspective, looking at the practical visual evidence alone.

Right?

We-ell...there is something more going on here.

You see it, I see it, and those 20,000 people (plus Jesus's disciples) saw it too.

The impossible became possible. The unreasonable demand became an easily doable task. Five small loaves of bread and two fish—enough food for *one* meal for *one* boy—became thousands upon thousands of meals eaten by the mouths of many. And there was so much food at the impromptu banquet that it filled a dozen basketfuls with leftovers!

That's why—even though we know that Jesus didn't actually hand food to anyone in the crowd—we say with absolute certainty that *"Jesus fed the 5,000."* If He's not involved, everyone goes home hungry. No, He didn't lift a finger in the actual work of waiting tables (so to speak)—but *He alone* did the miracle that made the moment possible. The disciples simply cooperated with His power and direction. And you know the rest.

Now, when it comes to your daily Christian life, why would you assume it'd be any different?

Here's what we've got: Jesus has given us an impossible command, found in Matthew 5:48, *"Be perfect, therefore, as your heavenly Father is perfect."*

Does He really expect us to be completely sinless, entirely pure in all thought and every action, living out lifestyles of total unconditional love toward *everybody*, every second of every minute of every hour of every day, for the rest of our lives? Apparently so. But we're *incapable* of doing that! He knows this, better than you or I know it. Christ *knows* He's given an unreasonable demand, knows that He's insisting on an unattainable standard. He might as well have commanded that we jump to the moon in a single bound, and make tea and crumpets for Mary Poppins on our way up.

Yet He is undeterred.

Why?

Because He also knows that, sure, we'll participate in the work. We'll get up each morning and schlep through each day doing our best to achieve His command...But *He alone* will do the miracle that makes it possible for us to increasingly live the perfection He requires. Our responsibility is simply to cooperate with His power that's already at work within us.

This is what it means when I say to you, unequivocally, that God's Holy Spirit works with you to live out your daily faith.

Let's discover more about this, now.

THE HOLY SPIRIT HELPS YOU THINK RIGHTLY

(See Romans 8:5; 8:6; 1 Corinthians 2:15–16; Galatians 5:17–18; Hebrews 9:14.)

Now, I want to ask you to do this one thing:

Don't think about puppies.

No puppies at all, please. No cute, little, round puppies or tail-wagging, fuzzy puppies or happy puppies climbing all over each other as they play. Particularly avoid thinking about dalmatian puppies, with their adorable black spots and bouncy, playful attitudes.

Not even one dalmatian puppy, OK?

Or 101 dalmatians, or any number of dalmatians in between.

Just do me this favor: *Don't think about puppies.*

OK…

I don't have to be a mind reader to know that you failed miserably at my request. The moment I mentioned "puppies," some version of an image of them flashed reflexively into your head—your mind was simply working to understand the text you were reading. The more I repeated that word, and described them, the more your attention was focused on those cute baby doggies. When your mind read "dalmatian," you couldn't stop it from thinking of adorable, black-and-white spotted pups—and maybe even the classic Disney movie, *101 Dalmatians.* Don't deny it, you know it's true. When you read, "Don't think about puppies," you couldn't do anything *but* think about puppies. It was an involuntary, predictable mental response.

You shouldn't feel too bad about that. It's just neuroscience, and I took advantage of the way your brain manages attentiveness. Honestly, you had no chance (sorry!). But I did this little experiment to make a point: Your thoughts, to a large extent, are not easy to control. You can't just decide not to think about something, or to always think about something else. Thoughts are centered in your physical brain, which is governed by electrical synapses that sort through your past experiences and present stimuli to create that ongoing, silent narrator inside your head—even the voice you "hear" as you read these words right now.[84]

However, your human brain also does some things that we don't see in the brains of other species, like mice or cats or animals in general—and that can't be attributed to simple physical function. Language, for instance, moral reasoning, philosophy, and religion. That has led scientists to differentiate between your "brain" (the physical functioning of your thinking) and the "mind" (your consciousness/self-awareness, language, moral judgments/conscience, perceptions of reality, and the soul).[85]

I find it interesting, then, that the Bible never once mentions the human brain, but speaks about the human mind and the human conscience close to two hundred times. More importantly, Scripture teaches us that *God's*

Holy Spirit is active in helping us direct the attention of our minds toward thoughts that are moral, healthy, good, and loving. Listen:

Those who live according to the flesh have their minds set on what the flesh desires; but those who live in accordance with the Spirit have their minds set on what the Spirit desires. (Romans 8:5)

The mind governed by the flesh is death, but the mind governed by the Spirit is life and peace. (Romans 8:6)

For the flesh desires what is contrary to the Spirit, and the Spirit what is contrary to the flesh. They are in conflict with each other, so that you are not to do whatever you want. But if you are led by the Spirit, you are not under the law. (Galatians 5:17–18)

How much more, then, will the blood of Christ, who through the eternal Spirit offered himself unblemished to God, cleanse our consciences from acts that lead to death, so that we may serve the living God! (Hebrews 9:14)

I'm particularly attracted to that phrase in Romans 8:6, "*the mind governed by the Spirit,*" because it tells me two things.

First, the Holy Spirit doesn't act as a dictator on my mind, but offers to govern it, meaning I am to cooperate with His leadership as the one who is governed. He acts in partnership with my will to lead my thoughts toward His life and peace. His "government" requires my good "citizenship" for me to gain the best benefit.

Second, my thinking can only be governed by the Spirit because the Spirit Himself is an ever-present companion in my mind. Here's how Paul described it in 1 Corinthians 2:15–16:

"The person with the Spirit makes judgments about all things, but such a person is not subject to merely human judgments, for, 'Who has known the mind of the Lord so as to instruct him?' But we have the mind of Christ."

This *"mind of Christ,"* then, makes it possible for us to avoid *"merely human judgments"* and to instead choose more easily the healthy, holy, loving lifestyle that honors God and others. How does the Spirit accomplish that in our thinking? Surprisingly, it's most often simply a matter of *attention*. That which we attend to mentally, we do physically. In other words, *you are what you think about.*

Remember when I told you not to think about puppies? That was a trivial example of how attention influences thinking, which then dictates attitude and action. All I had to do to get you thinking about dalmatian puppies was to draw your attention in that direction, and then you took care of the rest.

Magicians are masters of controlling your attention in this way, and thereby governing what you think about. World-famous entertainer David Copperfield reveals, "We've figured out that, with some skill and misdirection, we can get an audience to *focus its attention* in the right place and at the right time so that we can create the illusion of magic. In fact, these illusions are created not on the stage, but in the brain."[86] This is the power of attention direction. It can actually define reality for you and me.

Neuroscientists tell us there are three types of human attention: *overt, covert,* and *joint.*

Overt attention is when you're thinking about what you're doing, such as watching a TV show or aiming at a target with a bow and arrow.

Covert attention is when you're doing one thing but thinking about another. For example, when Patrick Mahomes throws a no-look pass, he's looking toward the right side of the football field but thinking about the open receiver in his peripheral vision on the left side of the field.

Joint attention is what I did to you earlier, when one person draws another person's attention toward a mutually shared object.[87] (Puppies, puppies, puppies!) That can be as obvious as pointing toward that object, or as subtle as raised eyebrows or a whispered cue. Curiously, joint attention can be either overt or covert—it's not limited to either one.

Now listen to this:

*"Those who live in accordance with the Spirit **have their minds set on what the Spirit desires**,"* Paul told us, and what he's talking about here is

joint attention that's expressed in both overt and covert ways. Think of it as spiritual neuroscience, almost as if the Holy Spirit is whispering into your soul, "Hey, look over here. That's the better choice, right?"

What a relief that is! No longer do we have to depend on our own limited intelligence or insubstantial attention spans to discern by ourselves the best ways to live and love and follow Christ. We can instead get into the habit of turning our attention to the governance of God's Spirit in our lives—teaching our minds to follow where He leads instead of trying to blaze a new trail toward righteousness every time we get up in the morning. In this way we experience firsthand the promise of Romans 12:2, *"Be transformed by the renewing of your mind. Then you will be able to test and approve what God's will is—his good, pleasing and perfect will."*

Are you starting to see where I'm going with this?

When you participate with God's attention-directing work that's always active inside your mind, *Christ's Holy Spirit will help you to think rightly* about the way you live your Christian life. With His power to guide, we can actually accomplish what Philippians 4:8 encourages us to do, *"Finally, brothers and sisters, whatever is true, whatever is noble, whatever is right, whatever is pure, whatever is lovely, whatever is admirable—if anything is excellent or praiseworthy—think about such things."*

This raises an important question: How can you and I better participate with Jesus in this attention-focusing way? Here are a few suggestions from my own life and from my friends.

First, get into the habit of reading the Bible regularly. I recommend spending time in the Book every day. Some people prefer memorizing, but I've never been able to do that, so I just read and re-read until I'm familiar with what's in the Bible and, generally speaking, where to find it.[88] Because we know that thinking is a combination of experience and stimuli, making Scripture a habitual (daily) activity means there's more in your "experience bank" for God's Spirit to bring to mind. In that way you're literally teaching yourself to think the thoughts of God, as expressed in His Scripture.

I've found that when the Holy Spirit is turning attention to what helps us to live well and love better, He'll often bring to mind passages and stories that have been generously given to us in the Bible.

Second, consider using desire to overcome desire. Hey, we're all tempted by many things, many times, all day long. But typically, there are just a few persistent temptations that lead to a ruined life. The top three tend to be sexual temptation, the temptation for power, and the temptation for greed. If you're like me, you might also add the temptation to act with pride and arrogance to that list.

The pull on those kinds of recurring sins can be very strong and, honestly, you won't always be able to resist if you're depending on your own strength of will to do it. Human nature will always pursue what the human person desires; you can't simply "just say no" and decide not to sin over and over again. So here's something I've found to be helpful in this regard:

With God's help, I try to use "higher desires" to overcome base desires.

First, I identify that persistent sin that repeatedly trips me up in my Christian life. Then I make a list of five or six things I desire more than I desire that sin. For instance, when my wife was living, I was tempted on a few occasions by pretty women who made it clear that they were interested in a sexual fling with me. But on my list of things I desired more than having an affair were items like:

+ frequent, happy sex with my wife;

+ my own self-respect;

+ never making my son feel ashamed of me,

+ an honest, transparent life;

+ and so on.

So when a sexual temptation presented itself, I'd ask the Holy Spirit to point my attention away from the woman in front of me and toward the things I desired more than that temptation. After that, it was always pretty easy to think, *Eh, I can get better than this at home,* and walk away. Then I'd make love to my wife that night and remember again why I was the luckiest man in the world. Does that make sense?

So, I'd suggest that you try making a list of your "higher desires" in life. Then, when you face that inevitable, persistent temptation, ask the Holy Spirit to govern your attention, drawing your thoughts away from that temptation and toward the things that really matter to you. In this way, you can partner with the Spirit to use your higher desires as motivation to overcome your base desires and choose rightly in a temptation situation.

Third, try to get into the habit of praying at all times. Just keep a running conversation with God going in your head. "What do You think I should eat for lunch, God?" And, "This guy is really annoying me right now, Jesus. What would You suggest I do about it?" Because I've had a history of chronic bowel disease, I've even gotten into the habit of thinking "Thank You, Jesus!" every time I sit on the toilet. (You can make that one optional, I guess, but if you really knew what a miracle your digestive system is, you might decide to join me in those kinds of potty praises!)

There are more things you can do, but I'm guessing you can come up with new ideas of your own. The important thing to remember is that, when you willingly cooperate with Him, the Holy Spirit will use joint-attention opportunities to help you think rightly in your day-to-day Christian experience. I guarantee you're going to like that.

THE HOLY SPIRIT HELPS YOU ACT RIGHTLY

(See Romans 8:4; Galatians 5:16; 5:25; 6:1; 6:8.)

I was driving home from the library recently when I pulled up to a stop sign. Two other cars had already stopped, and after a moment, I realized no one else was moving. I soon saw why.

In the middle of the crosswalk, a frail, elderly homeless man had fallen and was struggling to pull himself up by his walker. But no matter how hard he tried, he simply wasn't strong enough to stand by himself.

I sat there a moment and then thought, "I should go help that man."

Before I could move, though, a car passing by on the cross street screeched to a halt. Two other men leaped out, leaving their doors swinging open. They came *running* into the crosswalk to help the homeless man. They lifted him gently, one on each side, then walked him to a nearby bus bench, where he could sit down to recover. Only when they were done did this thought cross my mind:

"Well, crud. Why wasn't I the one who *ran* toward the opportunity to help a person in obvious need?"

I mean, I saw the need, and I was willing to help. I actually wanted to help. But the transition time between my thought and action took too long, so I missed my chance to add a small act of kindness into my world. Guess Mikey still needs a lot of work. *Sigh.*

The next day, I mentioned this incident (OK, whined about it) to a friend of mine over lunch, and he said something important. "Mike," John said, "those guys were most likely off-duty first responders. Firefighters, police, EMTs, or something. They're trained to help—it's just a habit ingrained in who they are by now. That's why they could react more quickly than you."

Now, I don't know if they were truly off-duty firefighters, but John raised an idea I hadn't considered before: helping can become a natural habit, ingrained in who we are as people. That makes even more sense when I think about how the Holy Spirit helps us to act rightly each day— so much so that I think that's what God's doing when He's training us for righteous behavior.

Richard Shotten is a behavioral science expert in Britain. He's known for marketing and advertising insight, not so much for theology—but I think he's onto something spiritual when he talks about a process he calls "The Choice Factory." His basic premise is that choices prompt action, and that everyday decision-making is overwhelmingly influenced by biases already set within each of us. With that in mind, he cites a Duke University study that revealed, "Nearly half of behavior is habitual...Across a range of areas from exercising to travelling, from eating to socializing, a full 45% of behaviors [are] habitual—the same decisions being made at the same time and place without full conscious thought."[89]

In other words, Shotton's research reveals that we're mentally prone to do what we've always done, to choose what we've always chosen, to live the familiar rather than the unknown. If you don't believe it, then ask yourself this question: When was the last time I changed toilet paper brands? Or took a different route to work?

The great "Aha!" moment for me from the Duke study was the realization that *God's Holy Spirit is a habit-maker* in our souls.

It's by the Spirit that we first learn, and then can repeat, the choices that prompt actions of holiness, hope, and love. As these choices and actions become more frequent, by God's grace, they also become habitual. It becomes easier to quickly answer God's call to righteousness because righteousness becomes what we've always done, a choice that we're used to making, a familiar lifestyle rather than something new and unknown. We don't even have to think about it anymore—we just *act rightly* because that's the habit our Holy Spirit has built within us, and so it's what we've grown accustomed to doing.

Scripture calls this habit-forming experience "living by the Spirit" (see Romans 8:4; Galatians 5:25; 6:1), "walking by the Spirit" or "keeping in step with the Spirit" (see Galatians 5:16; 5:25), and "sowing to please the Spirit" (see Galatians 6:8). I think my favorite of those biblical images is the one in Galatians 5:25, where Paul encourages, "*Let us keep in step with the Spirit.*" It reminds me of a dancer leading a partner in a way that creates beauty through movement.

I think I mentioned earlier that I'm not a great dancer. Well, that's an understatement. I've actually been known to frighten small animals with my dancing! (But, as my wife used to say, what I lack in skill I make up with enthusiasm.) Despite my own insufficiencies, I'm mesmerized by truly talented dancers on a stage. This past Christmas, for instance, I went to see my granddaughter perform in a professional ballet production of *The Nutcracker*. There was a point where the entire stage was filled with dancers twirling and leaping and moving in such captivating symmetry that it brought tears to my eyes.

This, then, is how I picture the idea of keeping in step with the Spirit: Following His example, doing what He does, letting Him lead the movement while I stay in symmetry with Him nearby. And by working together with Him, I get to see Him create something beautiful in my life.

"*Whatever the Father does,*" Jesus said of Himself in John 5:19, "*the Son also does.*" Likewise, what we see the Holy Spirit doing, we also can do. This is how we live out lives of meaning and righteousness. We fixate on Him and joyfully articulate His movement in the whole of our being and behavior. This is defined by motion, by activity, and kinesthesis—by things *happening* as an expression of God in our lives. The ancient Romans had a common saying that's helpful when we think about this: *Facta non verba,* which is Latin for "Deeds, not words."[90] That's reminiscent of the brother of Jesus when he said, *"Faith by itself, if it is not accompanied by action, is dead"* (James 2:17). We don't just talk about symmetry with God's Spirit, we get to live it in breathtaking, heart-pumping ways each day.

Now, since we're talking about behavior here—*acting rightly*—we must take a moment to distinguish between behavior modification as a means to earn righteousness, and behavior imitation as a response to righteousness.

It's popular to assume that the road to God's approval runs through your own self-discipline. That is, you act right first (deeds), and then God loves and blesses you for it (faith). This is a persistent theme that extends from the days of the Pharisees in Jesus's time into our own Bible studies and church sermons today. Without diminishing the biblical call for us to be people who pursue God's standards, I want you to clearly understand that this kind of deeds-first legalism is a foolishly backward way to try to live your Christian life.

The apostle Paul dealt with a significant threat of legalism in his day. It was personified by "Judaizers" who taught that one couldn't become Christian without first becoming a Jew. Specifically, they insisted that all Christian men had to be circumcised to earn Christ's free gift of salvation. Paul's reaction to those Christian leaders was *not* polite. In his letter to the church at Philippi, he called these legalists *"dogs,"* (i.e. "dirty, flea-infested, disease-ridden scavengers")[91] *"evildoers,"* and *"mutilators"* (Philippians 3:2). So if you think I'm being rough on the idea of a deeds-first Christianity, remember that Paul was much more profane about it!

The fact of the matter is:

We do not act to earn; we respond because we've already received.

Gratitude is the motivation for all Christian action. *"Give thanks in all circumstances,"* Paul directed in 1 Thessalonians 5:18. Additionally, John clarified the way things work when he said, *"We love because he first loved us"* (1 John 4:19).

Because God has already loved and blessed, our natural response is gratitude (*"give thanks"*) which motivates us to treat others the way Christ has already treated us (*"because he first loved us."*) If we mix up that understanding, reordering the process so that our actions take primacy over our gratitude (for instance, "We must be pure before the Holy Spirit will bless"), we crudely push God's Spirit into the backseat of the Christian life. Then we spend our days in grudging obedience rather than in joyful partnership with God. That's when *"all our righteous acts are like filthy rags"* (Isaiah 64:6) and all our so-called pure and holy deeds are worth nothing more than *"dung"* (Philippians 3:8 KJVER) in God's eternal economy.

Christian history has shown what happens when we take that backward approach to Spirit-life—and it's neither pretty, nor "Christian." People starve themselves. They force themselves into isolation—literally living in caves in the desert to supposedly avoid sin. They spend decades living atop small pillars several stories high, never coming down for food, and flinging their excrement toward the people below because there's no room for it in their "holy" place up high. They castrate themselves. They wear "hair shirts" intended to scrape festering sores into the skin, supposedly as a reminder of sin. They wear painful "pelvic chains" (chastity belts) to physically prevent them from sexual activity. They live voluntarily in prison cells (again, supposedly to prevent sin). They start wars. They drink bowls of pus.[92] I could tell you more stories, of bloody flagellation and extreme self-deprivation, of torture and war and cruelty and atrocity... but I'm too grossed out about that whole pus-bowl-situation to keep this paragraph going.

My point is this:

We do not act to earn; we respond because we've already received.

This is how living in the Spirit, walking by the Spirit, and keeping in step with the Spirit work in you. Don't let your own guilt and need for self-salvation ever let you forget that truth. Instead, lean into the gift of God's habit-forming Spirit at work in you. Let that be the thing that leads you toward the choices that help you act rightly today.

THE HOLY SPIRIT HELPS YOU SERVE RIGHTLY

(See Romans 7:6; Philippians 3:3.)

When we talk about *acting rightly* by the Spirit, the idea of *serving rightly* bears special mention—even though, really, it's part and parcel of acting rightly. But service is such a key element of the Christian life, I thought you wouldn't mind if we explored that a little more deeply in this final section.

"By dying to what once bound us, we have been released from the law so that we serve in the new way of the Spirit, and not in the old way of the written code," Paul wrote in Romans 7:6. And to the church at Philippi he reminded, *"We...serve God by his Spirit...*[we] *boast in Christ Jesus, and... put no confidence in the flesh"* (Philippians 3:3).

One thing I find thought-provoking about these two Bible verses is that the word the NIV translates as *"serve"* is different in each Scripture. In Romans 7:6, it's from the Greek root, *douleuó*, and was used exclusively of slaves, as in, "having all personal ownership-rights assigned to the owner." Philippians 3:3, on the other hand, uses the Greek root, *latreuó*, which most often referred to a free man hired to do a work—and which could carry a connotation of worship, as in, hired to perform service to a god. (In fact, some modern translations gloss over the literal meaning of *latreuó* and render it as "worship" instead.)

Whether we serve God as free persons or slaves, Paul seems to be saying, *all of our service is accomplished by the Holy Spirit* acting out in our lives. So *"we serve God by his Spirit"* and *"we serve in the new way of the Spirit"*—but the power to serve always comes from the Spirit.

And what does that kind of supernatural service look like? I see two scriptural examples that inform my perception. The first is found in John 13:1–17.

It's the Last Supper, the night before Jesus is crucified. After the meal, Christ does the unthinkable. He gets up, puts a dirty towel around His waist, and commences to washing His disciples' unpretty feet. And yes, He washes Judas the betrayer's feet too. When He's done, He sits back down and says, *"Since I, your Lord and Teacher, have washed your feet, you ought to wash each other's feet. I have given you an example to follow. Do as I have done to you"* (John 13:14–15 NLT).

He was speaking figuratively, of course, commanding them to serve others as if they were the lowliest of slaves—the foot-washers. No ego or pride allowed.

In that time and place, Jesus's request would've been hard to swallow. Not only was the foot-washer a slave, but he or she was a *debased* slave. In fact, in a Jewish household, only a gentile slave would be given that job—Hebrew slaves were considered too good for something so degrading.[93] Roman law also stipulated that any free person *acting* like a slave could legally be *made* a slave and barred from claiming his freedom.[94] That means when Jesus told His disciples to do as He'd done, He was telling them not only to swallow their pride, but also to risk their freedom to serve like He did.

I see a second example of supernatural Christian service *"in the new way of the Spirit"* in Acts 3:1–10.

It's after Christ's resurrection, and after the Holy Spirit's eventful appearance on the day of Pentecost. Peter and John are walking into the temple in the afternoon when they see a lame man begging for money. Peter pauses to take a look, then says, *"Silver or gold I do not have, but what I do have I give you. In the name of Jesus Christ of Nazareth, walk"* (Acts 3:6). *"Instantly the man's feet and ankles became strong. He jumped to his feet and began to walk"* (vv. 7–8).

I love this, and I'm so glad that Luke included it in his historical account of the disciples after Christ. It reminds me of something important about service: All God expects you to give is what you have—what He's already given to you. You don't need money, fame, or a ton of social media followers. All you need is a willingness to give what God has already placed in your care.

So, I think these two things are what it means to participate in supernatural service, empowered by the Holy Spirit. First, to rely on Him for strength to make yourself humble, and second, to rely on Him to provide the kind of service you will freely give.

One last story, and then we'll be done with this topic.

A few years ago, I briefly took on the role of assistant manager at a retail operation. It didn't pay much, but I liked the work, enjoyed the people, and found it helped to get my mind off my everyday troubles. Then, one day, my manager unexpectedly quit.

I was passed over for the promotion, and they hired someone else. He was fine—but then he also quit after only a month or so. I was passed over again, and this time they hired a new manager without any retail experience. The first thing she wanted to do when she came in was to impress on me that *she* was the boss, and I definitely was *not*.

On her first day, she ordered me to clean the bathroom. I think her actual words were, "Deep clean that disgusting bathroom, right now." My first instinct was to tell her to stuff her head in the toilet and use that to clean it herself, because it wasn't in my job description. But before I could pop off, I felt the Holy Spirit whispering inside my soul. "Don't fight this battle," He seemed to say. "Come on, I'll help you." So I got out the cleaning supplies and started scrubbing that disgusting toilet. I was annoyed at first, but pretty soon felt at peace with my situation, and almost (*almost*) enjoyed seeing the results of my work.

Because the new manager didn't trust me (I was just a lazy foreigner to her), she insisted that I leave the door to the bathroom open while I cleaned, so she could watch me work, which she did. I spent a good half hour in there, cleaning up the muck, shining the porcelain, and not throwing up even one time. Afterward, I went back to doing my real job.

About four hours later, the new manager started scolding me about the bathroom, demanding to know why I hadn't cleaned it yet. I was dumbfounded; she had *watched* me clean it. So I opened the bathroom door to remind her. She didn't apologize. She just sniffed, said, "Oh, right," and walked away.

To tell the truth, I didn't last much longer in the job after that. But no matter what demeaning task she gave me over the next month, I just did it—something so out of my natural personality that it surprised even me. No matter how unfairly she treated me or insulted me—she once made me *literally* go stand in a corner for fifteen minutes because she didn't want me to be near where she was working—I found I could just smile and refuse to retaliate. Believe me, this wasn't because I am such a polite, non-offensive guy (ahem, no comments from the gallery, please!). But I had supernatural help from the Holy Spirit, who guided me into *serving rightly*, even in a difficult situation.

On my last day, before I left, the manager cornered me again. I expected her to chew me out, just for old times' sake. Instead, she said, "I've been watching you, and I have to admit that you've done a good job. You've made this a better place with your ideas and hard work. So I just want to say thank you." Then she walked away, and I've never seen her again.

My point with this story is not that, "Hey, I won her over," or that she was a total wad of a boss, and I was supposedly some great example of service. It's that I didn't have to serve on my own, in my own strength, by the grit of my will and the grumble in my grinchy heart.

Instead, *God deliberately partnered with me so that I could serve in the new way of the Spirit.* It was an attitude adjustment as much as a task ability. It just didn't matter that my boss and I couldn't get along, or that she was demeaning and mildly racist toward me; what mattered is that Jesus helped me to serve her as if I were serving Him anyway. That, for me, was close to a miracle—but it should be the norm of our everyday Christian lives. Why? Because *this is the kind of thing the Holy Spirit does,* day in, day out, and beyond. So I'll say it one last time:

The Holy Spirit helps you serve rightly.

Maybe you and I should try to remember that.

How would I react, I wonder
If You [Lord] pointed to a basin of water
And asked me to wash the calloused feet
Of a bent and wrinkled old woman
Day after day
Month after month
In a room where nobody saw
And nobody knew.
—Ruth Harms Caulkin[95]

FOR FURTHER REFLECTION AND SMALL GROUP DISCUSSION:

1. Based on what you read in this chapter, what do you think it means for the Holy Spirit to live your daily faith?

2. The author says that God's Holy Spirit is a habit-maker in our souls. Do you have any evidence from your own life to back up that claim? Describe it.

3. Knowing what you know now, how would you react if the Lord pointed to a basin of water and asked you to wash the calloused feet of a bent and wrinkled old woman, day after day, month after month, in a room where nobody saw, and nobody knew?

SIX

THE HOLY SPIRIT ENERGIZES YOUR PASSION IN WORSHIP, SONG, AND PRAYER

When your heart longs for God, the Holy Spirit ensures you find
Him. He energizes your pursuit of Christ through:
Activating and facilitating your worship experience;
making music that resonates in your soul; and offering
unobstructed prayers on your behalf.

Richard Sherman just needed to take a walk.

The seventeen-year-old was stressed, depressed, and worried. His older brother, Robert, was back from service in World War II, and now both were headed to their first year of college together. Bob knew exactly what he wanted to do; he would major in literature and get on with a life of purpose. Richard, though, felt lost. He knew he had to choose a major soon, but what would it be? Finally, he just went outside to get some fresh air.

"As I walked, I was hearing music," he reported later. But he couldn't locate the source. He kept walking, trying to figure out where that music was coming from. Then, he says: "I realized it was coming from my own head." It was a surreal moment, but unmistakable. Richard's mind was creating music that only he could hear.

"I darted back to the apartment," he said, "where we had a little piano, and started picking it out on the piano, this feeling I had. I'd never done that before. Never."

The boys' father heard the commotion and came to see what was going on. "What are you doing here? What is this?" he said.

"This is something I felt," Richard told his dad. "I had to say it. This is what I feel."

His father listened a moment, then said, "You're going to be a music major." And suddenly Richard knew that was right. He'd found his purpose, his passion—and that changed everything.[96]

Richard Sherman (along with his brother, Robert) went on to great acclaim as a songwriter and lyricist working for Walt Disney himself. He and Bob created some of the most memorable Disney soundtracks of the twentieth century, including *Mary Poppins*, *The Jungle Book*, *The Aristocats*, and the now-classic earworm song at Disneyland, "It's a Small World (After All)."

You may not be destined for melodic Disney glory like Richard Sherman, but you can discover inside of you a passion for God that gives great purpose to your life. It's something the Holy Spirit works within the heart of every believer: *He energizes your desire and ability to express yourself to God* in worship, song, and prayer. In other words, with Christ's help, "You're going to be a worship major"—and that's going to change everything for you.

THE HOLY SPIRIT ACTIVATES AND FACILITATES YOUR WORSHIP EXPERIENCE

(See John 4:23; 4:24; 1 Corinthians 14:16.)

First of all, you must understand that you were made to worship.

Like it or not, we're all created to worship. Something within us wants to—no, *needs* to—lift up, admire, praise, and follow a power greater than us. My friend, Ron, brought this home for me once during an after-dinner conversation many years ago. Citing a performance he'd attended featuring a favorite rock band of his, Ronny suggested that next time I went to a concert or a sporting event that I should watch the crowd instead of the show. So I did. Know what I saw?

People raising their hands in exultation. Joyful shouts and singing. Dancing. Hand-clapping. Hugging, laughing, crying, trembling, and praising. All the things Ron told me I'd find. How did he know?

Because all of those actions are, in one way or another, expressions of worship. We do them naturally—not necessarily because we want to worship a rock star or an athlete, but because they spring from humanity's common need to reach toward something greater than ourselves. Because we *need* to worship, and unless we direct that worship to our eternal God, we can easily be distracted into acting out a pseudo-worship of other, temporary things.

So, how do we worship God authentically, meaningfully, in ways that fulfill the universal craving within us? Jesus gave us the first understanding of that during a conversation with a sinful Samaritan woman at a well.

"God is Spirit," He said, *"and his worshipers must worship in the Spirit and in truth"* (John 4:24). Paul also shed light on this in 1 Corinthians 14:16. He mentioned it almost as a throwaway statement, during a larger discussion about speaking in tongues, as if, *of course*, everyone knew this already: *"When you are praising God in the Spirit..."*

The thing that jumps out to me in both these Scriptures is the repeated phrase, *"in the Spirit."* Jesus even goes so far as to say that worship of God must be *en Pneumati*, that is, in the Spirit. God's Holy Spirit is *not* an optional component of authentic worship; He is the sole activator and facilitator of that experience.

Remember when we talked about *en Pneumati* in chapter 4? *"In the Spirit"* is a term that references being filled with God's Spirit. It's the continual indwelling of God within an individual person in a way that's an ongoing process, experienced on a regular basis, includes heightened awareness of the nearness of God, empowers heightened spiritual authority, and infuses heightened desire and ability to pursue authentic, daily Christian living.

Do you notice that this worship *en Pneumati* isn't simply a weekly moment of singing a few choruses at church and then being done? Far from it. When I tell you that God activates and facilitates your worship experience, I mean the totality of it that, yes, includes corporate singing, but also encompasses the whole of your life. Paul defined it this way:

> *Therefore, I urge you, brothers and sisters, in view of God's mercy, to offer your bodies as a living sacrifice, holy and pleasing to God—this is your true and proper worship.* (Romans 12:1)

I like the way Pastor Costi Hinn describes it: "Worship is a lifestyle. It is not merely music. We must stop thinking of worship as the moment when the band plays and the lights go out. Worship is praying, preaching, singing, serving, giving, receiving, fellowshipping, counseling, baptizing, remembering, loving, and more. We are to live for the glory of God. We are worshippers in every moment of every single day."[97] Or as the poet E. E. Cummings once wrote, "now the ears of my ears awake and now the eyes of my eyes are opened."[98] No wonder we need someone as all-encompassing as the Holy Spirit to activate, facilitate, and accomplish that within us!

"Why does God want to be worshipped?" a friend asked me once. "I mean, is He that insecure in who He is that we have to keep reminding God of His supposed greatness? Or is He just some cosmic egomaniac who's not happy unless everybody in the world recites compliments to Him?"

The questions may seem harsh, but they are valid, and the person who asked them of me is one of the most committed Christians I know. He wasn't trying to insult God, simply trying to understand Him. Sadly, I had no answers for my friend that day, but the questions stayed with me through the years, through days of prayer and nights of studying Scripture and weeks and months of growing, ever so slowly, into a deeper relationship with God.

Then one day, I read (for probably the thousandth time) the story of Jesus as He talked with a woman at a well. The account is found in John 4:1–43, but I'll just summarize it here for you.

A Samaritan woman (despised by Jews because of her race) came to a well to fetch water in the middle of the day. She came alone, because she was also known to be a woman of ill repute; promiscuous and looked down upon by those in her own community. Although she was obviously an ostracized person, Jesus Himself approached her and struck up a conversation.

During their talk, Jesus revealed that He knew all about the woman's past and challenged her to move forward to a greater destiny with God.

Now, there's such depth in the record of John 4:1–43 that I actually once wrote a whole book on this passage alone. But here I want us to focus on one seemingly obscure reference within this story, the words of Jesus in verse 23:

"True worshipers will worship the Father in the Spirit and in truth."

We've already talked about worship *"in the Spirit,"* but what strikes me about this verse now is Jesus's reference to *"truth"* in worship. Why did He tack on that emphasis about truth?

Here's my theory:

Because truth is the central element of worshipping God.

Does God need us to worship Him because He's insecure? Of course not. Does God want our worship because He's simply a cosmic egomaniac? Ludicrous. Does He need a "daily quota of compliments" before He can feel good about Himself? That's absurd.

So why does God want our worship? Perhaps it's because when we worship God, when our minds and hearts see and recite the wonders of His being, we acknowledge eternal Truth (with a capital "T"). We finally remove our eyes from our flawed, self-absorbed, sinful perceptions of reality, and accept the truth of eternity that God is spectacularly who He says He is. We state what is already known so that we can bring our spirits into alignment with the truth of the unseen world around us—and thus into alignment with God.

Are you getting the implications of this? Do you see what this means?

Worship isn't some crutch for God to use to feel better about Himself; worship is infinitely more for us than it is for God. Jesus doesn't need your puny compliments (or mine, for that matter), but *we* need to speak and act them toward Him, because in doing so we become united with the way things really are; we become partners with the truth and thus are changed, ourselves, more into His likeness, more into truth.

The fact is, God is awesome, powerful, loving, joyful, compassionate, all-knowing, all-encompassing, all-everything, whether we tell Him so or not. The absence of our worship takes zero away from God, just as night-time doesn't stop the sun from shining in its heavenly spot. Lack of worship doesn't stop God from being God. He is God, whether we admit it or not. *We* need to worship Him simply because of the truth of who He is, and we are made the better for it.

God, knowing our need for worship, gratefully makes it both possible and meaningful for us through the energizing, indwelling activity of His Holy Spirit. All we have to do is follow His lead in truth.

THE HOLY SPIRIT MAKES MUSIC RESONATE IN YOUR SOUL

(See Ephesians 5:18-19; Colossians 3:16.)

One exhilarating way that the Holy Spirit energizes our passion for Him is through song. This has been so at least since the time of Moses (see Exodus 15:1) and likely long before. In ancient Israel, this kind of praise was the required opening for attendees at synagogue meetings, later written in the Talmud as this instruction: "[We] should always first utter praises, and then pray."[99] Jesus also sang hymns (see Matthew 26:30; Mark 14:26), and most likely sang from the Psalms as part of His normal activities in the temple and at the synagogue.

Paul and Silas, in the worst of circumstances—in prison, after being beaten severely—found music in the Spirit to be a comfort, so they sang to God. (See Acts 16:25.) The Corinthian church made a habit of singing (see 1 Corinthians 14:26), as did the churches in Ephesus and Colosse. So clearly, God speaks to us in song, as we speak back to Him.

Although songs aren't the only way to worship God, they do provide a unique avenue into the awareness of His presence—I think because music prompts the whole gamut of emotions within a human being, from joy to sorrow, from comfort to peace, from thankfulness to enthusiasm and more. When it comes to worship, the Holy Spirit activates music to engage the soul in the truth about God. That's why Paul could say with confidence:

Be filled with the Spirit, **speaking to one another with psalms, hymns, and songs from the Spirit.** *Sing and make music from your heart to the Lord.* (Ephesians 5:18–19)

*Let the message of Christ dwell among you richly as you teach and admonish one another with all wisdom through **psalms, hymns, and songs from the Spirit,** singing to God with gratitude in your hearts.*
(Colossians 3:16)

I'm not sure why God uses singing *"psalms, hymns, and songs from the Spirit"* to activate worship in us—but I've certainly been the beneficiary of that kind of grace, so I'm not complaining. Perhaps you, too, have experienced moments in singing, whether in a group or by yourself, where it felt almost like a barrier between heaven and Earth had been thinned enough that you could practically smell the presence of God in the room. Or you just let yourself join in a song and felt your muscles relax and your soul sigh with relief simply because it felt good to turn your attention toward God instead of letting it dwell on your problems.

One thing I know is that, sometimes (maybe more often than we recognize), God's Spirit communicates to us through that common combination of lyric and sound. King David famously experienced that when he "[danced] *before the* LORD *with all his might*" (2 Samuel 6:14–22). Eighteenth-century composer George Frideric Handel also had a dramatic encounter with God through song.

In 1741, George took on a new project. Using Scriptures compiled and organized by Charles Jennens, Handel was to compose a new musical work, which he titled *Messiah*.

While it's no big deal for a composer to take on a job, what happened to Handel while he worked on the piece was *not* what he expected. He took on the work because he wanted the money and ended up meeting God in the process.

It's said that while Handel was composing the musical masterpiece, the "Hallelujah Chorus," his servant walked in and found the otherwise arrogant man broken, sobbing over his work. As Handel had been writing a chorus of simple praise to Christ that primarily repeated the word "Hallelujah" time and again, something happened inside him. For a few brief, yet precious moments, the chorus in his heart echoed the song of heaven, and he was changed because of that worshipful encounter.

As tears streamed down his aristocratic face, Handel sat humbled before his servant and could only explain, "I did think I did see all Heaven before me, and the great God himself." When asked later to describe what had happened, he could only paraphrase the Apostle Paul and say, "Whether I was in the body or out of my body when I wrote it I know not."

Handel's *Messiah* debuted on April 13, 1742, in Dublin, Ireland. Proceeds from the performance were used to free 142 men from Debtor's Prison. A year later, Handel staged a performance of Messiah in London, with King George II in attendance. At the start of the "Hallelujah Chorus," the king was moved with emotion and stood. It was customary at that time for people to stand when the king did, so everyone in the audience rose to their feet and remained standing for the entire song. As a result, standing during a performance of the "Hallelujah Chorus" became a tradition that's still practiced today.[100]

It's been nearly 300 years since George Frideric Handel wrote "The Hallelujah Chorus," but even now this aria of praise evokes a sense of wonder and worship in the ears of its hearers—and performers. Simply stating the truth of God's awesome power through the combination of orchestra and voices is still enough to facilitate a peek at our "great God Himself."

This is the kind of gift God's Spirit gives to us with *"psalms, hymns, and spiritual songs."* He makes music to resonate in our souls so that we can worship, and then, glimpse the truth about God and the universe around us. Song is a Spirit-given tool that helps us order our souls around the unfathomable truth of His great being. In doing that, we reap the reward ourselves.

THE HOLY SPIRIT OFFERS UNOBSTRUCTED PRAYERS ON YOUR BEHALF

(See Romans 8:26; 8:27; Ephesians 6:18; Jude 1:20.)

I don't know exactly what it means that the Holy Spirit prays on our behalf, because Scripture is clear that the Spirit of God is God Himself—that what we call the Trinity is still one Person in a mystery of eternity. So it seems odd to me that God would intercede with God in the spiritual realm to communicate my prayers. Regardless, here's what I do know: The Bible teaches us plainly that our Holy Spirit is active, even proactive, in the context of our prayers—interceding, helping, groaning, requesting, praying with and for us. Listen:

*The Spirit helps us in our weakness. We do not know what we ought to pray for, but **the Spirit himself intercedes** for us through wordless groans.* (Romans 8:26)

*He who searches our hearts knows the mind of the Spirit, because **the Spirit intercedes for God's people** in accordance with the will of God.* (Romans 8:27)

***Pray in the Spirit** on all occasions with all kinds of prayers and requests.* (Ephesians 6:18)

*But you, dear friends, by building yourselves up in your most holy faith and **praying in the Holy Spirit**, keep yourselves in God's love as you wait.* (Jude 1:20–21)

Dr. Lloyd John Ogilvie has a helpful perspective on this, I think. He emphasizes the two-way nature of prayer by pointing out that God is the initiator of any and all prayer conversations. Our first words in any prayer are actually the second in a dialogue that Jesus began within us.

This is refreshing for me to hear because, too often, I fall into the mistaken assumption that God is simply waiting—bored, somewhere up in the ether—for me to speak. The ignorant child inside me assumes He's probably frowning, constantly annoyed that I haven't come to Him sooner, tired of hearing my frequent whining and pitiful whimpers of faithlessness. I need to be reminded that God is *not* like that at all, and prayer is nothing like what I sometimes, depressingly, imagine it to be! So I thank Dr. Ogilvie for this reminder:

"Long before we talk to God, he talks to us. He calls us into conversation. Gently, but persistently, the Holy Spirit stirs our spirit. He creates a hunger and thirst for God. A sense of loneliness for God is a gift produced by the Spirit."[101]

Eugene Peterson sees a beautiful parallel to this Spirit-initiated conversation in—of all places—ancient Greek syntax. In modern English, our language relies on "active" and "passive" verbs. In active voice, we ourselves are the ones doing (acting), as in "I spoke to him." In passive voice, the doing (action) is being done to me, as in "I was listening to him." That's all we have—but ancient Greeks had one more option called "the middle voice." Here's how one Greek textbook describes that: "In the middle voice, the subject is acting so as to participate in some way in the results of the action. There is no English equivalent for this Greek construction."[102]

Eugene Peterson sees that as reading much like a definition of prayer. He observes, "[In prayer] I do not control the action...I am not controlled by the action...I enter into the action begun by another, my creating and saving Lord, and find myself participating in the results of the action. I neither do it, nor have it done to me. I will to participate in what is willed... Prayer takes place in the middle voice."[103]

I've never enjoyed Greek language studies (hated them, actually), but I have to admit I find this understanding of prayer as a "middle voice" conversation with God to be meaningful—and accurate. So with that in mind, let's look at the two primary ways the Holy Spirit's ever-present ministry energizes our prayer lives.

First, Ephesians 6:18 and Jude 1:20–21 inform us that we are always able to "*pray in the Spirit.*" As we discovered earlier, that phrase "*in the Spirit*" (*en Pneumati*) refers to being uniquely *filled* by God's Spirit in everyday situations. In prayer, this infilling presence of God serves as a source of power, wisdom, faith, and authority for us. When we pray *en Pneumati*, we go beyond our simple desires for God to act. We're empowered to see glimpses of how God intends to act—and can pray in unity with His will.

Like you, people often ask me to pray into their life circumstances or related situations. And like you, I'm happy to oblige; after all, speaking out to God on behalf of a friend is pretty easy, and uniquely satisfying. (Bonus: When people come back later to tell me how God answered our prayers, I get to feel like I had a little part in that answer from God.) For most of my life, when asked to pray, I'd pause to listen to my friend tell me what he or she wanted me to pray about, then I'd just dive right into a monologue toward God.

About ten years ago, there was a point in my life when something changed in the way I pray. It was a difficult season for me, emotionally, and I no longer had words always at the ready to speak to God. It was then that I started doing something that I still do today: In addition to asking my friend to fill me in on what to pray, I now ask God to do the same.

Before I dive into my requests and hopes, before I pray with others or in the privacy of my own room, I ask Jesus privately, "What would You like me to pray in this moment?"

And then I wait.

You'd think there might be awkward silences as a result, but I've not found that to be the case. Sure, my friend and I will wait a minute or two before I start speaking, but always, *always*, I begin to get an impression of how to direct my prayers. Sometimes it's just images that flash into my mind; other times, I feel certain words or themes are important. And once I have a direction to go, well, you know Mikey. Get me started talking, and I can't seem to shut up, right?

A few years ago, I joined a group at church praying for a young woman. She was in a bitter custody battle for her teenage son, after her marriage had disappointingly ended. Her court date was the following week, and she was stressed about it. "Jesus, how would You like me to pray for this woman?" I asked. And I waited. Pretty soon, I felt as though the Lord said to me something like this, "She will win the case. Go ahead and start thanking Me for that." So I said to her, "You don't have to worry. You're going to win the case." And then I spent a few minutes thanking Jesus for His kindness.

We all went our separate ways, and honestly, I forgot about it. Until last month. The woman's mother (the boy's grandmother) stopped me in church. "Mike," she said. "You remember back when you prayed for my daughter and her son?" I must've had a blank look in my eyes, because she recounted the moment for me. Then she said, "You were right, she won the custody hearing. And now my grandson is graduating from high school!" So I celebrated with her and tried hard to remember what I'd prayed!

This is the kind of advantage we receive from "praying in the Spirit." It's a ministry of God where He makes known to us things we might otherwise never know, so we can pray with confidence *"on all occasions with all kinds of prayers and requests"* (Ephesians 6:18). C. W. F. Smith explains it this way, "The Spirit interprets the mind of the God who knows what we need before we ask (see Matthew 6:8), and therefore prayer is in itself the discovering of what we really need."[104] That, to me, seems an incredible gift from God.

The second way that the Holy Spirit involves Himself in our prayer life is through constant intercession on our behalf.

"The Spirit helps us in our weakness," Paul wrote. *"We do not know what we ought to pray for, but the Spirit himself intercedes for us through wordless groans. He who searches our hearts knows the mind of the Spirit, because the Spirit intercedes for God's people in accordance with the will of God"* (Romans 8:26–27).

Christian author and editor Jody Brolsma is a friend of mine, and someone you might call an "unrecognized theologian." By that, I mean, she's spent the bulk of her life doing nothing but studying and teaching the Bible. As a result, Jody knows more about Scripture than most of us will ever attempt to discover. (She's also "unrecognized" because she works in a Christian world dominated by men who often look down on women who are Bible teachers...but that's a topic for another day.)

I love the perspective Jody offers about the Holy Spirit's ministry of intercessory prayer with us. So, as we move toward the end of this chapter, let me share with you some of her insightful commentary on Romans 8:26–27 (italics hers)[105]:

Praying for loved ones *isn't* about having all the right words to say. It's about admitting that our heart has a language only God knows...and that's OK. Communication and intercession can be a communion of spirits—ours with the Holy Spirit. Sometimes we simply need to abide in Jesus and let him carry our heart's message to the Father. *He* knows the words we struggle to find.

Jody learned this kind of faith in the Spirit's intercession firsthand, the hard way, watching helplessly while her sister lost a battle with terminal illness.

I simply couldn't wrap my head around what was happening, let alone my words. Prayer became inner groans, sighs, or concentrated emotion. I steeped my heart in God—just soaking in his presence and releasing pain, need, confusion, and frustration. Sometimes I'd manage one word, prayed again and again for hours.

Comfort.

Peace.

Heal.

Wholeness.

Mercy.

Jesus...

I found comfort in the truth that I had a Father who "knows all hearts."

And while we may notice Him more easily in times of grief, Jody reminds us that God's Spirit is always helping, always interceding, beyond just that kind of experience.

Wordless prayer isn't just for times of heartbreak or sadness. Joy is sometimes inexpressible! Have you ever witnessed a "God moment," a peek into heaven that left you wide-eyed in wonder? Perhaps the first time you saw the Grand Canyon your jaw dropped and you felt an overwhelming sense of love for our creative Lord. Or when you held your child or grandchild your heart bent with a breathtaking perspective of God's love. It may have been a moment during worship when the spirit of community with other Christians took your breath—and words—away. Those are times when our soul reaches out to God in wordless awe, and we simply *are*...

Wordless communion with God, whether in anguish or awe, is beautiful.

I know, I know, Jody's insights are wonderful, and we've really only begun to scratch the surface of the Holy Spirit's ministry in our spiritual expressions! But the time has come to draw this chapter to a close. So,

Friend, I just want you to remember that, in the ways you worship, sing, pray—even in those spiritual activities that you sometimes think are your own—God's Holy Spirit superlatively works *with* you to *energize* your passion for Him. Those things are not solely your responsibility.

When you feel dry and spent, spiritually, when you feel tired and beaten down by life, you don't have to fix those feelings on your own. Jesus will help you. He will activate and facilitate your worship, songs, and prayers (the ones with words, and the ones without). You can ask for help, and the Holy Spirit Himself will persistently renew your passion for God.

Let's face it, that feels pretty good.

FOR FURTHER REFLECTION AND SMALL GROUP DISCUSSION:

1. Why do you suppose it was important for you to read this particular chapter, this particular day? Explain.

2. When was a time you felt God's Holy Spirit energizing your passion for Him?

3. How do you expect your life to be different in the coming week because of what you discovered in this chapter? Be specific.

SEVEN

THE HOLY SPIRIT EMPOWERS YOUR ABILITY TO LIVE FOR CHRIST

What the mind thinks, the body does—and so we need help from God to choose rightly day by day, minute by minute. The Holy Spirit is up to that task, empowering you to live for Christ by: Helping you discern truth; bolstering your faith, hope, and love; and providing your strength for daily living.

To us, he's just sweet Uncle Ken. The rest of the world knows him as Ken Wakefield, probably the kindest, most genuine man you'll ever meet. At the time of this writing, Uncle Ken is ninety-one years old and, judging by his health and mental alertness, none of us will be surprised if he skates past one hundred years without any problem. Smiling all the way.

What most people don't know is that Uncle Ken is a raging alcoholic.

Well, he was a raging alcoholic before Jesus got involved.

When Ken was a teenager, he lived with his grandparents on a farm near Wheeling, West Virginia. The transition to adulthood wasn't easy for the boy. Soon, he discovered alcohol. A couple of drinks chased away his shyness and insecurities, making him feel ready to tackle anything. What Ken didn't realize was that one day alcohol would take over his life. By the time he recognized the danger, he was trapped—a slave to the addictive power of the bottle. It dictated what he thought about, where he went, whom he associated with, and how he behaved.

He finally had to speak the horrifying words: "I am an alcoholic."

"All I could picture," he recalls, "was that I was on a very high slide, going down real fast and soon I would hit bottom."

By now, Ken was in his thirties, married with a house full of children. One particular Saturday, his wife was ill, in the hospital. Coming home from a visit with her, he was deeply depressed—and contemplating suicide. For him, it seemed the only realistic solution.

Suddenly, unexpectedly, Ken had a distinct sense of the Holy Spirit speaking to him. The words he heard in his heart were, "If you do what I ask, I'll get you out of this mess."

He was both scared and excited at the same time. He immediately went to see his Christian neighbors, Vi and Ab, to tell them what had happened. They prayed with Ken, and he went home, but he was actually a little disappointed.

Nothing happened, it seemed. No skyrockets, no lightning flashes, or earth trembling. Ken felt just the same. Almost. Shrugging his shoulders, he went to bed. Next morning, he got up, and...no, wait. I'm going to let Uncle Ken tell you what happened next:

> When I got up, I decided to visit Vi and Ab's church. I went into the bathroom to shave. When I looked in the mirror, I realized that this was the first morning I could remember when I didn't have to have a drink.
>
> I started to feel a warmth that began at my feet and rose slowly to the top of my head. I felt as though I was being unzipped from head to toe, and someone was hosing me out with a big hose.
>
> I felt clean! (And I still have the feeling.)
>
> From that day on, a glass of beer had the same appeal to me as a glass of motor oil![106]

It's been over half a century since Uncle Ken stood in front of the shaving mirror that Sunday morning, and he still hasn't had another alcoholic drink in all that time.

What's surprising to me about this is that Ken's experience is *not* surprising. God's Holy Spirit frequently intervenes in the lives of His children to empower their ability to live for Him. And that's what the rest of this chapter is about.

THE HOLY SPIRIT HELPS YOU DISCERN TRUTH

(See Luke 2:26; John 16:13; Acts 10:19; 20:23; 21:4; Romans 9:1; 1 Corinthians 2:10–11; 2:14–15; 7:40; 1 John 4:2; 4:6. Also: Acts 6:3; 13:9; Revelation 1:10–11; 4:2; 17:3; 21:9–10.)

Let's play the game, "Two Truths and a Lie."

Here's how it goes: I'll make three statements. Two of them will be true, and one will be a lie. Your job will be to use what you know about me (from this book or other sources) to determine which one is the lie. Ready? Let's go!

1: I once met Marvel Comics legend Stan Lee for about forty-five seconds at a comic book convention.

2: My wife, Amy, and I got engaged to marry only ten days after our first date.

3: When I was a younger man, I spent two years as one of the lead vocalists in a Black gospel choir.

All right, what do you think?

Fact is, all three of those statements are true: I was lying when I told you one of them would be a lie!

I know, that was sneaky of me, and not playing by the rules—but (hopefully) it highlights for you the importance of being able to discern truth in a world overrun by untruth. After all, this planet of ours is filled with much misinformation, disinformation, and outright deception—both in the spiritual realm and in our physical and social environments. Being able to navigate between truth and untruth can be the difference between life and death, health and illness, hope and despair, and…well, you get the idea.

"When the Spirit of truth comes," Jesus promised 2,000 years ago, *"he will guide you into all truth"* (John 16:13 NLT). The Holy Spirit has been

fulfilling that promise, day in and day out, ever since. Remember when God first drew you to Him, and you understood that you needed Jesus? That was the Holy Spirit guiding you into truth. (See John 6:44 and 1 Corinthians 2:14.)

Additionally, the Holy Spirit reveals truth to Christ-followers in many other ways, including:

+ heightening understanding of current circumstances (see Acts 10:19; 13:6–12; 20:23; 21:4),

+ granting awareness of future facts (see Luke 2:26; John 16:13),

+ providing insight into spiritual matters (see Romans 9:1; 1 Corinthians 2:10–11; 2:14),

+ sharing wisdom to make good judgments (see Acts 6:3; 1 Corinthians 2:15; 7:40; 1 John 4:2; 4:6), and

+ giving supernatural perception of the heavenly realm (see Revelation 1:10–11; 4:2; 17:3; 21:9–10.)

All these things are part of the Holy Spirit's truth-telling ministry to your soul—and most often, you're probably unaware that He's working in this way within you.

Remember when you were engaged in a conflict with a family member, and suddenly you saw what to do to get that resolved? Or when you wanted to give good advice to a friend and just the right Bible verse came to mind? Or you wanted to predict the outcome for a particular action, and you "guessed" the right thing to do? Or during worship last week when you felt that unmistakable presence of God nearby? Or when you exercised good judgment in regard to your relationships at work? *All* those moments (and more) were the Holy Spirit at work in you, helping you to discern truth for daily Christian living. If He weren't constantly active in guiding you into truth, it'd be impossible for you to find it on your own.

So this raises an important question: What exactly is "truth," from the heavenly point of view?

In our world today, it's easy to speak about "your truth," or "their truth" or even "alternate truth." Those can be valid perspectives—for instance, a person with claustrophobia is living a personal truth that legitimately makes an empty closet frightening for them, even though that's not typi-cally scary for others. However, those kinds of subjective truths aren't uni-versal, and therefore aren't actually "truth" in the biblical sense.

The term for truth used in John 16:13 (which is also the standard expression throughout the New Testament) is from the Greek root word, *alétheia*. It doesn't mean simply presentation of facts, but *accuracy of reality* in all phases of life—temporal, moral, spiritual, physical, eternal, and so on. The ancient poet, Homer, showed a glimpse of this in practice by using the term in reference to someone judging a race. That judge was charged with telling the *alétheia* (the accurate reality) of who won and who lost the race.[107]

This idea of the Holy Spirit revealing the *accuracy of reality*, rather than just understanding facts, is extremely important, because we're human beings with a sinfully flawed ability to consistently perceive what is and isn't real. After all, there was a time when it was "fact" that the world was flat, and another era when smoking tobacco was "factually" safe. Furthermore, during the Jim Crow era and up into the time of the civil rights movement, a common argument in favor of racist discrimination against Black people was based on a logical progression of the following (supposedly) factual statements:

1. All men are made in the image of God.

2. God, as everyone knows, is not a negro.

3. Therefore, the negro is not a man.[108]

People claimed these were incontrovertible facts and used those "facts" to justify the idea of Black sub-humanity as biblical truth. But those selec-tive, manipulated "facts" are *not reality*, and never were, and thus are *not truth* at all. Truth can only be the accurate perception of authentic reality, as seen from God's eternal perspective.

This ancient idea that truth is reality (temporal, moral, spiritual, eter-nal, and so on) is also paramount to the way we live out our faith in Jesus today. As Paul put it, *"For we walk by faith, not by sight"* (2 Corinthians 5:7 KJVER). Because of that, in some situations we must act on the spiritual reality we can't see rather than the temporal facts we can.

We see this happening time and again in Scripture, but my favorite is the moment we talked about earlier, when Peter and John healed a lame beggar. *"Silver or gold I do not have,"* Peter said, *"but what I do have I give you. In the name of Jesus Christ of Nazareth, walk"* (Acts 3:6). The miracle here is made by Peter's understanding of the truth. The actual reality of this situation was contrary to the facts and unseen to anyone (except Peter and John). Fact: This man's physical lameness was permanent. Truth: Peter possessed the invisible ability to make that man walk again, regardless of the facts. So that's what he did.

The Holy Spirit's willingness to help you discern truth (*reality*) in this way is critical to your daily Christian life. So I want to encourage you to try an experiment for the next week: Every day, several times a day, pray this prayer: "Holy Spirit, please show me the truth of this current situation; make clear to me the reality that only You can see. Amen." Then, see what happens!

OK, we should move on to the next section, or I'll keep talking for days...

THE HOLY SPIRIT BOLSTERS YOUR FAITH, HOPE, AND LOVE

(See Acts 6:5; 11:24; Romans 15:13; 15:30; Galatians 5:5; Colossians 1:8.)

Anne Graham Lotz was, ah...let's call it *perturbed.*

In case you're not familiar with Anne, she is Billy Graham's daughter, and the one he called "the best preacher in the family." For decades, she's been a spiritual leader and role model for millions of Christian people, including me. On this day, though, she was just an angry woman ready to vent her rage at the person who'd set her off.

Seventy-two hours prior, a decision had been handed down to her that she felt was both unfair and terribly unjust. The more she thought about it, the more she seethed inside. "I was white-hot angry," she reveals. "I experienced the unfamiliar emotion of deep-down rage that seemed almost uncontrollable." For three full days, she stewed before finally venting her frustration to Jesus in prayer. Afterward, there was quiet for a moment, then what she felt to be a whispered rebuke from God. She rocked back from her knees to a sitting position on the floor before admitting, "He was right. As always."

Here's what happened next:

So I began to confess my anger to the Lord. In the end, I told him I would rather live with the injustice than offend him with my anger. I told him he would have to remove my anger, as I didn't have the ability to release it in my own strength. I was willing to give it up, but I couldn't…

When I got up off my knees, the anger was gone. Gone! The dramatic difference on the inside of me was actually stunning. I knew it was the supernatural work of the Holy Spirit within my heart… Through an invisible yet powerful miracle, he replaced my anger with a quiet, gentle peace."[109]

What Anne experienced in prayer was a supernatural bolstering of three things in her soul: *faith, hope,* and *love.* Faith that God would listen and act, hope that He would forgive and strengthen, and love in spite of hurt and anger. The result was unnatural peace and an eventual resolution of the problem. No surprise, then, that these three qualities, faith, hope, and love, are specifically mentioned in Scripture in clear association with the active presence of the Holy Spirit. Consider:

- Stephen is described as *"a man full of faith and of the Holy Spirit"* (Acts 6:5).

- Barnabas, we're told, was also *"a good man, full of the Holy Spirit and faith"* (Acts 11:2–24).

- Paul reminded Christians in Galatia to find both faith and hope through God's Holy Spirit: *"For through the Spirit we eagerly await by faith the righteousness for which we hope"* (Galatians 5:5).

- Paul also told Christians in Rome they could *"overflow with hope by the power of the Holy Spirit"* (Romans 15:13).

- Scripture teaches that *"by the love of the Spirit"* we can be moved toward prayer and unity with other Christians facing a struggle (Romans 15:30).

◆ Epaphras, a coworker with the apostle Paul, reported that *"love in the Spirit"* was a genuine characteristic of the Christian church in Colosse (Colossians 1:7–8).

These Bible passages seem to indicate that faith, hope, and love in the life of a believer are the *natural outgrowth* of Jesus's ongoing work in us— part and parcel of the infilling presence of God's Spirit. It's not a mere coincidence that Paul, when talking about specific gifts of the Spirit in 1 Corinthians 12 and 13, springboards from that discussion into a beautiful oratory that ends with this Spirit-driven statement: *"Now these three remain: faith, hope and love. But the greatest of these is love"* (1 Corinthians 13:13).

Listen to me now: *These three qualities are your birthright in God's Spirit.*

Do you lack faith, long for hope, and struggle to love? The answer for you isn't simply to try to "become a better person." Like Anne Graham Lotz, you just don't have the ability to do that in your own strength. So your call is to continually draw yourself nearer to Christ and invite the Holy Spirit to activate and increase those supreme character qualities in your very being.

So, what is faith, and what's the Holy Spirit's role in that?

Of course, entire books have been written on this subject, so I won't try to duplicate centuries of that conversation here—but I will try to give you an overview that you can take to heart.

At its core, faith is summed up in these two verses of Scripture:

*Now faith is the **substance** of things hoped for, the evidence of things not seen* (Hebrews 11:1 KJVER)

And Abram believed the LORD, and the LORD counted him as righteous because of his faith (Genesis 15:6 NLT)

In other words, faith, in the biblical sense, is *believing that God is telling the truth—and acting accordingly.* The Greek word that we translate as "faith" in Hebrews 11:1 is *pistis.* This, scholars tell us, conveys "placing confidence in a person, trusting in a person, or believing in a person...[it] is correlated to considering the person or object of trust, belief, or confidence as reliable—'faithful.'"[110]

So we have faith—but *not* in any specific circumstance or desired outcome. Instead, our complete trust is placed in God Himself, because He is faithful to us in every circumstance or outcome, regardless of what happens—most especially, faithful to us in the heavenly security He promises after this life is over. This is what faith is.

One other thing that's worth mentioning here: You do not, and cannot, *create* your faith. God gives you the privilege of cooperating with His Holy Spirit to practice faith and help it grow—but He's the one who makes faith in you. Romans 12:3 advises that we are to think of ourselves *"in accordance with the **faith God has distributed to each of you**."* Additionally, the author of Hebrews in the Bible reveals unmistakably that it's Jesus who is *"the author and finisher of our faith"* (Hebrews 12:2 kjver). The *New Living Translation* (nlt) relates that idea this way, *"Jesus, the champion who initiates and perfects our faith…"* and that sums it up well.

Jesus, by His Holy Spirit, creates, sustains, expands, and completes the faith that grows daily within you. He does the work, you follow His lead, and you both enjoy the result.

Now, what's hope, really, and how does that work within you and me?

In our modern view, we tend to view "hope" as an expression of anticipation, longing, or desire for a certain, favorable outcome. "I hope my team wins this weekend." "We hope to go to Disney World next summer." "My son hopes to get a new job before the end of the year."

In Scripture, though, Christian hope almost always is a reference to either Christ Himself, or the saving work that Jesus has accomplished for us. For instance, we hope in His Word (see Romans 15:4), in His gospel—the good news of Jesus's life, death, and resurrection (see Colossians 1:23), in His grace (see 2 Thessalonians 2:16), in His promise of salvation from judgment (see 1 Thessalonians 5:8), in His gift of eternal life (see Titus 1:2; 3:7), in His righteousness bestowed on us (see Galatians 5:5), in His glory infused in us (see Romans 5:2; Colossians 1:27), in His glorious second coming, promised to us (see Titus 2:13), and in our future resurrection from the dead (see Acts 23:6).

This ever-increasing hope in Jesus and what He's done for us is the catalyst for gratitude that prompts our joyful obedience to His desires for us. His life-changing hope reminds us that our existence means more than the short number of days we inhabit this earth—that we were indeed meant for eternity. It's why ancient Christians could walk to their deaths in the Roman arena singing with joy, and why people like Mother Teresa and Pedro Claver could happily spend themselves in service to the poorest of the poor and the weakest of the slaves. And it's why you and I can get up tomorrow and know we serve a purpose bigger than ourselves, and a God who gives us continuous, eternal hope.

Finally, what is love? And how does Jesus's Spirit grow His love in your soul?

It's impossible to adequately define love in words because love is so much more than any word can mean! First John 4:16 reminds us that "*God is love.*" If this is true, then love can't be neatly defined, because God Himself is indefinable. We can't know Him in His entirety because of His inherent limitlessness and our shockingly limited comprehension. (See Romans 11:33–36). So when speaking about love, all we can do is what Paul talked about in 1 Corinthians 13:12, "*For now we see only a reflection as in a mirror; then we shall see face to face. Now I know in part; then I shall know fully.*"

Regardless, each of us does have *some* understanding of what love is, even if we can't put it clearly into words. The Greek term for love used in Romans 15:30, Colossians 1:8 (above), and 1 John 4:16 is *agapé*. This is understood to be the highest expression of love and goodwill—a pure, selfless, unconditional thing that always seeks the best interests (i.e., the welfare) of the one who is loved.[111]

The apostle Paul, in his now-famous treatise, also describes love by what it does: "*Love is patient, love is kind. It does not envy, it does not boast, it is not proud. It does not dishonor others, it is not self-seeking, it is not easily angered, it keeps no record of wrongs. Love does not delight in evil but rejoices with the truth. It always protects, always trusts, always hopes, always perseveres. Love never fails*" (1 Corinthians 13:4–8).

So in that context there are two things we can intuit about what love is and how the Holy Spirit increases it in our souls: (1) Love is being like

Jesus—the only one to love with true *agapé*, and who Himself possesses all the qualities of 1 Corinthians 13:4–8; and (2) the Holy Spirit works to grow love within us by accomplishing Romans 8:29 (NLT) in the core of our being: "*God knew his people in advance, and he chose them to* **become like his Son.**"

We become better at love through both Christ's example and our supernatural transformation into imitators of Jesus.

That's pretty awesome—but God's Spirit doesn't stop there.

THE HOLY SPIRIT HELPS YOU FIND STRENGTH FOR DAILY LIVING (ADVOCATE/COMFORTER)

(See John 14:16; 16:7–11; Romans 8:13; Ephesians 3:16; 6:17; 2 Timothy 1:7; 1:14.)

Science, of course, is not the defining word on the Christian faith. Still, I think it's interesting that reams of research have shown that "religious" people possess significant, positive behavioral differences from their un-Christian peers.

Michael McCullough and Brian Willoughby, at the University of Miami, conducted a landmark study on religion and daily life that analyzed data from hundreds of studies over eighty years. The results? They found that religious people are less likely to engage in risky sex or take illicit drugs. They're less likely to smoke or get drunk. They're more likely to practice healthy habits (such as wearing seat belts or taking vitamins), which makes sense for someone who views the body as God's temple in flesh. They maintain better social connections and emotional support. They cope better, psychologically, with setbacks and misfortunes. They exhibit better self-control and even live 25% longer than non-religious people. [112]

There's more, but I think you get the point.

For many scientists, the explanation for these kinds of lifestyle benefits must be due to things like positive peer pressure, or hyper-controlling churches, or social support groups, or fear of punishment, or better accountability with others, or a panacea effect from praying—even though no one is really listening, or a heightened focus on willpower and behavior monitoring, or blah, blah, blah.

If the Holy Spirit were uninvolved in your daily Christian life, I might be tempted to believe some of those hypotheses. If God's not an option, then you have to blame something else, right? Trouble is, I've seen first-hand, time and again, what Jesus can do in a person's life.

I've experienced what Paul described to his protégé, Timothy: "*The Spirit God gave us does not make us timid, but gives power, love, and self-discipline*" (2 Timothy 1:7). I've lived and seen the truth that, "*By the Spirit you put to death the misdeeds of the body*" (Romans 8:13), and "*From his glorious, unlimited resources he will empower you with inner strength through his Spirit*" (Ephesians 3:16 NLT). I've known the truth of Jesus's promise in John 14:16–17, "*I will ask the Father, and he will give you another **advocate to help** you and be with you forever—the Spirit of truth.*" When Christ calls the Spirit our advocate, the ancient meaning of that word carries all the ideas of: comforter, counselor, helper, encourager, supporter, carer, and one who takes responsibility for another's well-being.[113] And I've experienced and witnessed the Holy Spirit's redeeming ability to bring conviction over sin and righteousness, and judgment. (See John 16:7–11.)

So it doesn't bother me at all to say, without hesitation:

God's Holy Spirit helps you access His strength for daily Christian living— and science appears to back up that promise of Scripture.

These ideas of inner strength and divine help are talking about a Christian person's *strength of will*, supernaturally amplified by the Spirit of God Himself. Like a daddy helping a toddler walk, He holds our hands up and steadies us so we can toddle along after Him. We pump our legs to take each new step—but He provides the strength and guidance that makes us move. Without Him, we simply fall down.

Now, I've read a number of books about willpower, and they all seem to say pretty much the same thing: If you work hard enough, for long enough, if you sacrifice and suffer, if you create a detailed plan of self-denial and stick to it, then someday in some glorious future, say when you're ninety years old or so, you might make slow progress toward training your will to do the right thing. As one twentieth-century expert put it, "It is the will which builds up the will by willing."[114] Which, of course, is a honeypot full of hooey. Self-made men (and women) are just disfigured statues pretending to be beautiful.

Yet, we can't deny that our natural human tendency is always toward sin (see Isaiah 53:6; Romans 3:10–12 7:18–20), and something must be done to build up the human will within each of us. So if you or I are to *"Love the Lord your God with all your heart and with all your soul and with all your mind and with all your strength,"* and *"Love your neighbor as yourself"* (Mark 12:30–31), we've got to have help. We need an Advocate to empower us with inner strength of will so we can actually, authentically put to death the misdeeds of the body. And that's exactly what we have.

Let me give you an example of what I mean.

This story begins on January 27, 1956, in Alabama. It's near midnight in the King home when the phone rings. Coretta and the baby are fast asleep.

Martin quickly picks up the receiver and hears this vile, derogatory promise: "Listen, n----r, we've taken all we want from you; before next week, you'll be sorry you ever came to Montgomery."

It's been nearly two months since Rosa Parks refused a white man's order to move to a seat at the back of the bus. The ensuing bus boycott by the Black population of Montgomery, Alabama, sparked hatred on both sides, white and Black people alike. A leader in the movement, Martin Luther King, Jr., has been a target of this kind of threat and harassment for weeks. And this, it seems, is the final straw.

Discouraged, frightened, feeling alone, Martin begins to pace in his kitchen. He's ready to give up. Then, he later reports, "I decided to take my problem to God." Head in his hands, he bows over the kitchen table and prays out loud. "I am afraid..." he speaks into the room. "I am at the end of my powers. I have nothing left. I've come to the point where I can't face it alone."

And in that weakness, strength appears. The Holy Spirit has come to do what he does best: *Help.* Here's how Martin described it:

At that moment I experienced the presence of the Divine as I had never experienced him before. It seemed as though I could hear the quiet assurance of an inner voice saying, "Stand up for righteousness, stand up for truth; and God will be at your side forever."

Almost at once my fears began to go. My uncertainty disappeared. I was ready to face anything.

Three days later, on January 30, "anything" came. Martin was speaking at the First Baptist Church of Montgomery. He didn't even hear the bomb go off on the front porch of his home, had no idea his wife and baby Yolanda were inside during the explosion. He found all of this out later, after the fact. He rushed home to find his house a shambles—but his family safe (thank God).

"Strangely enough," he reported, "I accepted the word of the bombing calmly. My religious experience a few nights before had given me the strength to face it."

On his front lawn, hundreds of angry people had gathered. Already, conflicts were brewing between white police officers trying to keep order and a crowd of outraged supporters of Dr. King and his family. Going into his home, Martin heard a Black man arguing with a white cop: "You got your .38 [gun], and I got mine; so let's battle it out."

The crowd outside was getting larger by the minute—and angrier. A powder keg was about to burst into a full-blown race riot. Then Martin spoke to everyone:

We must love our white brothers, no matter what they do to us. We must make them know that we love them. Jesus cries out in words that echo across the centuries: "Love your enemies; bless them that curse you; pray for them that despitefully use you." This is what we must live by. We must meet hate with love...

Martin later wrote:

Things remained tense the whole of that night...This could well have been the darkest night in Montgomery's history. But something happened to avert it: The spirit of God was in our hearts; and a night that seemed destined to end in unleashed chaos came to a close in a majestic group demonstration of nonviolence.[115]

When I tell you that *God's Holy Spirit helps you find strength for daily living*, this is the kind of thing I'm talking about—being able to supernaturally resist the natural, sinful action in favor of God's loving intention. You see, you and I have the same Holy Spirit that Martin Luther King, Jr., did, and the same one that raised Jesus from the dead. (See Romans 8:11.) He can, and will, strengthen us to be able to follow Him. All we have to do is be willing to participate in the work He's already doing inside us.

This week, when you need help to resist a temptation, when you feel afraid or alone, when you want to give up or lash out in anger—in all those moments and more, remember that *the Spirit of Jesus is working in you to strengthen your will*, to help you face whatever you may have to face. Do as Dr. King did and "decide to take your problem to God."

That's when the real adventure begins anyway, isn't it?

FOR FURTHER REFLECTION AND SMALL GROUP DISCUSSION:

1. What makes it hard for you to rely on God's Holy Spirit for help in your daily Christian life? Why?

2. How have you seen God's Spirit boosting your own faith, hope, and love? Be specific.

3. This week, what lesson do you want to take from the example of Martin Luther King, Jr.? Write it down so you won't forget it.

EIGHT

THE HOLY SPIRIT WALKS BESIDE YOU

God leads from alongside—He does not simply point and hope you get to His destination. The Holy Spirit guides your steps in this way: Teaching you all necessary things; reminding you of Christ; instructing you in faithfulness; and leading you into His purpose.

Historically speaking, Cleopas rates near the bottom.

I mean, if not for a passing mention by the gospel writer, Luke, no one would even remember his name. Despite that, we do know a few things about him:

His name, Cleopas, was a shortened form of the Greek *Cleopatros*, which meant "of a renowned father."[116] He was a disciple of Jesus (Luke 24:9–35)—not one of "the twelve," nor part of the in-crowd with Mary Magdalene, Joanna, and Mary the mother of James. Still, he was among *"the others with them"* (v. 10) who gathered after Jesus's death. On the morning of Jesus's resurrection, he heard firsthand the report from the women that the tomb was empty, and also heard Peter and John confirm that as well (vv. 22–24). Then, for unknown reasons, after hearing that news, he left Jerusalem with a companion (his wife, maybe?) to walk roughly seven miles to nearby Emmaus. The general assumption is that sturdy Cleopas was a minor businessman and, crushed messianic hopes or not, he still had work obligations in that city.[117]

It was a clear Sunday afternoon. While walking along the road, he was soon joined by another traveler, who was Jesus, though Cleopas didn't recognize Him.

They got to talking about the recent crucifixion and the crazy reports that Christ's tomb was empty. *"We had hoped that he was the one who was going to redeem Israel,"* Cleopas told the stranger mournfully. In response, Jesus promptly, emphatically, insulted the poor son of a renowned father: *"How foolish you are, and how slow to believe all that the prophets have spoken!"* (vv. 21, 25). At that point, Cleopas did the smart thing: he shut up and listened while Christ *"explained to them what was said in all the Scriptures concerning himself"* (v. 27).

When they all sat down to dinner in Emmaus, Jesus revealed himself to Cleopas (vv. 30–31), then disappeared, apparently to go meet Simon Peter. (See verse 34.) The two stunned travelers sitting at the dinner table said to each other, *"Were not our hearts burning within us while he talked with us on the road and opened the Scriptures to us?"* (v. 32). Unable to contain their excitement, they ran back through the night, going over all seven miles again, to Jerusalem to report that yes, Jesus was indeed alive! (vv. 33–35).

History barely remembers Cleopas. He was pretty much a nobody among the first followers of Jesus. He apparently wasn't very bright; he was actually foolish, and slow to believe, according to Christ. But Cleopas still rated the deliberate, personal attention of Jesus Himself, who walked beside him for miles just to make sure he understood the most important things.

I like that.

It makes me feel good to know that Jesus refused to overlook the stupid guy in the group because, let's face it, all too often I'm that foolish follower who's painfully slow to believe. And I relate to the feeling he described when he said, *"Were not our hearts burning within us while he talked..."*

Yes, Cleopas, my heart burns with His presence too, from time to time.

I'd like to find Cleopas in heaven one day and thank him, because his brief story in Luke 24 gives me hope. He reminds me that while we don't have Jesus in physical form to walk beside us anymore, we do have His Spirit. And like Christ did for that foolish follower on the road to Emmaus, He's determined to stay near so that we, too, can know what's important.

Even today, our Holy Spirit teaches us all necessary things, reminds us of Christ, instructs us in faithfulness, and leads us into His purpose.

THE HOLY SPIRIT TEACHES YOU ALL NECESSARY THINGS

(See Luke 12:12; John 14:26; Acts 6:10; 1 Corinthians 2:12; Ephesians 1:17; Colossians 1:9.)

Now seems a good time to me to bring up the subject of ancient espionage.

(Stick with me—you'll see where I'm going pretty soon!)

Spy work in antiquity required both patience and ingenuity. For instance, one time when the Greek king Histiaeus wanted to send secret orders to a military commander, he tattooed them onto the bald head of his messenger. Then he waited for the man's hair to grow back before sending him on his mission. The ancient Demaratus wanted to alert Sparta that the massive army of Xerxes was marching their way. But how to send the warning? He hid it under the wax of a writing tablet, unseen until it got to its destination. Ovid, the famous (and sometimes scandalous) poet, liked to use milk as invisible ink for his clandestine love letters. The liquid would appear invisible until sprinkled with coal dust, which would adhere to the milk and reveal the mash notes.[118]

Why do I tell you of the subterfuge of Histiaeus and Ovid? Because some of us live under the assumption that learning about Jesus and the Christian life is a lot like trying to uncover secret messages. We feel God is so intent on keeping us in the dark that He's hidden His truth from us behind layers of (figurative) wax or written it in something as hard to read as raw dairy. Well, I'm not saying there are no mysteries to God, but I am going to tell you straight up that you don't have to live your life in the dark like others do. *The Holy Spirit is your tutor for anything you need to know about your Christian life.*

Here's what Jesus said about this teaching role of the Spirit:

*"The Holy Spirit, whom the Father will send in my name, will **teach you all things**"* (John 14:26). He also promised that, when facing opposition to faith in Him, *"**The Holy Spirit will teach you** at that time what you should say"* (Luke 12:12).

These aren't simply promises, but explanations of how our Christian lives work. Every new day, the Spirit shares with us His wisdom and understanding for living well in Christ. With His help, we can grow in our knowledge of God, in the gifts of God at work in our lives, and in our ability to share the messages of God we speak to others.

For instance, Acts 6:8–10 records that Stephen got into a debate with people from the Synagogue of the Freedmen who were opposed to Jesus. However, *"they could not stand up against the wisdom the Spirit gave him as he spoke."* Similarly, the apostle Paul explained to believers in Corinth that we've received *"the Spirit who is from God, so that we may understand what God has freely given us"* (1 Corinthians 2:12). To the Christians in Ephesus, Paul wrote that his prayer was for God to *"give you the Spirit of wisdom and revelation, so that you may know him better"* (Ephesians 1:17). And to the church in Colosse, he promised continual prayers for *"God to fill you with the knowledge of his will through all the wisdom and understanding that the Spirit gives"* (Colossians 1:9).

So we can see pretty clearly that the intent of Christ's Holy Spirit in "teaching us all things" is to give us God's own wisdom and understanding for use in our daily Christian experience: to know Him better, to discover more intimately what He's given freely to us, to increase our knowledge of His will and good desires for us, and to help us be able to speak well on His behalf.

The question that arises, then, is how does the Spirit accomplish this teaching ministry of His?

The most common answer is through the "spiritual disciplines" that can enrich a Christian life immeasurably. We often hear the Spirit's teaching in times of biblical study, in prayer, in meditation and service, through fasting, and so on. In fact, when we cooperate with God's Spirit, He'll most likely turn these disciplines into habits that can bring both knowledge and comfort, as well as joy, into our daily lives. This is normal for followers of Jesus. As Richard Foster points out, these basic spiritual habits are "for ordinary human beings: people who have jobs, who care for children, who wash dishes and mow lawns...the Spiritual Disciplines are not hard...The primary requirement is a longing after God."[119] So if you want to learn from the Holy Spirit, you can be confident He *will* teach you through these fundamental disciplines.

There is one other aspect to God's teaching ministry that I want to make sure you're aware of, though, in case you haven't heard of it yet. This is something called "spiritual temperament," and I'm indebted to Gary Thomas and his book, *Sacred Pathways*, for this insight.

History has shown that God loves us all equally, but like any good parent, He doesn't treat us all the same. He relates to us as individuals in ways that communicate His love to each of us in personal, profound ways.

For instance, I have a friend whose answer to everything is "get alone with God, get alone with God!" For him, solitude is the place where his spiritual experience thrives. I see the value in that as an occasional practice, but a life spent in solitude is definitely *not* what my soul craves. I find that God speaks more frequently to me in the noise—in crowds, at artistic and theatrical events, in group discussions, and so on. Meanwhile, I have another friend for whom both solitude and crowds are distractions from a spiritual experience. For him, God whispers loudest during religious rituals, while he's lighting candles or chanting psalms and the like. No surprise that he, after a long life as a protestant, turned to the Catholic church and became a priest when he was over fifty years old.

Which of us is right? Well, we all are, and none of us are. God is meeting each of us in ways that are meaningful according to our spiritual temperaments. The variety of methods He uses to communicate with each individual soul is part of the wonder of a relationship with Him.

"People have different spiritual temperaments," Thomas says. "What feeds one doesn't feed all." After studying both biblical and historical examples, he reported, "I discovered various ways in which people find intimacy with God: by studying church history or theology, by singing or reading hymns, by dancing, by walking in the woods. Each practice awakened different people to a new sense of spiritual vitality."[120]

So when you're thinking about how the Holy Spirit's teaching ministry best connects with you, don't worry about it if one of your friends seems to hear God in a way that doesn't really do much for you. Find your own "spiritual temperament," and pursue that sacred path to discover what God's Spirit wants to teach you. To get you started, here are the nine primary temperaments that Thomas identifies in his book:

+ *Naturalists.* This person is drawn to the outdoors and finds it easy to worship in secluded, natural settings like wooded areas, mountain highs, open skies, streams, valleys, oceans, and so on.

+ *Sensates.* This person finds God in beauty, in sound, smell, sight, and all five senses—experiencing the voice of God in the noise of a concert, the voices of children's laughter, or the breathtaking view of a work of art.

+ *Traditionalists.* This person encounters God in the performance of religious rituals, celebration, and observances. "High church" is a breath of fresh air for this one.

+ *Ascetics.* This person craves simplicity, the removal of all distractions. Solitude, austerity, and restrictions make it easier for this one to hear God.

+ *Activists.* This person is energized by action; he or she connects *hearing* from God with *doing* on His behalf.

+ *Caregivers.* This person feels closest to God when helping the afflicted, such as the poor, the sick, and the elderly.

+ *Enthusiasts.* This person is drawn to the mystical nature of experiencing God, and to celebrating Him in that mystery.

+ *Contemplatives.* This person connects best with God through meditation, adoration, and prayer.

+ *Intellectuals.* This person's soul is brought to life through biblical study and academic pursuits.

THE HOLY SPIRIT REMINDS YOU OF CHRIST

(See John 14:26; 15:26; 16:14–15.)

Another crucial element of the Holy Spirit's walking beside you in life is that He will daily *remind you of Christ*. In so doing, He gives a flawless example for you to follow, as well as guidance for your life and relationships, and comfort of His unending love lavished freely on you.

Christian tradition tells us that the apostle Peter and his wife were martyred at the same time, in Rome, under the persecution of the deranged emperor, Nero. Peter's wife was led out first to be crucified, and there was nothing he could do about it except shout one last encouragement in her direction. As the love of his earthly life was being taken to her sadistic execution, I might've expected the old apostle to say something like, "I love you," or "I'll see you in heaven," or "Be strong," but he didn't say any of those things. If the records are correct, Peter called out her name and, when she turned to hear, the last words he spoke to her were:

"Remember the Lord!"[121]

This strikes me as odd until I remember that bringing Jesus actively to mind is actually a great gift of the Spirit for each of us, even in the worst of circumstances.

In this way:

+ The Holy Spirit reminds us of everything Jesus has said in the past (see John 14:26)—including His ironclad promises, His revelations about heaven and eternity, His hopes and callings for us, His words of comfort and truth, and more.

+ The Holy Spirit reminds us of what Jesus has done and will do (see John 15:26)—testifying to the greatness and kindness of Jesus, of the unfathomable sacrifices He made for us, and of His death-destroying power that brings resurrection and new, eternal life.

+ The Holy Spirit reminds us of the messages Christ has for each of us within our own lifetimes (see John 16:14–15)—making known to our innermost souls everything Jesus speaks into the heart now, in the present, to communicate His strength and love.

Seeing it that way, I understand why Peter said what he did. I have no doubt that his voice and that call provided strength, hope, and encouragement to his wife—even after the first nail pierced her wrist. And I hope, with more than hope, that when my moment comes, someone near to me (you maybe?) will encourage me with those magnificent words:

Remember the Lord.

THE HOLY SPIRIT INSTRUCTS YOU IN FAITHFULNESS

(See Acts 1:2; 11:12; Philippians 1:19.)

As God's Spirit walks beside us, He is not silent. It's His nature to be helpful, and so it shouldn't surprise you to discover that He's fairly good at communicating instructions for all of life's circumstances. Examples of this in Scripture are interesting, sometimes broad-ranging, and sometimes very specific.

For instance, Acts 1:2 reports that the resurrected Jesus, until the day He was taken up into heaven, was continually *"giving instructions through the Holy Spirit to the apostles he had chosen."* We can safely assume those instructions were broad in scope, likely preparation for the coming of the Holy Spirit in power (see Acts 2), and for their future mission to spread the good news of Jesus to the world. Additionally, Acts 11 tells of a time the Holy Spirit gave very specific instructions that applied to a one-time situation. Three gentiles (non-Jews) had come to Peter, asking him to come to Caesarea to tell a household about Jesus. Peter later testified that, *"The Spirit told me to have no hesitation about going with them"* (Acts 11:12).

Another time, when Paul was under arrest, the Holy Spirit gave instructions for him to trust God's sovereign work, help, and hope for future release because, Paul wrote, *"Everything that has happened to me here has helped to spread the Good News...The Spirit of Jesus Christ helps me, this will lead to my deliverance"* (Philippians 1:12, 19 NLT).

In our modern lives today, the Spirit still gives instructions, both broad-ranging and sometimes very specific. Most often, this happens when He reminds us of Christ's example and teaching so that we can apply those to a daily situation. Frequently, He'll bring to mind specific Bible passages or events to help instruct our attitudes and behaviors. And sometimes He'll speak guidance into our souls and expect us to follow, regardless of what the outcome might be—or whether we even see the eventual result. This can be fairly uncomfortable at times, to say the least!

For example, in the early 1980s, there was a man (let's call him Sam) who felt very strongly that God was instructing him to move his family to war-torn Uganda, where they'd work as missionaries. So he traveled to that country to check out the situation. His first night, he found himself

142 IT DOESN'T HAVE TO BE THIS HARD

in a dingy hotel room when a six-foot, five-inch-tall Ugandan man burst through the door and shouted, "What are you doing in my room?"

Sam tried to explain that their room had apparently been double-booked. Then the man asked, "What are you doing in my country?" Sam was still flustered and a little afraid, but he tried to explain anyway. Suddenly, the man shouted, "Praise God, praise God!" and lifted him up in a bear hug, dancing around the room with Sam in his arms.

Turns out that man had been praying for two years for God to bring someone from the US to come and help him share the gospel in Uganda. He and Sam became friends, coworkers, and then best friends. With his help, Sam was able to learn the language, move his entire family into the country, and spend many years in a thriving ministry to the Ugandan people. All because Sam was willing to follow the Holy Spirit's deeply uncomfortable instructions.[122]

Another example that's not quite as extreme, but also a moment of uncomfortable instruction, happened to me once during a Sunday morning church service. We were singing praise songs, just enjoying the time. At one point, my eyes drifted to the person standing in front of me. Immediately, I felt sharp pain in my lower back. When I looked away from him, the pain disappeared. I didn't think much about it until a few minutes later when I glanced at the guy in front of me again. Once more, sharp pain in my lower back. At that point, God had my attention.

"All right, Jesus," I prayed. "What are You trying to tell me?"

The pain in my back faded, and I studied the man in the next row. I noticed he seemed to be shuffling uncomfortably back and forth on his feet. Then I felt like God's Spirit spoke into my mind, "He's injured his back, and I want you to pray for him."

"Sure, no prob"—I started, but the Spirit wasn't finished.

"But," He spoke, "I'm not going to heal him today."

Huh?

I suddenly started to sweat. What was the point of God prompting me to pray for healing when He had no intention of answering that prayer with healing? Still, I swallowed my discomfort and, during a break in the service, I introduced myself and we swapped names. "So, Joshua," I said awkwardly, "what's wrong with your back?" He was surprised at first, then said he'd hurt his back a few months ago at work and it still hadn't healed. I stumbled, hemmed, and hawed, but finally got out, "I feel like Jesus wants me to pray for your back, but, ah, um, well, He's not going to heal you today. Is it OK if I pray anyway?"

Joshua generously said yes, and I prayed a pitifully weak, unconvincing prayer. Then the teaching started up and we both went back to our seats. After the service, I complained to God about feeling like an idiot. By the way, did God notice how fast Joshua rushed out of church, probably just to get away from that weirdo sitting behind him? Then I felt a tap on my shoulder. Joshua had come back.

"Mike," he said, "I just want you to know it's OK that God didn't heal me today. Jesus used you anyway, and your prayer was just what I needed. God accomplished His purpose, so thank you for praying for me."

Huh, again.

I have no idea what God did or didn't do for Joshua—I've never spoken to him since. But the Holy Spirit gave me an uncomfortable instruction, I followed it, and that was apparently what that man needed at that time.

So I think it's OK when we don't know exactly why God's Spirit instructs us to do something, or when we obey and it seems like nothing happens (yet), or even when we feel foolish for following God's guidance expressed intuitively within. What's important for us to remember is that *the Holy Spirit actively instructs us toward lives of faithfulness.* Our job is just to listen for that, in Scripture, in prayer, in worship, and more—and to be open to obey when we recognize it happening.

THE HOLY SPIRIT LEADS YOU INTO HIS PURPOSE

(See Matthew 4:1; Mark 1:12; Luke 2:27; 4:1; Acts 8:29; 8:39; 13:4; 16:6; 16:7; 20:22; Romans 8:14; 2 Corinthians 12:18; Galatians 5:18.)

The final aspect of the Holy Spirit's walking beside us is that He leads us through this life. Honestly, this idea is so common nowadays as to be almost boring. Still, we see Scripture teaching us that the Spirit leads us into lives of integrity so we can join with Paul and Titus in saying, "We *have the same spirit and walk in each other's steps, doing things the same way"* (2 Corinthians 12:18 NLT). He leads us into experiencing God's grace so that *"if you are led by the Spirit, you are not under the law"* (Galatians 5:18). He takes leadership responsibility over us as a parent does, so we can affirm by our own lives that Romans 8:14 is true, *"Those who are led by the Spirit are the children of God."* None of these things are new or radical ways of thinking about the Holy Spirit's leadership in our lives.

What I find interesting—and a little bit frightening—is that the Holy Spirit's leading is often not safe, nor sensible (from our human perspectives), and is sometimes even obstructionist, preventing us from doing a work on His behalf. Listen to some of these examples of the Holy Spirit's leading:

Scripture teaches that God's Spirit forced Jesus into the wilderness to face temptation by the devil. (See Matthew 4:1, Mark 1:12–13, Luke 4:1.) We tend to assume this harassment was limited to a short time, maybe one day at the end of several weeks. But Luke reveals *"he was tempted by the devil for forty days"* (Luke 4:2 NLT). Mark 1:12–13 reports the same thing. So, Jesus followed the Spirit's leading into the wilderness, and straight into an ambush by the enemy, where Christ had to endure *for forty days* the devil's provocation and lies. That's what the Holy Spirit's leading produced for Jesus here.

Another time, the apostle Philip had started a thriving outreach ministry in Samaria (see Acts 8:4–13), but then an angel cut short his life-transforming work and sent him walking on an almost-empty desert road. (See Acts 8:26.) That doesn't make sense, right? But God's Spirit led him to speak to an Ethiopian man, which turned out well. That man immediately gave his life to Jesus (see Acts 8:34–38)—and it was a new kind of cross-cultural, evangelistic success for Philip's ministry. Then, just when everything was starting to ramp up, *"The Spirit of the Lord suddenly took Philip away"* (Acts 8:39). Again, from a human strategic standpoint, that seems senseless. Why end a great work of God that was just beginning? But the Holy Spirit led Philip away anyway; He had other plans.

God's Spirit led Paul to become a traveling missionary (see Acts 13:2–4), which was a great thing—but also, in turn, forced Paul to endure many hardships that included beatings, imprisonment, and violent opposition.

Still, he was doing a significant work…except when he started to go into Asia. Scripture reports, the Holy Spirit actually *interfered* to stop his dynamic mission work. Acts 16:6 tells us that Paul and his companions were specifically *"kept by the Holy Spirit from preaching the word in the province of Asia."* (Did you ever think you'd read that the Holy Spirit would keep anyone from *"preaching the word"*?) Regardless, Paul turned away from Asia and toward a place called Bithynia (part of present-day Turkey). He was ready to spread the good news of Jesus throughout that region. Once again, though, he was obstructed by the Holy Spirit: *"They tried to enter Bithynia, but the Spirit of Jesus would not allow them to"* (Acts 16:7). How frustrating! You're doing a great work that God Himself told you to do—and His Holy Spirit prevents you from doing it? Twice? But, as usual, the Spirit of Jesus knew what was best.

Later in his ministry, Paul reported that he felt *"compelled by the Spirit"* to return to Jerusalem (Acts 20:22), even though *"in every city the Holy Spirit warns me that prison and hardships are facing me"* (v. 23). God's Spirit was determined to lead Paul into terrible, violent circumstances. Do you find that comforting? Does it make you feel safe in the way God leads you today? Regardless, and to his credit, Paul was determined to follow the Spirit's leading anyway.

So, despite the one-sided propaganda some modern Bible teachers love to passionately proclaim to us, you can see that when the Holy Spirit leads, it sometimes is *not* safe. He may be leading you straight into hardship and suffering that He intends to use in ways you can't even conceive. He may be intentionally placing you in situations that are demoralizing, difficult, and frustrating. God may actually obstruct or redirect your efforts to do what He told you to do in the first place. On occasion, it won't make sense, like when the Spirit sent Philip *away* from evangelistic success. Sometimes we just won't understand the "why" behind what the Holy Spirit asks of us; we have to learn to be OK with that, if we're going to be God-followers in our daily Christian lives.

What we do know, though, is this: *the Holy Spirit leads with purpose and into His plans.*

He's never guessing or playing haphazard games with your life. Whether He leads you to success or failure, joys or hardships, He's always working out His good will for your life and the lives of those you touch—even the ones you may never see. Remember, Paul never met you or me or any of us living today, and yet his courage to follow Christ into *"prison and hardships"* has made him one of the most influential men in all of Christian history.

Do you think Paul knew that would be the outcome, back when the Holy Spirit led him directly into the hands of his enemies in Jerusalem? Doubtful. But he followed anyway, and you and I are beneficiaries of his obedience.

This is our honor and privilege, then. When we speak of the Holy Spirit's leading in our lives, the question isn't really *how* He does that. We see that happening all the time, through Scripture and prayer, in worship and service, by teaching and mentors, in relationships and acts of integrity, and more. We know from biblical example that the Holy Spirit is often willing to subordinate our comfort to His eternal purpose when He leads—that in fact, He will pretty regularly deliberately lead us into hardship, sacrifice, suffering, frustration, and sorrow. So the real question for us today is the same one that Jesus faced, and Paul, and Philip, and the millions upon millions of other believers who are our brothers and sisters throughout the centuries:

When the Holy Spirit leads, will we have the courage to follow?

FOR FURTHER REFLECTION AND SMALL GROUP DISCUSSION:

1. Why do you suppose it was important to Jesus to walk beside Cleopas on the road to Emmaus?

2. What does it feel like to you when God's Holy Spirit walks beside you? Describe it.

3. What's one important insight from this chapter that you want to take with you each day of the coming week? Why?

PART 3

WHAT THE HOLY SPIRIT DOES *THROUGH* YOU

EXPLORING THE VISIBLE THINGS THAT DEMONSTRATE OUTWARDLY THE
HOLY SPIRIT'S INVISIBLE WORK IN YOUR LIFE.

NINE

THE HOLY SPIRIT COMMUNICATES CHRIST THROUGH YOU

God makes you a partner to speak His truth. The Holy Spirit
helps you do that by: Bringing Scripture to life in your world;
testifying of Jesus and His work in your life; explaining spiritual
mysteries; and speaking blessing to those in your reach.

"**I** didn't say you were stupid."

What do you hear when you read that sentence above? The fact is,
there are at least six different meanings, depending on which word you
emphasized in your head when you read it.

For instance, if your mind stressed the first word, as in "*I* didn't say
you were stupid," you probably understood it as communicating, "Well,
Mikey himself didn't call me stupid—but someone he knows sure did!"
If you emphasized the third word, "I didn't *say* you were stupid," then the
meaning was obvious: "Mike didn't say out loud that I'm stupid, but he was
definitely thinking it!" How about accentuation on the fifth or sixth words,
as in "I didn't say you *were* stupid," or "I didn't say you were *stupid*"? Those
would mean, respectively, "Mikey didn't think I was stupid before; he sure
thinks I'm stupid now," or "Mike isn't calling me stupid; he's saying I'm
something worse, like a complete idiot!" You get the idea.

This "stupid" little demonstration is an exercise in *communication*—
and it reveals how easy it is for us to mix up messages between us.

Humans are astonishingly good at misunderstanding each other. We think we say what we mean, but find out it doesn't mean what we said. We speak the right words, but they're canceled out by the language of our bodies, or even the tone of our voices. We believe lies and distrust the truth. It's amazing we're able to communicate anything at all.

This human failing becomes more significant when we realize that *God has chosen to communicate His truth through immensely fallible people* like you and me. If I were on God's council of advisors, I'd strongly recommend against that. I'd tell Him He should find another way because, let's face it, we're generally ill-equipped for a task of that magnitude. Fortunately, God's not asking me how to run His kingdom, nor is He caught off guard by the limitations of human communication. You see, God's got an ace up His sleeve: The Holy Spirit.

In parts 1 and 2 of this book, we've seen that God's Spirit works *in us*, and *with us*, to accomplish the Christian life for us. With that as the basis, we can now begin to explore how the Spirit works *through us* to make Christ known to our world. Although we get to cooperate with Him in this effort, He's the one who accomplishes it—making it supernaturally possible for us to articulate His message with clarity, compassion, and consistency.

To put it another way, *the Holy Spirit communicates Christ through you,* using everything He's constantly doing in and with you each day.

Let's explore four specific ways He does that.

1. THE HOLY SPIRIT BRINGS SCRIPTURE TO LIGHT IN YOUR WORLD

(See Matthew 22:43; Mark 12:36; Acts 1:16; 4:25; 28:25; 2 Timothy 3:16; 2 Peter 1:21. Also: Acts 1:8; 4:31; 2 Corinthians 3:3; 1 Peter 1:12; John 3:34.)

The main way the Holy Spirit communicates Christ through you is to bring Scripture to light for you. This is typically a two-step process that is repeated throughout your entire life.

First, the Spirit illuminates Scripture to you. This began ages ago when, as the apostle Peter explained of the Old Testament, *"Prophecy never had its origin in the human will, but prophets, though human, spoke from God as they were carried along by the Holy Spirit"* (2 Peter 1:21). Paul also emphasized the Holy Spirit's role in the creation of Scripture, saying, "*All Scripture is God-breathed and is useful for teaching, rebuking, correcting and training in righteousness*" (2 Timothy 3:16). The Greek word for "God-breathed" in that verse is *theopneustos*, a compound word based on *pneuma*, the designation used for the Holy Spirit. Additionally, Jesus and His disciples at various times credited the Holy Spirit with speaking through the Bible. (See Matthew 22:43; Mark 12:36; Acts 1:16; 4:25; 28:25.)

Having created Scripture for you, God's Spirit is thus a master at helping to reveal practical and theological meaning to you through the Bible. This is why it can often seem that, when you read the Bible, there's always something new to discover and/or learn about faith in Christ for your life. The Holy Spirit is continually bringing new understanding of Himself to light for you, in the pages of your Bible.

Second, the Spirit figuratively opens up the aperture of your life's camera so that light of biblical understanding going on inside you also illuminates—and speaks to—people in your world. I love the imagery Paul used to describe this in 2 Corinthians 3:3, "*You are a letter from Christ, the result of our ministry, written not with ink but with the Spirit of the living God, not on tablets of stone but on tablets of human hearts.*" The Greek term translated "letter" by the NIV is *epistolé*. That's the word we know in English as "epistle," as in "The Second Epistle of Paul to the Corinthians"—which may appear as the title of that book in your translation of the Bible. In essence, Paul was saying to the Corinthian believers, "You are, to those around you, what this letter (*epistolé*) is to you: a living message of Christ to your world."

It's important to understand that your "letter" to this world isn't something you're writing; notice the emphasis Paul made to clarify that your example and witness are "*written not with ink **but with the Spirit of the living God.**" This is God's work, happening through you, and in cooperation with you. It's a natural outgrowth of your relationship with Jesus. Because of that, you can speak the words of God (see John 3:34), speak God's word boldly (see Acts 4:31), with the power of God's Spirit (see 1 Peter 1:12), as a faithful witness of Christ (see Acts 1:8), in both word and deed (a living *epistolé*) as an example to those in your circle of influence. (See 2 Corinthians 3:3.)

Let me see if I can explain this better for you with an image from the world of art and authorship.

In ancient days, parchment and canvas were readily available, but also rare enough to be used with judicious care. It simply wasn't cost-effective to waste a canvas or toss out a sheet of parchment. So it became common practice to erase unwanted text on a parchment and reuse it to write something new, or to simply paint over one work of art with another, newer one instead. These reused parchments and canvases became known as *palimpsests*, from a Greek word meaning "scraped again."

What's interesting about *palimpsests* is that some of our most prized historical pieces have been discovered underneath other, generally worthless works. For instance, a medieval prayer book had actually been created by erasing and then writing over two priceless, lost texts from the classic inventor Archimedes, dating hundreds of years before Christ. They were rediscovered using ultraviolet light to reveal shadows of the original iron gall ink that couldn't be fully erased.[123]

Likewise, the famous painting, *Salvator Mundi* by Leonardo Da Vinci, was a lost work of art. Historians knew it had once existed from notes and preliminary sketches of it in Da Vinci's records—but no one knew what had happened to the final work. That previously lost painting was rediscovered after someone bought a relatively cheap, different painting at an auction. During a cleaning, it came to light that the cheap painting had covered over elements of a much older work, disguising it from modernity. Yep, someone had painted over the *Salvator Mundi*. Once restored and with its authorship verified, it eventually sold for $450 million—the most expensive artwork ever sold.[124]

Now, if you'll allow me to use the *palimpsest* as allegory, then...

Scripture at work in you is the Holy Spirit's masterpiece within you—a picture of Christ He's painting in heart, soul, and personality. But God's Spirit doesn't stop there. He uses your voice and actions to (figuratively speaking) shine an ultraviolet light on the sin-stained paint-overs of your life to reveal His original, perfecting artwork inside you, to those around you. He works *through* you, by changing you into a likeness of Jesus, to bring Scripture to light in your world. In that way, this work of the Spirit is similar to the fantastic revealing that happens when a palimpsest is redis-covered after being hidden for centuries beneath other, inferior work.

2. THE HOLY SPIRIT TESTIFIES OF JESUS AND HIS WORK IN YOUR LIFE

(See Matthew 10:20; Mark 13:11; Acts 5:32; 1 John 5:6–8; Hebrews 3:7; 10:15.)

In addition to bringing Scripture to light, the Spirit also works through you to spread the testimony that Jesus is alive and well and active in your daily life. According to the New Testament's teaching, this happens in both natural and supernatural ways—and really, it's not up to you which of those methods God uses. The Spirit works in both ways, according to whatever He prefers in that moment.

Take, for example, the experience of James Fell and Clay Walker.

Mr. Fell is a self-described atheist, as well as a bestselling author and journalist. He wanted to study the idea of how lasting change can happen in a person, so he spent months researching and conducting a number of in-depth interviews. One of his interview subjects was country music star Clay Walker, who has had multiple number one hits on the Billboard Hot Country Singles & Tracks chart. Clay, he found out, had been diagnosed with multiple sclerosis and told he'd "be in a wheelchair in four years, dead in eight." Then Clay told James what happened. He'd been devastated at the diagnosis, and he'd dropped to his knees in prayer. Fell reports: "He said God answered, speaking the words, 'I have you,' and delivered an over-whelming sense of peace to the man...More than two decades later, Clay is still touring, still bringing joy to his fans."[125]

Although unwilling to credit Christ with any real influence (atheist, remember?), Fell can't dismiss Clay Walker's testimony (the natural) and the apparent miracle of healing (the supernatural). So now, *atheist* James Fell offers his readers this somewhat reluctant advice:

> You may have minimal or perhaps significant belief. Alternatively, you may have none. Regardless, consider two things:
>
> 1. Prayer can result in massive change in a person...

2. Approximately one-third of those who experienced a life-changing epiphany were engaged in prayer at the time...

And so, taking those two realities into consideration, I ask you to think about the use of prayer for helping achieve a life-changing insight.[126]

This is the kind of thing that happens when the Spirit works *through* you to spread the testimony that Jesus is alive and well and active in your daily life. It's not that you must do anything out of the ordinary, or that you have to manipulate circumstances to slant them in God's favor. All you have to do is the same thing that Clay Walker did:

Tell what happened.

Be open to sharing what God's Spirit does in your life, whether it's natural or supernatural. This kind of transparent lifestyle has power when the Holy Spirit gets involved—so much so that the book of Revelation reveals that, in the last days, we who follow Christ will overcome the enemy *"by the blood of the Lamb* [Jesus] *and by the word of their testimony"* (Revelation 12:11).

When the Holy Spirit testifies of Jesus through you in natural ways, it may involve:

+ Talking about things you've witnessed. (See Acts 5:32.)

+ Talking about truth you've found in Scripture, where *"The Spirit... testifies."* (See 1 John 5:6; Hebrews 3:7; 10:15.)

+ Talking about the *"three that testify: the Spirit, the water, and the blood."* These are emblems for the life and gospel of Christ, as in: the Spirit's working in Jesus's earthly life, Jesus's water baptism by John, and the sacrificial, redeeming death of Christ on the cross.[127] (See 1 John 5:7–8.)

+ Talking about coherent arguments (sometimes called "apologetics" or even courtroom testimony) in favor of the Christian faith and life. (See Matthew 10:19–20; Mark 13:11.)

Max Lucado tells a story about that last item above that's so normal— yet almost miraculous—that I have to share it with you here, too.

Samuel Justin is a pastor in India, which has become increasingly intolerant of non-native religions (like Christianity). At one point, the Indian police came to see him, demanding that Pastor Justin answer their questions. One of the officers took out a notebook to write down notes of Samuel's potentially incriminating statements.

"By what authority are you doing these things?" the police officer demanded. Samuel shrugged and opened his Bible to Matthew 28:18. He read, *"Then Jesus came to them and said, 'All authority in heaven and on earth has been given to me.'"*

The officer wrote it down. And he waited. So Pastor Justin kept reading.

"'Therefore go and make disciples of all nations, baptizing them in the name of the Father and of the Son and of the Holy Spirit, and teaching them to obey everything I have commanded you. And surely I am with you always, to the very end of the age'" (Matthew 28:19–20).

The policeman studiously copied down every word. Then he left to report his findings to his superiors.

After that, Samuel Justin reported, the police didn't bother his church anymore. In fact, on occasion, they even provided some protection for the church when others wanted to interfere with their work of spreading the news of Jesus in India![128]

There's more, of course, because sometimes the Holy Spirit testifies of Jesus through you in supernatural ways. When that happens, it may involve:

+ Prophesy (See Luke 1:67; Acts 2:17–18; 19:6; Revelation 19:10.)
+ Foreign languages/speaking in tongues. (See Acts 2:4; 19:6.) Note that in this context, *"speaking in tongues"* seems to refer specifically to human languages that can be interpreted by others—not to "prayer languages" as indicated elsewhere in Scripture.
+ Visions and dreams. (See Acts 2:17.)

Some of you may feel uncomfortable that I included this short "supernatural" list above. Others may feel I didn't emphasize enough these more mystical methods that the Holy Spirit uses. To paraphrase Monty Python,

"I yawn in your general direction." I've heard too many fiery arguments from both of those extremes, and now they just bore me (as, I think, they should you too).

Scripture is clear that God's Spirit works in these supernatural ways, and Christian history testifies to that as well, so it'd be foolish of me to omit them. History has also proven that we humans are very good at corrupting these supernatural expressions to fit our own aggrandizing desires, so it'd be unwise of me to overemphasize God's natural supernaturality. Listen: This is *what God does through us*, not something you or I manufacture. So let's just live in readiness for when He chooses to testify, regardless of whether He uses natural or supernatural means. Make sense?

3. THE HOLY SPIRIT EXPLAINS SPIRITUAL MYSTERIES YOU CAN SHARE

(See Acts 4:8–12; 1 Corinthians 2:13; 12:3; 14:2; Ephesians 3:5; 1 Timothy 4:1; Hebrews 9:8; 1 Peter 1:11.)

When you think about it, the gospel of Jesus Christ is really intellectually hard to swallow.

God himself is born into a helpless infant body? A virgin is the mother? A Man is sinless, and He makes miracles into everyday occurrences? Then, that sinless Man is tortured to death for…telling people to love each other? And finally, hardest to believe of all: That Man raises from the dead and is still alive today?

I understand why some people I know think that's all just historical fiction, written by fanatics with something to gain by deluding people. It does sound absurd…

Unless it's true.

Then it's transformative, eternal, and demanding of our awe and gratitude.

But not everybody gets to understand that truth; in fact, it's a deliberate mystery to most. I don't know why that's so, but I do know that 1 Corinthians 1:18 tells us, *"The message of the cross is foolishness to those who are perishing, but to us who are being saved it is the power of God."* I also know that Jesus purposefully hid much of His truth behind stories. When His disciples asked why He taught in parables, He told them honestly, *"Because* *the knowledge of the secrets of the kingdom of heaven has been given to you, but **not** to them*" (Matthew 13:10–11). And I know that Jesus once prayed, "*I praise you, Father, Lord of heaven and earth, because **you have hidden** these things from the wise and learned, and revealed them to little children*" (Matthew 11:25).

Do you see what this means for you and me? God, who has intentionally hidden truth from many, has revealed certain mysteries of His kingdom to you, and to me, and to us. And then, because He chooses to do it that way, *we* get to be the people who explain those mysteries to others He brings into our orbits. I mean, that's also absurd, right? And pretty fantastic.

There are a number of examples of this kind of mystery-revealing in Scripture, such as Peter (*"filled with the Holy Spirit"*) explaining the fundamental necessity of Christ's work on the cross to the religious leaders in the Jewish Sanhedrin: "*Salvation is found in no one else, for there is no other name under heaven given to mankind by which we must be saved*" (Acts 4:8–12). Other examples include Paul teaching that no one can authentically say "*Jesus is Lord*" without the Holy Spirit (1 Corinthians 12:3), or revealing to Timothy that "*The Spirit clearly says that in later times some will abandon the faith…*" (1 Timothy 4:1), or the Spirit *"explaining"* or *"pointing"* or *"showing"* and so on (1 Corinthians 2:13; 1 Peter 1:11; Hebrews 9:8). But I also want to share an example of this I've seen, myself, recently.

I'm going to tell you about a good friend of mine now, but I'm going to change his name because you might know him, and I don't want to embarrass him. I'll call this guy "Saint Nicholas," mostly because I think that'll make him laugh when he reads this book.

St. Nick is an older guy, a Christian writer and editor—retired, and he loves to travel. Prague, Czech Republic, is one of his favorite destinations. During lunch about a year ago, he said this to me:

"You're not going to believe what happened to me in Prague."

He was right, but he told me the story anyway, and I laughed the whole time. (Nick's a good storyteller!)

As with many older men, my friend has a variety of chronic aches and pains. Chief among them is persistent back trouble. So, here in the US, he regularly gets therapeutic massages to ease the pain. On this particular trip to Prague, the strains of travel aggravated his back to the point where he could barely walk. So he found a therapeutic massage office nearby, made an appointment, and went to get his back straightened out.

The office was smaller than he'd expected, but the therapist (let's call her Sofie—not her real name) was professional and seemed to know how to treat his back pain. As is common, Saint Nicholas stripped down to his skivvies, then lay face down on the table while she started the massage. They made small talk and then, about fifteen minutes in, Sofie climbed onto the table and stretched her whole body across his back as part of the massage.

"That was when I realized she was completely naked," Nick told me.

First, he panicked—Prague is a sex tourism destination for some Americans, but definitely not for an old married codger like Nicholas. Then he collected his senses and calmly asked what the heck she was doing.

"You wanted a sensual massage, right?" she said.

No, my friend informed her. Just the "massage" part. She shrugged agreeably and put on her clothes.

Now, at that point, you or I probably would've vehemently condemned the masseuse, called down fire from heaven, and raced out of the office before God's lightning could strike...right? Well, not Nicholas. Now he was curious. He'd learned that she was an intelligent, educated business-woman who spoke three languages. It seemed unusual that she'd want to add "stripper" to her job description as a massage therapist. So he asked her why she'd chosen sensual massage as an occupation.

First, she told him, she was no prostitute. She had a (common law) husband, and they had a child together. Sex was something she simply wouldn't do for any customer. But stripping off her clothes while she gave a massage? That was just good business, she said, because men paid her more if she was naked than when she was clothed.

They spent the rest of the hour talking (and yes, she kept her clothes on the whole time). Afterward, Nicky left and assumed he'd never see her again.

Fast forward a year or two, and Nick's health had deteriorated enough that he figured he wouldn't be returning to Prague. His wife, though, talked him into taking one last trip—one final vacation to his favorite destination. So, last year, my good friend spent three weeks of springtime visiting Prague.

As expected, he needed a therapeutic massage again.

"Did you see Sofie?" I asked when we had lunch. "And did she keep her clothes on?"

"Yes," he laughed. "And yes." She remembered him, and this time even introduced him to her husband and their adorable child, now preschool age.

"Here's the interesting part," he said. "We talked the whole time she gave the massage, and she was very interested in my career as a Christian writer." As he was telling her about that, she asked the question that was pressing on her heart.

"So you are a Christian, then?"

Yes, Nicholas told her, and she nodded. Then she started asking him all kinds of questions about his faith. Although Christianity is known in the Czech Republic, it's just not as common as it might be in the US, and Sofie didn't know anyone she could talk to about it. But she was hungry to know about God.

"So we spent the entire time talking about Jesus," my friend told me.

When they were done, Sofie asked if any of his books were available in Czech, because she really wanted to learn more. He said no, but that he'd written a children's devotional book all about Jesus, to answer questions kids asked about Christ. The English language in the book was simple and straightforward, and he offered to send it to her. She clapped her hands together and beamed with joy.

"So here's what we're going to do," Nicholas told me. "I sent her the book. She should get it in the next few days. Then we're going to read it together, and discuss it through email, exploring answers to any more questions she has about Jesus."

And that's what they're doing.

Will the stripper/massage therapist become Christian by the time they're done? I don't know—but it wouldn't surprise me if she did. God's Holy Spirit does have a way of working through his people to explain spiritual mysteries to those around them—even in Prague. It also makes me grateful for a guy like Saint Nicholas. Where other Christians would've attacked, condemned, and ostracized Sofie, he was patient and kind. He was interested in the person, not just her skin, and someday—maybe?—there could be another rejoicing of angels in heaven as a result.

4. THE HOLY SPIRIT SPEAKS BLESSING TO THOSE IN YOUR REACH

(See Matthew 12:18; Luke 1:41–45; 4:18–19; Revelation 14:13; 22:17.)

I've read some who say that God's Holy Spirit is "forgotten," or overlooked, or sits in miserable silence watching helplessly while we all go astray. Although they don't say it specifically, He comes across a lot like the guy in the song, "Mr. Cellophane"—the hapless, unnoticed husband to Roxy Hart, in the hit musical, *Chicago*.[129]

For someone who's supposedly invisible like Mr. Cellophane, God's Spirit sure speaks with a loud voice!

Jesus is our first example of that, as in Matthew 12:18, which quotes an Old Testament prophecy about Christ that says, *"I will put my Spirit on him, and **he will proclaim justice** to the nations."* Similarly, Jesus Himself testified in Luke 4:18–19, *"The Spirit of the Lord is on me, because he has anointed me to **proclaim good news** to the poor. He has sent me to **proclaim freedom** for the prisoners and recovery of sight for the blind, to set the oppressed free, to **proclaim the year of the Lord's favor."***

And then we discover that the Spirit also speaks blessing through people like you and me. For instance, Elizabeth was an average person like us, and also a relative of Mary, the mother of Jesus. When Mary visited her, Luke 1:41–45 reports, *"Elizabeth was filled with the Holy Spirit. **In a loud voice she exclaimed**: 'Blessed are you among women, and blessed is the child you will bear!...Blessed is she who has believed that the Lord would fulfill his promises to her."*

Also, the apostle John spoke the Spirit's blessings down through the generations in places like Revelation 14:13, *"Blessed are the dead who die in the Lord from now on. 'Yes,' says the Spirit, 'they will rest from their labor."* Also in Revelation 22:17, John spoke the Spirit's blessing: *"The Spirit and the bride say, 'Come!' And let the one who hears say, 'Come!' Let the one who is thirsty come; and let the one who wishes take the free gift of the water of life."*

We who are being made into the image of Christ (see 2 Corinthians 3:18) get the great privilege of imitating Jesus in speaking God's blessings to those in our circle of influence.

Because the Holy Spirit is working *through* us, we too can:

+ proclaim His justice,

+ shout His good news,

+ declare His freedom, and

+ announce the year of the Lord's favor.

Because Christ's Spirit works *through* us, we can join in the legacy of the earliest believers like Elizabeth and John and say:

+ blessed is the one who believes that the Lord keeps His promises,

+ blessed are those who die in the Lord, and

+ let the thirsty come and take the free gift of the water of life.

Now, I want you to take a moment before we close this chapter. Bring to mind that person, that time, that place where someone once spoke hope and truth and honest-to-goodness *blessing* into your soul. Maybe it was the day you first became a follower of Jesus. Maybe it was a teacher who affirmed God's purpose and potential in you. Maybe it was your older sister who, after a loved one had died when you were young, held your hand and explained heaven to you. Whatever it was, you know that moment, you know that time.

Remember for us both right now.

This is what it means when I tell you that the Holy Spirit communicates Christ *through you*. He creates those moments for others, using *your* voice, *your* heart, *your* kindness, and faith—using all those things that He's creating and nurturing inside you. He makes it supernaturally possible for *you* to articulate His message with clarity, compassion, and consistency.

His work *in* you is also something He shares *through* you.

Now, what do you think about that?

FOR FURTHER REFLECTION AND SMALL GROUP DISCUSSION:

1. What's one thing in this chapter that makes you curious to discover more?

2. What's one thing in this chapter that you feel excited to share? Why?

3. How do you think something you've learned today will change what you think or do tomorrow (and the rest of this week)?

TEN

THE HOLY SPIRIT FLAUNTS CHRIST THROUGH YOU

Your life demonstrates Jesus to those around you—but not by your power alone. The Holy Spirit does the heavy lifting for you, expressing Christ to your world through: Growing His fruit in your life; expressing His gifts in your personality; and displaying His power and signs in your experience.

God, it seems, is a social marketer.

That feels like a strange statement, even for me—and I'm the one who wrote it. So let me backtrack a bit and tell you how I came to this conclusion.

It started when I read about some social psychologists who asked this question: *What happens when people look up?* They decided to find out. Stanley Milgram, Leonard Bickman, and Lawrence Berkowitz devised an experiment where they placed one man on a busy street corner with instructions to look up into an empty sky for sixty seconds. Most passersby ignored him and kept walking.

Next, they put five men on the corner, all looking up at the same time, for sixty seconds. Now, a number of commuters paused to stare upward with them—at nothing—as well. Then our intrepid psychologists tried putting fifteen men on the corner, all gazing into the empty, sun-bleached sky. Believe it or not, nearly half (45 percent) of the people walking by halted and stared along with them—again, at nothing. By the time Milgram, Bickman, and Berkowitz were done, they were able to get 80 percent of strangers passing by to stop and look up at a blank sky—just by increasing the number of their stargazing men on the corner.[130]

Hmm.

Then I read about Sylvan Goldman. You may not know his name, but you use his creation several times each month. You might even curse him when you get one of his contraptions that's got a squeaky wheel, or pulls inexorably to the right, or gets stuck fast in a long line of them at your local supermarket.

That's right, Mr. Goldman invented the shopping cart back in the 1930s. The problem was, he couldn't convince the customers at his grocery stores to actually *use* one, even after posting enthusiastic signs and clear instructions. Finally, he did what any good social marketer would do: He hired employees to wheel the carts around his store. Customers followed their examples, and voila! A staple of American consumerism was born.[131]

Then, of course, there's P. T. Barnum, probably the greatest social marketer of recent memory. It seems Mr. Barnum had opened the American Museum in New York City—his first solo venture in what would become a long and colorful career. Unfortunately, attendance at his collection of curiosities wasn't yet what he'd hoped, so P. T. hired a beggar to help out.

Barnum gave the man five bricks, with instructions to walk around several blocks near the museum until he'd made a full circuit back. He was to speak to no one, to acknowledge no one. Instead, he was told to periodically place one brick on the sidewalk and move on, always keeping one brick in his hand. The important thing was that he should *be seen* doing this. So the man walked. Every so often, he'd stop, pick up a brick, and replace it with the one in his hand. He continued showcasing this brick-laying routine until he arrived back at the American Museum, where he'd enter through the front door, then leave through the back door to start all over again.

People took notice.

Who was this plain man, flaunting his common bricks all over the neighborhood?

Pretty soon, curious groups began to follow him, inevitably ending up back at the museum. When he disappeared inside, well, they had to see what was in there, right? They bought tickets and were wowed by Barnum's marvels. On the first day of bricklaying alone, more than 1,000 people followed the beggar into the American Museum. Before the week was up, the New York Police Department had to order Barnum to cease and desist the beggar's conspicuous walks—the daily crowds were blocking traffic! The Greatest Showman had secured the success of his first big, solo venture.[132]

What these three stories teach me is what social marketers already know: People do what they see. Marketers call it social proof, which is what's given rise to careers as "influencers," celebrity endorsers, politicians, book endorsers, and more. When people see something that attracts others, they are also drawn to it.

And this is why I've come to the conclusion that God is a social marketer. In fact, social proof seems to be His entire strategy for reaching the world with the good news of Jesus. How? *The Holy Spirit flaunts Christ through us*, figuratively drawing eyes upward toward Him because people see so many of us looking in that direction—and they notice the difference it makes down here, below.

When our world sees Jesus displayed in the many of us who follow Him, they can't help but want to know more. Time and again, throughout history, you've likely witnessed it too: Christ makes Himself seen *through* us by the working of the Holy Spirit *in* us, and that attracts others to Him like lint to a belly button or smiles to teddy bears. It's social marketing (so to speak) on a grand, eternal scale.

Scripture indicates that the Holy Spirit flaunts Christ through us in three main ways: by His fruit conspicuously seen in our lives, using His gifts expressed in our personalities, and with His power displayed in our experiences.

Let's dig in.

THE HOLY SPIRIT GROWS HIS FRUIT IN YOUR LIFE

(See Luke 10:21; Acts 13:52; Romans 8:23; 14:17; 2 Corinthians 6:6; Galatians 5:22–23; 1 Thessalonians 1:6.)

I have an old pastor friend who once taught me a lesson I've never forgotten. "Mikey," he said to me, "go into my backyard and sit under that apple tree. And listen, just listen." Then he lowered his voice to a whisper. "If you're very quiet," he continued, "you'll hear that tree begin to grunt and groan and strain. After much effort and toil, that old tree will pop out an apple on the branch, right before your very eyes."

Then, with a twinkle and a grin, Pastor Kent patted me wisely on the shoulder and waited to see if I'd believe that theory, because we all know that, without a doubt, that's how fruit grows…right?

Of course not!

And that was my mentor's point. Fruit doesn't grow because a tree puts forth great effort to bring about change. Fruit grows on trees because *that's what fruit trees do when they're healthy*—when their roots go deep and they're nourished by sunshine, water, and soil. The fruit tree doesn't pop out apples as an act of its will. It simply drinks in the life that surrounds, fills, and feeds it. And then, in the fullness of time, that dependent cooperation with God produces fruit that we can see, taste, touch, and love.

This principle also applies to how we develop the fruit of the Spirit in our lives. *"I am the vine; you are the branches,"* Jesus taught His disciples. *"If you remain in me and I in you, you will bear much fruit; apart from me you can do nothing"* (John 15:5). In other words, the fruit of God's Spirit flows naturally into our attitudes and actions from being spiritually tethered to—and completely dependent upon—Jesus, our only authentic "Vine."

Interestingly, that word we translate as *"nothing"* in John 15:5 is *ouden*. Want to guess what it means when you parse the ancient Greek? Ahem: *Nothing.* As in, without Him you can do:

Not. One. Single. Thing.

That's not great for our collective self-esteem, but it's also extravagantly freeing, isn't it? To accomplish the fruit of the Spirit growing in our lives, all we have to do is go along with what He's already doing—and let him be the one who makes it easier and easier as we grow along.

Now, the classic Bible passage for the fruit of the Spirit is Galatians 5:22–23 (ESV), "*The fruit of the Spirit is love, joy, peace, patience, kindness, goodness, faithfulness, gentleness, self-control; against such things there is no law.*" When Jesus gave the warning, "*By their fruit you will recognize them*" (Matthew 7:16), He was talking about these kinds of qualities listed in Galatians 5. How could He be so sure? Because, "*Every good tree bears good fruit, but a bad tree bears bad fruit*" (Matthew 7:17). When the Holy Spirit inhabits, revives, and nurtures, He's incapable of growing anything in you but "*good fruit,*" and that's why Jesus could say with certainty, "*By their fruit you will recognize them.*"

What I love about this list of qualities in Galatians 5:22–23 is that it isn't a description of stuff to do, but a description of *Someone* who shows us who we can become. Every characteristic the apostle Paul included here can be connected to a specific event in Jesus's life as recorded in the Gospels. (Check it out for yourself—you'll enjoy the process of discovery!) So I think Paul wasn't necessarily trying to *define* the fruit of the Spirit, but was more likely describing the qualities he saw in Someone he knew very well: that is, Jesus.

The second thing I want to be sure to point out to you is that this list in Galatians 5:22–23 is *not* the complete tally of all the virtues of the Spirit growing in you. This passage offers a *representative* summary of the fruit of the Spirit, but not an *exhaustive* one. I know this because elsewhere in the New Testament are lists of character qualities the Holy Spirit creates in us that include some items from Galatians 5 paired with other holy attributes. For instance, Romans 14:17 adds "*righteousness*" to "*peace and joy in the Holy Spirit.*" Also, like Galatians 5, we see 2 Corinthians 6:6 associating the Holy Spirit with patience, kindness, and love—but then, unlike the Galatians verse, adding on purity and understanding.

In other words, it's a mistake to interpret Galatians 5:22 as saying, "*The fruit of the Spirit is* [only] *love, joy….*" A better understanding is, "*The fruit of the Spirit* [includes] *love, joy….*" God's Spirit is growing in you more than you can imagine or measure.

Regardless, the list in Galatians 5 serves as an excellent starting point. Before moving on to the next section, I'd like to provide a brief insight into those qualities within the context of the ancient Greek understanding at the time when they were written. Hopefully, this will help you begin to recognize the Spirit's ongoing work as He nurtures these qualities of Jesus in your mind, will, emotions, and actions.

LOVE.

We talked about this a little bit in chapter 7, but here's a refresher: The word Paul used here is *agapé*. It's understood to be the highest expression of love and goodwill—a pure, selfless, unconditional thing that always seeks the best interests (i.e., the welfare) of the one who is loved.[133]

JOY.

This is the Greek word, *chara*. It's characterized by the idea of "calm delight" and gladness and is associated with an awareness of God's grace in any circumstance. It's not to be confused with simple happiness or pleasure. As C. S. Lewis observed, "Joy is never in our power, and pleasure often is..."[134]

PEACE.

A beautiful word we now adapt for use as a woman's name: *eirēnē*. Although it certainly includes the idea of absence of conflict, the more complete meaning of *eirēnē* is that of "wholeness," including harmony, prosperity, and fulfilment.[135]

PATIENCE.

Here Paul wrote, *makrothymia*. This word indicates a willingness to wait, despite provocation, for a situation to resolve. The King James Bible translates this as "*longsuffering*," and it includes qualities of endurance, particularly in relation to physical or emotional pain.

KINDNESS.

The Greek word for this is *chrēstotēs*, and it speaks of moral virtue in relationships; it's an ability to be generously friendly and helpful to others, even enemies.[136]

GOODNESS.

This word is unique to the New Testament in ancient times: *agath-ōsynē*. It doesn't appear in non-religious, ancient Greek texts. Related to *chrēstotēs* above, it refers to a personal quality of overall virtue, or spiritual and moral excellence.

FAITHFULNESS.

For this word, Paul wrote *pistis*. That can be both active and passive in use. In the active, it means willfully trusting and believing; in the passive it indicates trustworthiness and unshakable reliability.[137]

GENTLENESS.

The term for this is *prautēs*, and it demonstrates a personality that's calm and nonthreatening—while possessing at the same time strength and authority to impose one's will. One with *prautēs* is neither weak nor passive, but is considerate and respectful.[138]

SELF-CONTROL.

This is the Greek word, *enkrateia*. It refers to mastery of one's actions that are related to desires, particularly in regard to exercising restraint in the face of temptation.[139]

PREFACE TO SPIRITUAL GIFTS

All right, for the rest of this—slightly extended—chapter, we'll be exploring what are known as "The Gifts of the Spirit." (Someday I want to write a book of silly cartoons called *The GIFs of the Spirit*. That'd be fun, right? But I digress, sorry…) When we speak about the gifts of the Spirit, I think it's important first to point out that Scripture mixes them all up with each other, never bothering to categorize any of them as "sign gifts" or "speaking gifts" or "administrative gifts" and so on.

The apostle Paul does rank some gifts as "greater" than others (see 1 Corinthians 12:28–31), but his ranking has nothing to do with categories. For instance, he ranks teaching above miracles, followed by healing and then helping—mixing the mundane and the miraculous without differentiating any as belonging to a certain "kind" of spiritual gift.

The reality is that all spiritual gifts are just abilities that the Spirit gives, *as He desires*, to His people. We're the ones who insist on sorting them into groups, mostly so we can elevate the gift groupings we prefer and de-emphasize the ones we don't. I've seen as few as two categories ("administrative" and "sign" gifts), and as many as five. Even then, the placement of a gift into a category is fairly arbitrary, depending, for instance, on whether a theologian thinks "prophecy" and "discernment" are sign gifts or whether things like "giving" and "mercy" are administrative gifts. Ugh.

In case you couldn't tell already, this imposition of a separation over the Scripture texts annoys me, as I firmly believe in *all* the gifts of the Spirit.

However...

Despite my snooty theological complaints, I'm going to follow the accepted practice of my peers in discussing them according to two categories—not because I like it, but because it's familiar and should make it easier for you to follow as we talk through them in this chapter. So, in the next section, we'll focus on "Personality Gifts," and after that, we'll dig into "Sign Gifts." (Be aware, though, that I'm one of those guys who lumps things like prophecy and discernment and word of knowledge in with "sign gifts" that include miracles and speaking in tongues.)

The second thing I want us to remember about spiritual gifts is that (like the fruit of the Spirit) the lists we glean from Scripture are not exhaustive. It is, I suppose, *possible* that all gifts of the Spirit that exist are found in the five New Testament passages most associated with them (see Romans 12:6–8; 1 Corinthians 12:8–10; 1 Corinthians 12:28–31; Ephesians 4:7–12; 1 Peter 4:10–11), but that's extremely unlikely. The fact that there are five summaries of these gifts in Scripture, and all are different from each other—even though four of them were written by the same guy—strongly suggests that what we've got are representative lists of gifts, not complete inventories of them all.

Third, every Christian (this includes you!) has received at least one spiritual gift or, more likely, a cluster of gifts which the Spirit uses to flaunt Christ through you. (See 1 Corinthians 12:7, 12:11.) Every gift given demonstrates publicly one or more unique aspect of Jesus's character and abilities at work in your life.

Which is, you know, pretty cool.

And just to clarify, being gifted in one area doesn't mean you are therefore completely devoid of any other spiritual ability. It just means that your gifted aspect of Christ comes more naturally for you, more easily, and is more frequently noticeable to others.

Also, although there may be maturity limitations, there doesn't appear to be an age limit on the Holy Spirit's gifting. (Some even ask the question of when a spiritual gift is given, at birth or at conversion, or at some other time?[140] But that's a discussion for a different book.) My wife often told the story of a time when she was a teenager and had somehow injured her back. She had pain for weeks, and then at a home-church meeting where her father was pastor, she asked for prayer. A child, a little girl about five or six years old, placed hands on her back and prayed simply for Jesus to heal. Amy said she immediately felt a release of the worst of the pain, and by the next morning, all pain was gone. So, you know, never underestimate the faith of a child.

One more thing and then we'll dive in. Scripture is clear that the gifts of the Spirit are not given for your benefit. The apostle Peter advised us that, *"Each of you should use whatever gift you have received **to serve others**, as faithful stewards of God's grace in its various forms"* (1 Peter 4:10). Paul backed this up as God's intention when he said, *"Since you are eager for gifts of the Spirit, try to excel in those that **build up the church**"* (1 Corinthians 14:12). And *"to each one the manifestation of the Spirit is given **for the common good**"* (1 Corinthians 12:7), and *"so that the **body of Christ may be built up**"* (Ephesians 4:12).

So please, as you read through the rest of this chapter, keep top of mind that the reason you're gifted by the Holy Spirit is *to serve others*—to be helpful and generous, not proud and demanding or self-satisfied. With your gifts, you're to be like Christ who *"did not come to be served, but to serve"* (Matthew 20:28).

OK, let's go.

THE HOLY SPIRIT EXPRESSES HIS GIFTS IN YOUR PERSONALITY

(See 1 Corinthians 12:4; 12:7–9; 12:11; 14:37; Hebrews 2:4. Also: Romans 12:6–8; 1 Corinthians 12:1, 7–11; 12:28–31; Ephesians 4:11–12; 1 Peter 4:10–11.)

Here's where we begin to look at what I call the "personality gifts" of the Holy Spirit. For this group, I've defined "personality" as any gift that:

a. is not a supernatural ability.

b. is public by nature, though it may not be intended for a crowd to see, and may often actually be unknown to the wider world.

c. is obvious testimony of Jesus at work.

There are nine gifts of the Spirit that I'd categorize as personality gifts. They are: Apostleship, Encouraging, Evangelism, Faith, Giving, Leading (also known as Guiding or Pastoring), Serving (or Helping), Showing Mercy, and Teaching (or Speaking).

Because personality gifts aren't obviously supernatural, people gifted in these ways are sometimes mistaken for just being talented or passionate about a unique interest. After all, many people may be good at something like teaching, without being gifted by the Spirit in that exercise. In my experience, though, it's usually pretty obvious when someone has a personality gift of the Spirit.

The gifted person has unusual confidence when exercising the gift, and that aspect of the personality comes through naturally, without needing to be forced. Sure, one can get more comfortable exercising the gift with practice, and can even learn more about how to use that gift well—but generally speaking, it's just easier for that person than for the rest of us. Also, people with personality gifts report a sense of joy when expressing them. Whether they're serving, speaking, showing mercy, or whatever, the exercise of the gift is energizing, not draining. It's that moment when someone gets the feeling, "I was made for this!" And, the results from this kind of gift expression tend to exceed normal expectations (and in that sense, they may demonstrate something of the supernatural).

For instance, I saw Billy Graham preach once when I was nineteen. We were in a convention center venue that held over 15,000 seats. As he was speaking, I was honestly a little bored. To me, it seemed a fairly basic gospel message: Jesus loves you, He died for you, and now offers eternal life to you. Then Reverend Graham said, simply and fairly dispassionately, "If you'd like to give your life to Jesus, I invite you to come forward now."

Bam!

Instantly (and I'm not exaggerating), thousands of people started streaming from their seats to become Christians. Some were even running to get to the front, weeping and ready to start new lives as soon as possible. I was stunned—and that's when I first understood that Billy Graham's "personality gift" was definitely evangelism. I've tried to never underestimate God's gifting like that again.

One other thing to note about personality gifts, from theologian Millard Erickson: "Some gifts, such as faith and service, are qualities or activities expected of every Christian; in such cases it is likely that the writer has in mind an unusual capability in that area."[141]

All right, let's talk briefly about each of these nine personality gifts.

APOSTLESHIP (SEE 1 CORINTHIANS 12:28.)

Surprisingly, the New Testament never gives a clear definition of "apostle." It was used to reference Jesus's inner circle of disciples, as well as Paul, but also other unnamed followers. (See 1 Corinthians 15:5–7.) The Greek word for this is *apostolous*, and it means simply "messenger." That seems the safest understanding of this gift—one who is uniquely gifted as a messenger of Christ. For that reason, missionaries are often considered to have an apostolic gifting.

ENCOURAGING (SEE ROMANS 12:8.)

People with this gift (also called "exhorting") are particularly good at coming alongside another to offer help, hope, comfort, strength, instruction, and, when needed, correction. These are the ones who seem to draw people to them and who inspire loyalty in others, because they always want the best for those they know. They're sometimes teachers, but more often "disciplers" who spend a lot of one-on-one time with others, encouraging all along the way. My wife, Amy, had this gift, and people from all walks of life were just irresistibly drawn to her in that way.

EVANGELISM (SEE EPHESIANS 4:11.)

Think of Reverend Billy Graham as a prominent example of this kind of gifting. In the days of the early church, a person with this gift was known as a "gospelizer," or (more literally) "herald of good news."[142] This person is just gifted at telling people about Jesus, maybe as a speaker, or a musician, or as your coworker at AT&T (or wherever). The person may not be particularly polished or exceptionally articulate, but people still seem to listen and respond, and that's the real sign of the gift of evangelism.

FAITH (SEE 1 CORINTHIANS 12:9.)

The gift of faith, in this context, appears to indicate a certain exceptionality of faith expression, as when Paul said, *"if I have all faith, so as to remove mountains"* (1 Corinthians 13:2 ESV). Interestingly, in all of history, no one has ever moved a mountain (yet)—but this gift indicates (a) an understanding of God's calling regarding a specific course of action or event, (b) complete trust that Jesus will accomplish that calling, and (c) acting accordingly.

I recall reading about a time when Mother Teresa insisted she would go into an active war zone in Beirut, Lebanon, to rescue thirty-seven stranded children. Despite many objections for her safety, she made arrangements to go. Although fighting had been going on nonstop for months, at precisely the time she was ready to go, the war zone fell silent. She went in, got the children, and came out again. As soon as she was back to safety, the war resumed.[143] That would be an example of the gift of (exceptional) faith.

GIVING (SEE ROMANS 12:8.)

Again, this appears to be referencing exceptional giving—not necessarily in the amount given, but in the generosity and selfless spirit of the gift. It carries the idea of giving without any thought of receiving in return, giving without pretense or obligation, giving freely, and with delight. People with this gift truly love giving things away, without concern for who gets the credit. The biblical example of this is the widow who gave two small coins—even though that was all she had. (See Mark 12:41–44.)

LEADING/GUIDING/PASTORING (SEE ROMANS 12:8; 1 CORINTHIANS 12:28; EPHESIANS 4:11.)[144]

Perhaps you've had to suffer in a church that had a pastor who just didn't have the gift of pastoring (also called leading and guiding). That's a hard, dry place to be. When your pastor is actually gifted in leading, it's water for a thirsty soul. A person with this gift plays the role of spiritual shepherd for a group of Christians who gather as a church. This person teaches God's Word, encourages spiritual growth, and creates a safe community where people can thrive spiritually and use their gifts to serve each other and those who live nearby.

SERVING/HELPING (SEE ROMANS 12:7; 1 CORINTHIANS 12:28; 1 PETER 4:11.)

The root word Paul used for this gift in Romans 12:7 is *diakonia*, and from it we get the English term, "deacon"—although this gift is never limited to only that official position in a church.[145] In fact, in ancient days, it referred to someone who waits tables or ministers supportively to others. The core concept of this gift is similar to giving, but it's expressed as *generous helpfulness*—assisting others in a way that offers relief and aid to them without pretense or obligation, serving freely, and with delight. Stephen and the other men chosen to wait tables in the early church are an example of this kind of gift. (See Acts 6:1–7.)

SHOWING MERCY (SEE ROMANS 12:8.)

I jokingly say this is the gift people get when they lose their sense of smell, because, I'm ashamed to admit, too often I've failed to show mercy simply because I couldn't take the odors associated with it. But seriously, I think the gift of mercy is the absolute most compelling way to demonstrate Jesus to our world. The person with this gift is filled with compassion for anyone who suffers—and is determined to do something about it.

These are the people you'll find in cancer wards, in AIDS hospices, visiting the sick, washing the weak, feeding the homeless, treating all with dignity and care—regardless of who they are or what condition they're in. Jesus is our biblical example of this (see Luke 18:35–42 and all of the gospel events). And yes, we need more people using this gift!

TEACHING/SPEAKING (SEE ROMANS 12:7; 1 CORINTHIANS 12:28; 1 PETER 4:11.)

This is a popular gift, simply because it's always expressed in front of a crowd. Unfortunately, many who claim this gift simply don't have it—they just like the status that comes with being up front. Biblically speaking, this gift is always about teaching truths of God to others. Typically, that includes studying and understanding the Bible, and communicating Scripture in ways that others find helpful and understandable. That communication doesn't always mean preaching; it can also be expressed through dialogue and discussion. (See Acts 17:16–34.)

Although one can be trained to improve teaching skills, the gift of teaching is something different than just oratorical polish or showmanship. In fact, many gifted teachers aren't particularly flashy or charismatic at all. As with the gifts of faith and giving, this gift indicates a certain exceptionality that's noticeable. These are speakers who teach without pretense or obligation, giving insight freely and with delight.

The best example I can give for this comes from Luke 24. After Cleopas and his companion had walked with the resurrected Jesus and listened to Him teach along the road, he said, *"Didn't our hearts burn within us as he talked…and explained the Scriptures to us?"* (Luke 24:32 NLT). That's what it feels like when you get to hear someone with the gift of teaching/speaking.

THE HOLY SPIRIT DISPLAYS HIS POWER AND SIGNS IN YOUR EXPERIENCE

(See Matthew 12:28; Luke 1:35; 4:14; 24:49; Acts 2:33; 10:38; Romans 1:4; 15:19; 1 Corinthians 2:4; 1 Thessalonians 1:5; 1 Timothy 3:16; Galatians 3:5. Also: Romans 12:6–8; 1 Corinthians 12:1, 7–11; 12:28–31; 14:2; Ephesians 4:11–12; 1 Peter 4:10–11.)

Now we'll begin to look at what are mostly known as the "sign gifts" of the Holy Spirit. For this group, I've defined "sign" as any gift that:

a. is an event of supernatural power,

b. is public by nature (meaning, it's intended for others to see); and

c. is obvious testimony of Jesus at work.

By my definition, Scripture identifies the following eight as sign gifts: Discernment (also called Distinguishing Between Spirits), Healing, Interpretation of Tongues or Languages, Word of Knowledge, Word of Wisdom, Miracles, Prophecy, and Speaking in Tongues or Languages.

Notice that I've included as sign gifts some that others wouldn't—so feel free to disagree with me on this and to mentally redistribute your preferences in either the "personality" or "sign" groupings. Honestly, it makes no difference to me. (Ha—see, I told you I didn't like forcing categories onto the lists of spiritual gifts!)

OK, here's a brief summary of each of the sign gifts as I understand them.

DISCERNMENT, OR DISTINGUISHING BETWEEN SPIRITS
(SEE 1 CORINTHIANS 12:10.)

The one with this gift has a unique ability to understand what's true and what's counterfeit in regard to spiritual matters. The biblical example of this is in Acts 5:1–11, when Peter knew instantly that Ananias and Sapphira were lying about the significance of their offering.

In the early church, this gift was almost always a reference to the ability to distinguish between authentic prophets and teachers of Christ, and those who were false, either by simple human error or by corruptive intent.[146] The Greek root word used for discernment (or "distinguishing") in 1 Corinthians 12:10 is *diakrisis*, and it certainly encompasses that idea of distinguishing prophecy, but it has wider application for us today as well. Its primary meaning is "the act of judgment," as in accurately determining the reality of a situation and then acting accordingly. In my experience, those with this gift seem to "see right through" other people and situations, even when there's no obvious evidence.

For instance, I remember a time when one of my friends was working in a retail shop, and a man came in who looked dirty and poor. One of his coworkers, a Christian, scoffed and said that they should watch that guy because he was probably a thief. My friend looked at him for a moment and then said, "No, I think he's a brother." He walked up to him and said, "I just have to ask, do you know Jesus?" The man broke into a wide smile and said, "Yes!" They talked happily together for a while—as Christian brothers. That's the kind of thing that happens with the gift of discernment of spirits, an unnatural recognition of what's true and what's not.

HEALING (SEE 1 CORINTHIANS 12:9; 1 CORINTHIANS 12:28.)

I think it's funny that those who are convinced miraculous healings no longer occur still pray for healing when they or their loved ones become sick. Of course, I don't fault them for praying—I expect that if they keep doing it, sooner or later, they're going to have to abandon their closely held disbelief in modern miracles.

Anyway…

The gift of healing is just what it sounds like—a supernatural ability to effect physical recovery in another person, typically through prayer and/or declaration of health in accordance with the unseen intention of God.[147] This can be recovery from illness or injury, and it's been a hallmark of the Christian faith since the very beginning, continuing to today.

Healings by Jesus and the apostles are well recorded in Scripture. Early church historian, Irenaeus (AD 130–202) once mocked two false teachers because they weren't able to heal the sick like authentic Christians were doing. Origen (AD 184–253) also recorded that he'd "seen many delivered from serious ailments, and from mental distraction and madness, [and] countless other diseases." [148] Church father, Augustine (AD 354–430), documented miraculous healings in his work, *The City of God*, because he said, "these modern miracles are scarcely known…although they are reported to the faithful by the faithful."[149] Even today, according to the Public Religion Research Institute, some 27 percent of Christians in America (more than one in four) report that they've "witnessed divine healing of an injury or illness."[150]

I could go on, but let me just say that healing miracles have happened in every era of Christian history, and I know personally some who've been healed—though I can't take time to document those here.[151] Regardless, the advice of Madeleine L'Engle regarding healing is instructive: "If Jesus of Nazareth was God truly become man for us, as I believe he was, then we should be able to walk on water, to heal the sick, even to accept the Father's answer to our prayers when it is not the answer we hope for, when it is *no*."[152]

INTERPRETATION OF TONGUES OR LANGUAGES
(SEE 1 CORINTHIANS 12:10.)

This gift, interpretation of tongues, is the only "dependent" one among all the listed gifts of the Spirit. By that I mean, this gift can't be used unless another one is being expressed—specifically, speaking in tongues.

The Greek reference in 1 Corinthians 12:10 is *herméneia*, and it's tempting to view that as meaning simply "translation," as in, I say something in a tongue and then you translate it. That's part of it, but the actuality of interpretation of tongues has more to do with the intent of the message rather than the individual words that are spoken. The HELPS word studies resource defines it this way, "Giving the gist of a message rather than a strict translation; an equivalent meaning, rather than a 'word-for-word' rendering." *Harper's Bible Dictionary* adds, "explanation, exposition, expression, [and] intelligible rendition."[153]

In my experience, this gift is very rare (meaning, I've never met anyone who authentically possessed this gift), and unique. If you are one to whom God has given interpretation of tongues, will you send me a note to tell me what it's like for you? You can reach me through the "Contact" page on Bible-Smart.com. Thanks.

WORD OF KNOWLEDGE (SEE 1 CORINTHIANS 12:8.)

Some see the word of knowledge as just another way to refer to the gift of teaching—but that begs the question as to why Paul would list those two things separately in 1 Corinthians 12 when he doesn't do that with any other listed gift. Others are reluctant to include this (and the word of wisdom below) as a "sign gift," but as I said earlier, it doesn't matter to me which category you prefer for a spiritual gift. Feel free to ignore my choice of grouping here if you're uncomfortable with it. (I don't really think we should put gifts in different categories anyway...but there's no need for me to get back on that high horse again, right?)

Anyway, this gift, along with "word of wisdom" is only mentioned in 1 Corinthians 12:8, and nowhere else in Scripture or early Christian documents, so our only biblical understanding is what we find here in this verse.

The Greek term for "word of knowledge" is *logos gnōseōs*, and it translates literally just like that, "word of knowledge." The word *gnōseōs*, though, has interesting connotations apart from our dry, academic understanding of "facts on file in the mind." It gives the indication of understanding gained by personal experience—as in the difference between knowing the stove is hot because someone told you, and knowing it's hot because you just burned your hand on it.

The commonly accepted understanding of this in practice is "a supernatural impartation of knowledge about some human need or situation."[154] This fits with my experience, where someone has knowledge about another that they couldn't possibly know without God whispering it to them. The assumption, of course, is that the unique knowledge is given so the one with the gift can be helpful with it.

I remember once sitting in a Bible study with a bunch of young adults, and when I looked at one of the girls, I saw sorrow and shame, despite her smile. So I told her, "I'm going to tell you a story, and I'm not going to tell you why because, if it's the right one, you'll know why." Then I told her a story about the necessity of failure as a stepping stone for success. She immediately burst into tears. She'd moved across the country to marry her boyfriend, and after moving, they broke up instead of getting married. She felt deep shame in the failure of that relationship—and I had understood that about her without anyone telling me about it. That's why I shared the story with her. It was, apparently, the encouragement she needed to hear. That's an example of how the gift of a word of knowledge might work.

WORD OF WISDOM (SEE 1 CORINTHIANS 12:8.)

The word of wisdom is similar to the gift of a word of knowledge, except that this appears to be a supernatural ability to apply specific truth of God to specific situations, especially when that kind of application isn't obvious.

In 1 Corinthians 12:10, the phrase is *logos sophias*, and the meaning of *sophias* is pretty straightforward: insight and intelligence. I think one of the associate pastors at my church may have this gift. Whenever I come to him with a question or seek advice, he immediately has just the right Scripture in mind to share with me. I joke sometimes that I think he must've memorized the entire Bible or something, but he only laughs and says that's just the way his mind works. According to him, he "sees" Scriptures pop up in his mind when he needs them. I don't know if he'd agree, but I think he's describing the activity of the Spirit supernaturally giving him the gift of a word of wisdom.

This is also a gifting that many pastors and speakers have, and if so, you've noticed it. After hearing them speak, you probably walked away saying things like, "I never thought of that before," and "That was just so helpful for what I'm going through right now." If you've got a pastor/teacher like that, be sure to tell them thanks for using their gifting to serve your church!

MIRACLES (1 CORINTHIANS 12:10; 1 CORINTHIANS 12:28.)

Scripture often describes this gift as the ability to do *"signs and wonders"* (see, for instance, Acts 2:22, 14:3, Romans 15:18–19, among others.) Second Corinthians 12:12 also indicates this gift is one of the *"marks of a true apostle."* The traditional definition is the ability to enact "a divine action that transcends the ordinary course of nature."[155]

The Greek root in 1 Corinthians 12 is *dunamis*, which strictly means "power," and isn't necessarily supernatural, so some interpret this as simply any impressive work of God. That'd be comforting for those of us without the gift of miracles, but the context of Scripture's use of this term always indicates some kind of supernatural, awe-inspiring event such as the ministry of Jesus. This kind of miraculous power is demonstrated in a viewable event, in a way that evokes a sense of awe in the viewers. Scripturally, it also includes the ability to cast out demons. (See Luke 10:7; Acts 8:5–7; 8:16–18.)

I've not known anyone with an authentic, reliably consistent gift of miracles, but I've heard stories of people like this. I look forward to meeting someone with this gift someday.

PROPHECY (SEE ROMANS 12:6; 1 CORINTHIANS 12:10; 1 CORINTHIANS 12:28; EPHESIANS 4:11.)

According to biblical history, a prophet was someone who "received supernatural messages from God and was commissioned to pass these messages on to God's people."[156] In this way, Jesus was considered a prophet in His time. (See Matthew 21:10–11). Prophecy is a significant part of the Old Testament and appears in the New Testament as well. It typically deals with messages of morality and predictions for the future (that is, both declarative and predictive messages). In fact, according to one source, about one-fourth of Scripture was predictive when it was first revealed."[157]

The gift of prophecy, then, is the ability to supernaturally understand a message from God and then speak it to a gathering of people, often to Christians. In Paul's day, prophets were foundational to the structure of the church (see Ephesians 2:9–20), and it was common for churches to have several prophets in residence. (See 1 Corinthians 14:29–33.) According to the biblical example, prophetic messages are given by God in a variety of ways, including visions, dreams, angels, trances, and inner understanding of God's specific intent. The unifying aspect is that any prophecy is always true and verifiable. In ages past, historical events verified a prophecy; in our day, prophecy is verified primarily through scriptural consistency (meaning, the message is fully in line with the teachings of the Bible, and can be completely supported by biblical texts), and sometimes by historical events.

Today, the gift of prophecy is more difficult to confirm in a person, even though nearly half of Americans (45 percent) believe that "God reveals his plans for the future to humans as a Prophecy."[158] Verification of the prophetic gift is especially difficult since we have so many self-proclaimed media prophets who tend to spout their own opinions (political and otherwise) as words straight from the mouth of God—and then make no apologies when their prophecies turn out to be wrong. Still, this is a legitimate gift of God's Spirit, and when you come into contact with someone handling this gift in a humble, everyday way (instead of a showy, send-me-the-money way), it'd probably be worth listening to that person.

SPEAKING IN TONGUES OR LANGUAGES (SEE 1 CORINTHIANS 12:10; 1 CORINTHIANS 12:28.)

This is simply a supernatural ability to speak in a language that the speaker does not understand, and is something that one in five (21 percent) of American Christians report seeing and/or experiencing.[159]

It may surprise you to discover that speaking in tongues is not limited to the Christian faith. Hindus, Muslims, Mormons, and more report speaking in tongues as part of a worship experience.[160] Ecstatic utterances like this were also common among the pagan religions of ancient Rome. In

Paul's day, particularly in Corinth, speaking in tongues was thought to be evidence of the presence of a god or goddess, and oracles were drugged so as to prompt mutterings that were viewed as divine messages from one of the random gods in the Roman pantheon.[161] Some use that cultic history as so-called "proof" that tongues are not from God, but that's a foolish perspective that deliberately ignores the testimony of Scripture and the fact that many of the gifts of the Spirit—both personal and sign—can be found in other religions.

Within the Christian faith, there appear to be two applications of this gift, one public and one private.

Public speaking in tongues serves either as a testimony to unbelievers (see 1 Corinthians 14:22) or as a message of encouragement for a gathering of Christians. (See 1 Corinthians 14:26–27). For example, my pastor tells the story of a time he and his wife visited a church in Canada many years ago. Suddenly, a man came onstage and started babbling in a strange language. My pastor and his wife were uncomfortable and talked about leaving. But afterward, the leader of that church asked if anyone knew what had been said. Another man, from the back of the room, came slowly forward. Dumbfounded, he said he was from a small village in China, and that he'd just heard the other speaking in his native dialect, telling him that today was the day for him to give his life to Jesus. And so he did.

That kind of tongues was a testimony to unbelievers. Tongues for the church would be those where an interpreter was ready to share the meaning of a message for a specific congregation, after someone spoke in a different language to that congregation.

Private speaking in tongues serves as a prayer of intercession, praise, or personal expression. (See 1 Corinthians 14:2.) Many associate this with the phrase we talked about in chapter 6 of this book, *"praying in the Spirit"* (see Romans 8:26–27; Ephesians 6:18; Jude 1:20). Theologian Wayne Grudem also offers this assessment, "Paul sees this kind of prayer as an activity that occurs in the spiritual realm, whereby our spirits speak directly to God, but our minds are somehow bypassed and do not understand what we are praying."[162]

When I was a teenager, it never even occurred to me to disbelieve in the Holy Spirit's gift of speaking in tongues—even though I didn't have that gift. My mother, on the other hand, was a staunch Southern Baptist who viewed tongues as dangerous and deceptive. We had a number of conversations that frustrated her because she thought I was going into error by saying that the gift of tongues was valid for today. Then, when I was in my mid-twenties, one day she came to me and said, "Mikey, how did you know?" I wasn't sure at first what she was talking about. "How did you know about speaking in tongues?" she asked. "I read it in the Bible," I said. She shook her head and told me, "Well, you were right." Turns out that one day, while she was praying, without expecting it, she began speaking out loud in another language. She didn't know what she was saying, but she understood what she was doing. At first, she was exhilarated, then embarrassed. Her own experience now forced her to admit her disbelief in the Holy Spirit's gift had been an error!

So remember, if you are one who doesn't have the gift of speaking in tongues—that's OK, but it doesn't mean that gift is nonexistent, dangerous, or deceptive. God's Spirit gives His gifts the way He wants to; might as well get used to that.

Obviously, I've left out other spiritual gifts (like dreams and interpretation of dreams, which Genesis records was a spiritual gift that Joseph had). That's not because I disbelieve in them, but only because they fall outside the scope of this book, which is to explore every time the New Testament mentions the Holy Spirit by name. Still, I have a friend who is something of an expert on spiritual gifts in both Old and New Testaments, so someday maybe we'll write a book together that's solely on that topic. Meanwhile…

The fruit of the Spirit and all the gifts of the Spirit are inescapably crucial to our everyday Christian lives—yet we must remember they are also "of the Spirit."

The means by which the Holy Spirit flaunts Jesus in us are conspicuously *not* "of the Mikey," or "of the Amy," or even "of the generic believer who shall heretofore go unnamed." As Pastor Francis Chan eloquently said of the fruit of the Spirit, "Grunting and *saying* through clenched teeth 'I *will* be patient' hasn't worked yet, and that isn't likely to change."[163] In regard to the Spirit's gifts, Dr. Millard Erickson adds, "The Holy Spirit apportions the various gifts *to whom and as he wills.*"[164]

It is God's Holy Spirit who brings these flamboyant qualities of Christ's character and activity into our being and then shows them off in our world. That happens when He wants, and how He wants. So we have to ask, what are we to do when it comes to this aspect of the daily Christian life?

First, I'd suggest that we *relax* and stop trying to do the Holy Spirit's job for Him. (Perhaps you've heard me mention that before? Ahem.)

Next, we can be grateful the Spirit has made us aware of His working within us, and even allows us to cooperate with Him to accomplish His purpose. When we are knowingly grateful, we can then *celebrate* and *participate* in the Spirit's flaunting of Christ whenever we want, as much as we want.

We will also benefit from maintaining a certain amount of humility in regard to the gifts that God's Spirit lavishes on us. We're followers in the exercise of His gifts, not leaders or masters. That's why Paul wisely gave us this advice millennia ago as a prelude to his writing on spiritual gifts, *"Don't think you are better than you really are. Be honest in your evaluation of yourselves"* (Romans 12:3 NLT). Similarly, R. A. Torrey's warning from more than a century ago still bears repeating: "One of the saddest things ever witnessed is the way in which some people who have entered by the Spirit's power into a life of victory become self-confident and fancy that the victory is in themselves...The depths to which such people sometimes fall is appalling."[165]

Further, we can be aware that the Spirit seems to be open to giving you gifts that you desire. Paul encouraged the Christians in Corinth to *"earnestly desire the spiritual gifts, especially that you may prophesy"* (1 Corinthians 14:1 ESV), and to *"earnestly desire the higher gifts"* (1 Corinthians 12:31 ESV). So I don't think it's wrong to ask Jesus for a particular gifting—but regardless of His answer, it'd be unwise to neglect the gift(s) He's already given you in hopes that He'll bestow something different.

Finally, and best of all, we can pour our energies into discovering greater intimacy with the Spirit of Christ given so freely to each of us. The key to using and enjoying our gifts is ever-increasing closeness with the Giver; when we know Him better, we know better how and when to use the gifts He's given. After all, sociologists tell us we become like those we spend the most time with, so why not take advantage of that part of human nature and hang out with God's Spirit every chance we get?

That seems like a solid plan to me.

FOR FURTHER REFLECTION AND SMALL GROUP DISCUSSION:

1. What resonated with you most in this chapter? Why?

2. What does it mean to you that the fruit of the Spirit and the gifts of the Spirit are *"of the Spirit?"* Explain that to the ten-year-old version of you.

3. What does this chapter make you want to pray about? What do you think would happen if you prayed about that every day this week?

ELEVEN

THE HOLY SPIRIT INCARNATES HIS CHURCH THROUGH YOU

The Holy Spirit unifies you with God's children. He plants you
with people and gives you grace to: Build each other up in His
church; thrive as one body of believers; and mobilize
His ministry to your world.

The first time Mary Karr ever prayed, she knelt on a cushion in her living room and said to the heavens, "Higher Power, where the f--k have you been?"

She didn't want to pray, not really, but everybody in her Alcoholics Anonymous group kept telling her it was a good idea. So she decided it was time for what she now calls her "prayer number one." As she expected, nothing happened. Except...that *feeling*. Was Someone listening after all? She started to stand, paused, then realized she wasn't done. Back on her knees, Mary said silently, sincerely, "Help me. Help. Me. Help me to feel better so I can believe in You, you subtle b-----d." She sighed and went back to bed.

But...she kept praying.

Every morning she'd wake up and pray, "Keep me sober." At night, after the end of each long day, she'd whisper to God and say, "Thanks."

Then something truly unexpected happened. One Sunday morning, her eight-year-old son, Dev, announced to her, "I want to go to church. I want to see if God's there."

So that's what they did, spending several months going to a parade of denominational gatherings, from an Episcopalian church to a Reformed church, to a hand-clapping Baptist church, and a few more mainline Protestant churches. Finally, Mary and her son settled on a Catholic parish where they had a few friends.

Of course, no matter what church they visited, she brought along a paperback book to read in the pews. She was there for Dev, after all, not for herself. But one week she forgot to bring her book—and didn't miss it. And then another. And before long, she didn't bother to bring it to church at all. She was too busy meeting people, becoming friends with these Catholic Christians. Watching. Listening. Even praying.

One Sunday, at Mass, she joined with a few others, now her friends, in prayer. She describes it this way: "I enter and get on my knees like everybody else, saying the prayers I usually say at home. Opening my eyes, I actually tear up. There's something different about praying in company—I can't deny it—once you get over feeling like a poser."

After a while, Mary couldn't resist meeting from time to time with the priest, Father Kane, to hash out all the reasons why she objected to organized religion and church and the pope and so on. She's an intellectual, you know. A prestigious professor at Syracuse University. A *New York Times* best-selling author. A Guggenheim Fellow in poetry, and winner of multiple Pushcart Prizes. Father Kane and Mary had become friends, though, and she figured he could take it.

One day, during their conversation, he just grinned and said to her, "God's after you. Struggle if you want."

Catholics aren't who I thought they'd be, she decided eventually, *not even close. It isn't the ritual of high Mass that impresses me, but the people—their collective surrender. If I can't do reverence to that, how dead are my innards?*

Mary Karr's struggle didn't last long, a little over a year at most. She finally turned herself over to Jesus, got baptized, and joined that Catholic parish. "If you'd told me even one year before I start taking Dev to church regular that I'd wind up whispering my sins in the confessional or on my knees saying the rosary, I would've laughed myself cockeyed. More likely pastime? Pole dancer. International spy. Drug mule. Assassin." But because of one congregation of Christian people, she's none of those things. Now, instead, she's on the great adventure of spending the rest of her life with Jesus.[166] Who knows what'll happen next?

In case you haven't guessed it yet, this story of Mary Karr is actually a story of your Holy Spirit—and the way He draws people to himself by *incarnating His church through you.* That, I'd like to say to Dr. Mary, is where God has been.

Now, let's explore this more.

THE HOLY SPIRIT HELPS YOU BUILD EACH OTHER UP IN HIS CHURCH

(See Acts 9:31; 11:28; 15:28; 20:28; 21:11.)

A quick glimpse in the book of Acts and we see the Holy Spirit actively using *people in His church* to help *people in His church.* In this way we receive from our brothers and sisters:

+ Encouragement (See Acts 9:31.)

+ Warnings (See Acts 11:28; 21:11.)

+ Help to lighten spiritual and emotional burdens (See Acts 15:28.)

+ Spiritual accountability, and mentors (shepherds) in the faith (See Acts 20:28.)

These are brief examples of what Paul meant when he said we're to use our spiritual gifts to *"build up the church"* (1 Corinthians 14:12), *"for the common good"* (1 Corinthians 12:7), and *"so that the body of Christ may be built up"* (Ephesians 4:12).

Listen: You and I were never meant to live out the Christian life in supposedly holy solitude, or to divorce ourselves from a local congregation of believers. Christianity, according to the Bible, is a team sport—and the Holy Spirit always meant it to be like that.

Last year I received an email from a reader asking me this question: "Do we really need to attend an actual church, or can we watch pastors like Dr. David Jeremiah and Greg Laurie and read our Bibles and pray daily?"

My first response was to groan. Because of who I am and what I do, people sometimes like to write to me because they want to start an argument on some random theological point or obscure doctrine—or they're just mad about something I wrote somewhere and they want to let me know about it. (Yes, I get a surprising amount of hate mail from otherwise loving Christian people, and I've learned to ignore it all.) So, in the beginning, I wasn't even going to respond to this woman; I figured she was just spoiling for a fight about the politicization of the modern church.

That night, though, I couldn't sleep. Sometime after midnight I realized why. God, it seemed, wanted me to know He'd prompted that woman to email that question to me—and He expected me to answer her. So I sighed, turned on the lamp beside my bed and stayed up way too late to write a short reply. I won't bore you with the entire email I sent (if you want to read it, check this footnote[167] where I've included a URL for you), but I'll tell you the gist.

First, I pointed out that one cannot "read our Bibles and pray daily" without quickly seeing in Scripture the dramatic importance and honor it is to be an active part of a local church. I shared with her a few Scriptures to emphasize that truth, and reminded her that Jesus indicated the church was His doing. (See Matthew 16:18). And I asked the question, if a local church community is an unnecessary thing, then why did the apostle Paul spend his entire adult life forming local churches in cities all over the world?

Then I yawned and finally went to sleep.

I'd like to say I forgot about it after that, but that wouldn't be true. The increasingly popular sentiment that the local church—founded and vitalized by the Holy Spirit Himself—is unnecessary to the Christian life weighed on my soul. It made my heart hurt, and I had a hard time letting it go. Look, I know there are problems in the church; I understand the intellectual appeal of divorcing the church sometimes—Christians can be really awful people. But if the body of Christ is sick, abandoning it to die seems an unfair cruelty for people who are supposed to be known for loving each other. (See John 13:35.)

Then, unexpectedly, I got to be on the receiving end of the Holy Spirit's encouragement through His incarnation in the church. Four months later—on my sixtieth birthday, as a matter of fact—I got another email from this same reader, through my website. She said:

I wanted to write back to give you the outcome of Mike's advice on attending a church. I reached out to a friend who invited me months ago to a local Church of Christ and started attending in September. The pastor and elders were wonderful and the services were Bible based sermons. I made covenant with the church today and Mike's email response to my inquiry was definitely a catalyst.

Please tell him I said thank you for helping me understand why an actual church membership matters.

This is just one example of how the Holy Spirit works through the church to build us up and strengthen each other in faith. He kept me awake late one night to share hope and accountability with my sister in Christ. Then, four months later when I was feeling discouraged, old, weak, and alone on my birthday, He prompted her to encourage my soul—just when I needed it.

When our Holy Spirit redeems us, He also draws us together in local congregations (see Acts 2:41), then incarnates various aspects of Christ Himself *in* each of us, *for* each of us, and expressing them *through* all of us. In other words, because of the Holy Spirit's persistent help and hope in the church, we can say confidently:

Helped people help people.

We are helped by God's Spirit, who then uses us—as a group of believers—to help people, both inside and outside His church. I feel like that's beautiful and extravagant. And an irreplaceable gift from the Spirit of God Himself. I'm grateful for that.

THE HOLY SPIRIT HELPS YOU THRIVE AS ONE BODY OF BELIEVERS

(See 1 Corinthians 12:13; 2 Corinthians 13:14; Philippians 2:1; Ephesians 4:3–4.)

When we talk about thriving as one body of believers, we're (of course) talking about unity—but even more than that, we're talking about actual *sustenance* of spirit, shared life itself flowing within community. Here's a picture of what I mean by that.

I first heard of the Pando forest from Rachel Held Evans, while reading her book, *Searching for Sunday*. "Each of its 47,000 trees are...one enormous, genetically identical organism," she said.[168] Wait a minute, I thought, 47,000 aspen trees are actually just one big tree? Much as I respect Rachel, I found this hard to believe. So I checked her facts with the US Forest Service and...whaddya know? She was right.

In case you've never heard of Pando, it's located in central Utah, about a mile southwest of Fish Lake on State Highway 25, and is considered one of the "40 Wonders of America." The US Forest Service describes it this way:

Pando is an aspen clone that originated from a single seed and spreads by sending up new shoots from the expanding root system.

Pando is believed to be the largest, most dense organism ever found at nearly 13 million pounds. The clone spreads over 106 acres, consisting of over 40,000 individual trees. The exact age of the clone and its root system is difficult to calculate, but it is estimated to have started at the end of the last ice age. Some of the trees are over 130 years old. It was first recognized by researchers in the 1970s and more recently proven by geneticists. Its massive size, weight, and prehistoric age have caused worldwide fame.[169]

This, I think, is a spectacular physical example of the metaphor the apostle Paul used to describe us, all followers of Jesus, who come from every tribe, race, nation, language, denomination, age, gender, economic status, career, family, and generation: *"We were all baptized by **one Spirit** so as to form **one body**—whether Jews or Gentiles, slave or free, we were all given the **one Spirit** to drink"* (1 Corinthians 12:13).

Each of us, individually, is like one of those stunning Pando aspen trees dotting the landscape out there in central Utah. Collectively, though, down deep where it matters, we're all one living organism—our unified lives held firmly within the single root system of God's Holy Spirit. Because Holy-Spirit-life courses continually through our shared spiritual experience, it really is true that in the church, *"There is neither Jew nor Gentile, neither slave nor free, nor is there male and female, for you are all one in Christ Jesus"* (Galatians 3:28).

192 IT DOESN'T HAVE TO BE THIS HARD

And so this is how the Holy Spirit makes us thrive in the Christian life—*together*, united in purpose, life, and familial devotion, by the Spirit, as one body of believers.

In Him we gather and find *koinónia*, or *"fellowship of the Holy Spirit"* (2 Corinthians 13:14; Philippians 2:1)—a concept that indicates intimate community, family partnership, sharing and help. In that way, by His working through a group of flawed believers, we gather and find strength in *"the unity of the Spirit,"* which bestows *"the bond of peace"* (Ephesians 4:3). How does this happen? Because *"There is one body and one Spirit"* (Ephesians 4:4) who fills us individually and collectively with His own life and purpose.

Philippians 2:2–4 describes, briefly, what this kind of divine *koinónia* looks like in a healthy church:

+ *"Being like-minded."*

+ *"Having the same love."*

+ *"Being one in spirit and of one mind."*

+ *"Doing nothing out of selfish ambition or vain conceit."*

+ *"In humility, valuing others above yourselves."*

+ *"Not looking to your own interests but each of you to the interests of the others."*

It's no accident that God's Spirit works to keep us in communion with others who worship and serve Jesus in these ways. In fact, it's as necessary to the soul as food, shelter, and clothing is to the body—and science has proved it.

The longest analysis ever of human happiness is the Harvard Study of Adult Development. Beginning in 1938, scientists have followed the lives of people from the same families for over eighty years—through three generations, into the twenty-first century. That includes 738 original participants and over 1,300 of their descendants. The goal? To find out what makes a happy life. That is, what makes a person feel like his or her life is one with meaning and purpose, "a sense that, outside of this moment, regardless of how pleasurable or miserable it is, your life is worth something, and valuable to you."[170]

The results of this multigenerational scientific study? Drs. Robert Waldinger and Marc Schulz summarize nearly a century of Harvard's research this way (italics theirs):

Scientific studies have told us again and again: human beings need nutrition, we need exercise, we need purpose, and we *need each other...*

When we really think about the consistent signal that comes through after eighty-four years of study and hundreds of research papers, it is that one simple message:

Positive relationships are essential to human well-being.[171]

It's almost as if our Holy Spirit *knew* that a local community of believers would feed the soul and protect the heart and mind of each one of us blessed to be part of a hometown church. Like He *knew* that in a family structure of positive relationships, we'd be better able to help each other be like-minded, to have the same love, to avoid selfish ambition, to serve the interests of others, and more. Go figure.

Yes, of course, there can be those who corrupt a local body with greed, hate, hypocrisy, or apathy—but when you find a place where people live out positive relationships in what Mary Karr called "collective surrender" to Jesus, well, that's the Holy Spirit's work. It's a unique blessing that empowers us to give and receive spiritual health and help, and more.

Ever wonder what happens when we isolate ourselves from the positive relationships found in a community of faith? Turns out we lose our moral and emotional bearings, and become skewed away from lifestyles of righteousness that characterize the Christian ideals.

Consider this: economic researchers used an "ultimatum game" to study moral decision-making in cultures all over the world. They found that when people interact directly with other people, they're more likely to act fairly, sympathetically, and even generously. But, "Once people become socially isolated, they stop simulating the feelings of other people. *Their moral intuitions are never turned on.* As a result, the inner Machiavelli takes over, and the sense of sympathy is squashed by selfishness."[172]

So you see, when the Holy Spirit helps you thrive as one body of believers, part of His work is in helping you avoid the disastrous consequences of social isolation. Instead, He's working to surround you with a community of people who share His goal of transformation into the likeness of Jesus. And He uses that living organism of relationships to incarnate His church *through* you, to your world. What a powerful resource that is—and what a kindness that He'd intentionally create that kind of place where we can thrive together in service to Jesus.

THE HOLY SPIRIT SPEAKS TO YOU ALONGSIDE OTHERS IN HIS CHURCH

(See Revelation 2:7; 2:11; 2:17; 2:29; 3:6; 3:13; 3:22.)

I have, on one of the many shelves in my home, a former library book titled, *Fabulous Fallacies*. I'm not sure why I have this—I don't even remember buying it. Chances are good it made me smile one day at a used bookstore, so I talked my wife into letting me bring it home. Regardless, I find it genuinely entertaining.

Among the "fabulous" errors chronicled in this book are the following:[173]

1. Elephants are afraid of mice.

This was actually tested with elephants, and mice, and found to be wildly untrue. When researchers introduced mice into a controlled environment of elephants, the massive pachyderms just sniffed at the rodents— then stomped them to death under their feet. Surprisingly, the little creature that did make elephants nervous was…a dachshund. [Insert eyebrow raise here!]

2. Ostriches hide their heads in the sand to escape predators.

This is pure myth that began (maybe as a joke?) among ancient Arabic tribes who passed it on to gullible Roman writers. When confronted by predators, ostriches will: a) Run—*very* fast—covering 10 to 12 feet in a single stride, and reaching up to 35 miles per hour. Or b) Kick the heck out of anything nearby; an ostrich kick is actually powerful enough to bend steel.

Ostriches do occasionally sleep with their heads lying on the ground, when they feel safe. Maybe that's where this myth started?

3. *Lemmings march into the sea to drown.*

It's true that lemmings migrate in groups to search for food, and some-times they cross bodies of water during those migrations. But hysterical rodents intent on mass suicide? No, not even close. These little vermin are actually really good swimmers, and more of them make it across the water than are lost in it. This legend appears to be founded in some hyperbolic sermon from a few hundred years ago, used to illustrate a parable of orig-inal sin.

Now, if you'll allow it, I'd like to add one more "fabulous fallacy" to our circus of errors. It's this:

4. *You must be alone for the Holy Spirit to speak to you.*

That, like lemming suicide and ostrich head-burial, is simply untrue. The fact is that God's Holy Spirit often speaks to us in community, making His intent known to and through the church. Our first example of this is found in a desolate cave, at a prison colony on a rocky island in ancient Rome.[174]

The aged apostle John had been banished to the island of Patmos, off the coast of modern-day Turkey (Revelation 1:9). *"On the Lord's Day I was in the Spirit,"* he reported, *"and I heard behind me a loud voice like a trumpet, which said: 'Write on a scroll what you see and send it to the seven churches: to Ephesus, Smyrna, Pergamum, Thyatira, Sardis, Philadelphia and Laodicea'"* (Revelation 1:10–11).

And so John proceeded to take dictation from heaven, writing seven short epistles from Jesus Himself to each of the churches in that list. What I find interesting about this is that each letter ends with this phrase: *"Hear what the Spirit says to the churches"* (Revelation 2:7; 2:11; 2:17; 2:29; 3:6; 3:13; 3:22). Seven times Jesus dictates that same phrase to John—indi-cating His Holy Spirit is speaking one message for many people in a con-gregation—and simultaneously, all messages for all the people in all His churches.

This is still how the Holy Spirit speaks—to local congregations and to the universal church as a whole—by giving messages meant to be shared with one and with all. In our time, this happens primarily through the frequent teaching and sharing of God's Word, the Bible; this is part of the reason why it's so important for each of us to be active and involved in a hometown church.

In these places, where we gather together in devotion to Jesus, we can hear, and discuss, and debate, and enact, and enjoy, and discover the actual words of the Holy Spirit being spoken in sermons, and Bible study groups, and affinity group meetings, and discipleship pairings, and worship experiences, and service projects, and so much more. When we do life together as the church, with Christian brothers and sisters gathered steadfastly around, *the Holy Spirit speaks to each of us alongside others*—drawing us all closer to him.

Our second example of how the Holy Spirit speaks to us through a community of believers comes from my friend, Len, and his friend, Pat.

Those two do life together because they belong to the body of Christ together—and sometimes the Holy Spirit uses one to speak His wisdom to the other, and vice versa. They're brothers in Christ and have earned the right to speak into each other's lives—and to share what's going on in their own lives too. Len describes Pat's input into his life this way (italics his):

"Sometimes his messages are *quirky*... Other times his messages are *encouraging*... Occasionally his words are *challenging*." Not long ago, Pat sent Len a "what if" kind of message that dealt with the frustrations of irritating people you meet every day—even at church.

"What if," Pat challenged his friend, "we all made it a practice to pray for the people around us? I mean, the people literally in proximity to us?" He gave a few examples: That bearded guy in the black truck in front of you—who hasn't noticed that the light is green. Or the impossibly slow cashier holding up your day while there's a long line of shoppers in front of you—including that tired-looking mom whose kids are just out. of. control.

"That would do a couple of things," Pat said. "First, it would change our attitudes. Instead of seeing people as obstacles, we'd see them as precious and unique. Second, people would be getting prayed for all over the place...So there's our opportunity to change the world."

You know what I hear when I listen to a Christian brother like Pat speaking a "what if" like that? Whispers of the Holy Spirit's voice in my ears—promoting, encouraging, and challenging me to become more and more like Jesus, even in the grocery store line.

Len hears the Spirit speaking in Pat's voice too, so much so that he's taking the challenge.

"I'm trying to cultivate the habit," he says, "of mentioning people to God—whoever he puts in my path—as I go about my day…What if we ran with my friend's idea and started a movement of 'guerilla praying'? Can you imagine?"[175]

Listen to what this means about who you are and the way God works through you:

In a way that's wildly irresponsible—and spectacularly gracious—the Holy Spirit incarnates His church *through you*. And as He does that, there'll probably be a time when He uses *your voice* to speak *His message* to others in His church, and when He uses other voices in His church to whisper His truth to you, and when He uses all of you as a group to say something powerful to all those people outside of His church.

Don't like that? Well, you'd better get used to it anyway—cuz that's what the Holy Spirit does.

One more thing…

THE HOLY SPIRIT HELPS YOU MOBILIZE HIS MINISTRY TO YOUR WORLD

(See Acts 13:2; 13:4; 2 Corinthians 3:8.)

All right, one more story and then I really need to move toward the end of this chapter or else my editor will give me a long lecture about brevity being the soul of wit and how I promised him a shorter book and yada yada and so forth. Yawn.

Anyway…

Have you heard, by chance, of The Singing Revolution?

You might say this revolution had its seeds planted in 1939, when Adolf Hitler made a pact with the Soviet Union, allowing the Russians to take over and occupy Estonia in exchange for allowing the Nazis to do the same to Poland. So 100,000 Soviet troops rolled into Estonia unopposed, and in the process trampled right over ethnic Estonian rights and identity, land and economy, and more.

In order to assimilate their new conquests under Russian dominion, the Soviet overlords outlawed singing. Well, not all singing, but it was definitely illegal to sing any of the historic, cultural, patriotic songs of the Estonian people. Punishable by prison or worse.

This forced subservience lasted through World War II, into the 1950s, 60s, and 70s. Then, in the late 1980s something began to stir in Estonia. People started singing again—literally.

In 1988, Estonians gathered for a music festival at the Song Bowl, a large venue between Kadriorg and Pirita in Estonia.[176] Spontaneously, a sing-along started among the crowd—and they were singing songs of patriotic Estonian history. The voices joined, and roared, some 300,000 strong. The revolution had begun.

Over the next three years, more "sing-alongs" happened, culminating in a cross-national show of unity when two million people across Estonia, Latvia, and Lithuania (the Baltic States) "joined hands and sang patriotic national songs to demand their independence" from Soviet oppression. Emboldened by their singing citizens, in 1991 the Estonian Congress formally declared the will of its musical people, and issued a declaration of independence.

The Soviets were not happy. They did what came naturally to them; they sent in tanks. The Russian soldiers were to target the radio towers and TV broadcast locations and destroy them. That way, the military brass figured, they'd nip this revolution in the bud. How could Estonians revolt if no one could hear about it?

When the Russian military arrived at their targets, they weren't met with bullets and guns—but with songs. "Masses of singing protestors put their bodies between the tanks and the radio towers and TV stations," one historian recorded, "forcing the Soviets to retreat."

Confronted by tens of thousands of unified voices, singing at them, they didn't know what to do until, finally, they just gave up. The tanks drove back to Russia, and history records, "It was through this Singing Revolution that Estonians gained their freedom."

As of the time of this writing, more than thirty years after that fateful showdown in 1991, Estonia is still free, governed by a parliamentary democracy, and is a successful member of the European Union (EU). In honor of their Singing Revolution, every five years the Estonian Song Celebration hosts some 30,000 singers to create the world's largest choir—still applauding the freedom they gained through the unity of their voices joined in song.[177]

This, I think, is a beautiful image of the way the Holy Spirit uses His incarnated church to mobilize His ministry to your world. He starts with one voice, figuratively (or literally!) singing of Jesus. That voice is joined by another, then more, and then all are sent out, together, to pursue the work for which He's called them. Slowly, but surely, our world is transformed.

This is the *"ministry of the Spirit"* (2 Corinthians 3:8) that expressed itself profoundly in the life, death, and unfathomable resurrection of Jesus, and which now continues to show its power, day after day, through the church of Christ in each of us. It first became evident with the formation of the church at the day of Pentecost. (See Acts 2.) It was seen again at a church gathering in Antioch, Syria (now in modern-day Turkey) while a group of Christians were worshipping. The Holy Spirit interrupted them and said, *"Set apart for me Barnabas and Saul for the work to which I have called them."* So they did, and that church body set in motion a missionary journey that would change their world—and ours. *"After they had fasted and prayed, they placed their hands on them and sent them off"* (Acts 13:1–4).

This Spirit-led mobilization of His people through the church has continued for millennia. D. James Kennedy and Jerry Newcombe once studied the impact of the historical church over twenty centuries, and here's what they found: "Despite its humble origins the Church has made more changes on earth for the good than any other movement or force in history." They list just a few, including: The abolition of slavery, hospitals, universities, literacy, and education of the masses, civil liberties, benevolence and charity, high regard for human life, codifying and setting into writing many of the world's languages, greater development of art and music, countless lives transformed, and (not least of all!) the eternal salvation of innumerable souls.[178]

So what am I saying to you, exactly?

200 IT DOESN'T HAVE TO BE THIS HARD

You, my friend, are part of something bigger than yourself—bigger than all of us put together. Actually bigger than all of history in its broadest, most expansive scope! Your Holy Spirit incarnates His church through you; and when He does that, He places you in a body of believers whom He will use to mobilize His ministry to your world.

So, you know, get ready for the revolution!

FOR FURTHER REFLECTION AND SMALL GROUP DISCUSSION:

1. "The Holy Spirit incarnates His church through you." How would you explain that to someone who's decided church is unnecessary?

2. What challenges you most in this chapter? What comforts you most?

3. The Holy Spirit uses your involvement in His church to mobilize His ministry to your world. How do you see that happening where you are?

AFTERWORD

HOW TO MAKE YOUR CHRISTIAN LIFE HARDER THAN IT REALLY IS

If you don't like that the Holy Spirit is doing so much in your Christian life, here's how to make it much, much harder for yourself: Quench the Holy Spirit; grieve the Holy Spirit; lie to and/ or test the Holy Spirit; resist the Holy Spirit; or blaspheme the Holy Spirit. (Any of those things should do the trick.)

Let's play the *Would You Rather...*game. You know how it goes: I'll give you a set of choices, and you get to pick which one you'd rather do (or be, or have).

We'll start off easy:

Would you rather...eat chocolate or asparagus?

OK, let's make it a little harder:

Would you rather...be rich or famous?

How about this one?

Would you rather...fly like Superman, or be able to stick to walls like Spider-Man?

Now, the most important one:

Would you rather your Christian life be harder, or easier?

Since you've read this book, I really, *really* hope you chose "easier" on that last one—because the Holy Spirit honestly does do the heavy lifting of the Christian experience for you. *However...*I know that some just like to make things harder than they have to be, for reasons I still don't understand. So, for those who feel that way about the Christian life, this "Afterword" is just for you.

If you'd like to make your Christian life harder than it really is, here are five things you can do.

1. QUENCH THE HOLY SPIRIT

(See 1 Thessalonians 5:19.)

The default understanding of "quenching" the Holy Spirit seems to be simply a generalized idea of committing "sin."[179] As in, if you don't want to quench the Holy Spirit, you should just stop sinning. You've probably heard this before, from the pulpit and from well-meaning Christian friends. Trouble is, that's just not what "quenching the Spirit" is.

The apostle Paul mentions quenching the Spirit only once in all of his letters, in 1 Thessalonians 5:19. The use here is specific to the gift of prophecy, and how to evaluate it. Here's Paul's whole thought:

> *Do not quench the Spirit. Do not treat prophecies with contempt but test them all; hold on to what is good, reject every kind of evil.*
> (1 Thessalonians 5:19–22)

In this context, *"Do not quench the Spirit"* and *"Do not treat prophecies with contempt"* form a pair of synonymous sentences, that is, different words meaning the same thing. It's one thought repeated for emphasis and clarification. In poetry we'd call that a couplet, or synthetic parallelism, and we find that kind of literary device often in the book of Proverbs (for example, Proverbs 3:1; 4:22; 17:4; 21:17; 31:9 and others). So in 1 Thessalonians 5:19–22 we see Paul using that same kind of wisdom literature structure to communicate the instruction not to dismiss prophecies, but to evaluate them for truth and then to *"hold on to what is good"* in them and *"reject every kind of evil"* in them. To do otherwise would be to *"quench"* the Spirit.

Additionally, the Greek root word Paul used for *"quench"* in 1 Thessalonians 5:19 is *sbennumi*, which describes actions taken to suppress or extinguish a fire. In this instance, Paul appears to be using the common symbol of the Holy Spirit as fire (see Exodus 3:2; 19:18; Ezekiel

1:13), and saying in effect, *The Holy Spirit is lighting a fire of prophecy among you; stop trying to suppress that.* Bible scholar Dr. David Williams, comments on that verse, "He [Paul] was speaking of the gifts of the Spirit, which the church in Thessalonica was attempting to 'dampen down,' particularly, as it appears, the gift of prophecy."[180]

So, if you want to quench the Holy Spirit, here's what to do: Spend your days disparaging the Word of God (which was given prophetically to the church); show contempt for your pastor's sermons as well as other spiritual expressions and teachings at your church; and dismiss general biblical and prophetic instruction as a whole.

2. GRIEVE THE HOLY SPIRIT

(See Ephesians 4:30.)

"Do not grieve the Holy Spirit," Paul wrote to the Christians in Ephesus (Ephesians 4:30). The Reverend Billy Graham puts this in perspective for us:

"Grieve" is a "love word." The Holy Spirit loves us just as Christ did…We may hurt or anger one who has no affection for us, but we can grieve only a person who loves us.[181]

So how would you or I grieve the Holy Spirit? The context around Ephesians 4:30 reveals the answer.

The general principle is that living like the pagans of Paul's day grieves the Holy Spirit: *"Having lost all sensitivity, they have given themselves over to sensuality so as to indulge in every kind of impurity, and they are full of greed"* (Ephesians 4:19).

In other words, be deliberately insensitive to the work of the Holy Spirit in your soul, and actively act against His intent for your life instead of cooperating with Him for your good. This, according to Ephesians 4, causes Him sorrow—something I'd guess that's akin to the feelings a parent has when watching a beloved child or teen live out self-destructive behavior.

As for specifics, here are a few self-destructive habits listed in Ephesians 4 that appear to grieve our Holy Spirit:

+ Embracing *"your old self, which is being corrupted by its deceitful desires"* (v. 22).

+ Refusing *"to be made new in the attitude of your minds"* (v. 23).

+ Refusing *"to put on the new self, created to be like God in true righteousness and holiness"* (v. 24).

+ Speaking falsehood and/or lying to your neighbor. (See v. 25.)

+ Letting anger become sinful (which gives the devil a foothold in your life). (See vv. 26–27.)

+ Stealing. (See v. 28.)

+ Refusing to be useful to others. (See v. 28.)

+ Unwholesome talk. (See v. 29.)

+ Not *"building others up according to their needs"* (v. 29).

+ *"Bitterness, rage and anger, brawling and slander, along with every form of malice"* (v. 31).

+ Refusing to *"be kind and compassionate to one another"* (v. 31).

+ Refusing to *"[forgive] each other as in Christ God forgave you"* (v. 31).

So, if you really want to hurt the One who loves you most—and make your Christian life immeasurably harder for no reason at all—pick a few things on this list. That should be enough to grieve the Holy Spirit today.

3. LIE TO AND/OR TEST THE HOLY SPIRIT

(See Acts 5:3; 5:9.)

The New Testament records only one instance of people lying to the Holy Spirit—but the results were tragic. The account is found in Acts 5. It seems that believers in the very first church were selling property and then donating the proceeds to the new congregation. (See Acts 4:34–36.) A husband and wife, Ananias and Sapphira, also sold a property. They apparently wanted to be acclaimed as generous, so they donated part of the proceeds from their sale, but they told the apostle Peter it was the full amount they'd received.

Peter knew the lie immediately, and said, *"Ananias, how is it that Satan has so filled your heart that you have lied to the Holy Spirit and have kept for yourself some of the money you received for the land? Didn't it belong to you before it was sold? And after it was sold, wasn't the money at your disposal? What made you think of doing such a thing? You have not lied just to human beings but to God"* (Acts 5:3–4). When Sapphira later continued the same lie, Peter said, *"How could you conspire to test the Spirit of the Lord?"* (Acts 5:9).

Peter clearly didn't care about how much (or how little) the couple donated, only that they lied about the amount. The result was sudden death for both Ananias and Sapphira. That seems a pretty harsh judgment for what, to me, is a mildly selfish lie—but I'm neither judge nor historian, so I can only tell you what happened. Still, it's apparent that lying to the Holy Spirit is a good way to sabotage your Christian experience, so if that's what you want to do, you might as well try it.

From the example of Ananias and Sapphira, it looks like the lie with the best chance of breaking off communion with God's Spirit would include: (a) premeditated deceit; (b) personal gain; (c) public hypocrisy; (d) pursuit of status as a result of your lie; and (e) speaking the lie to a leader of God's people. (See also 2 Kings 5:20–27.)

Hmm…this sounds a lot like some prominent pastors and Christian leaders we've all heard about in the news in recent years. So that'd be your company if you choose to lie to the Holy Spirit. I'm just sayin'.

4. RESIST THE HOLY SPIRIT

(See Acts 7:51; Hebrews 6:4–6.)

At first glance, the idea of "resisting" the Holy Spirit seems simple. He prompts you to do something—say, feed the hungry—and you say no. Mission accomplished, right? Well, not exactly. Biblically speaking, it turns out that resisting the Holy Spirit is significantly more drastic than that.

The two New Testament passages that speak of resisting (or turning away from) the Holy Spirit are:

+ Acts 7:51: *"You stiff-necked people! Your hearts and ears are still uncircumcised. You are just like your ancestors: You always resist the Holy Spirit."*

+ Hebrews 6:4–6 (NLT): *"For it is impossible to bring back to repentance those who were once enlightened—those who have experienced the good things of heaven and shared in the Holy Spirit, who have tasted the goodness of the word of God and the power of the age to come—and who then turn away from God. It is impossible to bring such people back to repentance; by rejecting the Son of God, they themselves are nailing him to the cross once again and holding him up to public shame."*

The first passage, Acts 7:51, is from Stephen, facing his accusers and actually blaming them for the crucifixion of Christ. (See Acts 7:52.) The next thing to happen was that those who *"always resist the Holy Spirit"* murdered Stephen by stoning him to death.

The second passage, from Hebrews, also accuses those who turn away from God of crucifying Christ, in a symbolic, spiritual way. And this passage condemns those people as destined for eternal judgment without possibility of repentance.

Both of these passages make reference to the "wilderness generation" of Israelites who, after miraculously gaining freedom from slavery in Egypt, created and worshipped a false god as their liberator. (See Exodus 32.) Those people were punished with a plague, and also eternal judgment. (See Exodus 32:33–35.) Bible scholars Gregg Allison and Andreas Köstenberger comment, "'Shared in the Holy Spirit' is not necessarily to be taken as actual reception of the Spirit but may refer to external observation of manifestations of the Spirit in the lives of others in the believing community...So denying and rejecting the Spirit's work in those around us in the age of the church may have severe ramifications."[182]

So, resisting the Holy Spirit is not just blithely saying, "Lord, I don't feel like doing that today." It's more like a militant adherence to ignorance, and a deliberate refusal to acknowledge the Holy Spirit's obvious involvement in the people and circumstances around you. Think of it like making an obscene, middle-fingered hand gesture to the Holy Spirit right after He's liberated you and your people from 400 years of slavery. Something like that.

5. BLASPHEME, OR INSULT, THE HOLY SPIRIT

(See Matthew 12:31–32; Mark 3:29; Luke 12:10; Hebrews 10:29.)

In Matthew 12:31 (NLT), Jesus is recorded as saying, *"Every sin and blasphemy can be forgiven—except blasphemy against the Holy Spirit, which will never be forgiven."*

This is the nuclear option—the "unpardonable sin." It's the choice you make when you know for certain you want absolutely nothing to do with God, now or in eternity to come. Fortunately, blaspheming the Holy Spirit is exceptionally rare, so much so that we don't even really know what it means. So, even if you really, really, really wanted to do this, chances are good you wouldn't know how, and couldn't do it anyway.

Still, ignorance has never stopped any theologian before, so here are some of the theories about *"blasphemy against the Holy Spirit"* that have been circulated over time:

THEORY 1: IT WAS A SIN SPECIFIC TO THE PHARISEES OF JESUS'S DAY, COMMITTED WHEN THEY CLAIMED JESUS WAS EMPOWERED BY SATAN.

This was the view of early church fathers such as Jerome and John Chrysostom. According to them, this sin could only be committed when Christ lived on the earth, and so would not apply to anyone after that time.[183]

THEORY 2: IT'S THE STUBBORN UNWILLINGNESS (*IMPOENITENTIA FINALIS*) TO REPENT, ALL THE WAY UNTIL DEATH.

Augustine of Hippo and other historic theologians were proponents of this view. Basically, this is the idea that the unpardonable sin is a refusal to accept Jesus Christ by faith for the entirety of one's life.[184]

THEORY 3: IT IS A "CONSCIOUS, MALICIOUS, AND WILLFUL REJECTION AND SLANDERING...OF THE TESTIMONY OF THE HOLY SPIRIT RESPECTING THE GRACE OF GOD IN CHRIST, ATTRIBUTING IT OUT OF HATRED AND ENMITY TO THE PRINCE OF DARKNESS."

This is the perspective articulated by influential Reformed scholar, Louis Berkhof. He adds that this sin is, "the audacious declaration that the Holy Spirit is the spirit of the abyss, that the truth is a lie, and that Christ is Satan."[185]

THEORY 4: IT IS A HARDENED, IRRATIONAL, IRREVOCABLE DECISION TO REJECT JESUS.

The idea here is that of apostasy, of a deliberate and decisive rejection of Jesus as Lord. This is a popular view among evangelical theologians. Dr. Lawrence O. Richards sums up this thinking when he comments on the Pharisees of Matthew 12:31, "Speaking against the source of Jesus's power was, first of all, a recognition of its supernatural origin, and second, a hardened rejection of Jesus Himself.... Their choice, made in the face of all the unique evidence which Jesus Himself had presented to them, was irrevocable; they had chosen to step beyond the possibility of repentance."[186]

THEORY 5: IT IS DELIBERATELY HONORING SATAN FOR THE WORK OF THE HOLY SPIRIT.

This is also a common view, as articulated by Anglican Evangelical scholar F. F. Bruce. He says the Pharisees were charged with blaspheming the Holy Spirit because "They deliberately ascribed the Holy Spirit's activity to demonic agency."[187]

So what exactly does it mean to blaspheme the Holy Spirit? I don't think anyone has yet come up with a complete definition—and I think that's OK.

However, Bruce seems to speak for all opinions when he says, "The nature of this sin is such that one does not repent of it." Thus, "The very fact of [one's] concern over having committed it proves that they have not committed it."[188]

Do with that as you will.

APPENDIX 1

246 DIRECT REFERENCES TO THE HOLY SPIRIT IN THE NEW TESTAMENT

References are translated in the NIV as: *Holy Spirit; Spirit; Advocate; Power (from on high); Promise; Gift; Anointing (from the Holy One).*

Matthew 1:18	Luke 1:41–45	John 3:34
Matthew 1:20	Luke 1:67	John 4:23
Matthew 3:11	Luke 2:25	John 4:24
Matthew 3:16	Luke 2:26	John 6:63
Matthew 4:1	Luke 2:27	John 7:38–39
Matthew 10:20	Luke 3:16	John 14:16
Matthew 12:18	Luke 3:22	John 14:17
Matthew 12:28	Luke 4:1	John 14:26
Matthew 12:31	Luke 4:14	John 15:26
Matthew 12:32	Luke 4:18–19	John 16:7–11
Matthew 22:43	Luke 10:21	John 16:13
Matthew 28:19	Luke 11:13	John 16:14–15
Mark 1:8	Luke 12:10	John 20:22
Mark 1:10	Luke 12:12	Acts 1:2
Mark 1:12	Luke 24:49	Acts 1:4
Mark 3:29	John 1:32	Acts 1:5
Mark 12:36	John 1:33	Acts 1:8
Mark 13:11	John 3:5	Acts 1:16
Luke 1:15	John 3:6	Acts 2:4
Luke 1:35	John 3:8	Acts 2:17

Acts 2:18	Acts 11:24	Romans 8:15
Acts 2:33	Acts 11:28	Romans 8:16
Acts 2:38	Acts 13:2	Romans 8:23
Acts 4:8	Acts 13:4	Romans 8:26
Acts 4:25	Acts 13:9	Romans 8:27
Acts 4:31	Acts 13:52	Romans 9:1
Acts 5:3	Acts 15:8	Romans 14:17
Acts 5:9	Acts 15:28	Romans 15:13
Acts 5:32	Acts 16:6	Romans 15:16
Acts 6:3	Acts 16:7	Romans 15:19
Acts 6:5	Acts 19:2	Romans 15:30
Acts 6:10	Acts 19:6	1 Corinthians 2:4
Acts 7:51	Acts 20:22	1 Corinthians 2:10
Acts 7:55	Acts 20:23	1 Corinthians 2:11
Acts 8:15	Acts 20:28	1 Corinthians 2:12
Acts 8:17	Acts 21:4	1 Corinthians 2:13
Acts 8:18–19	Acts 21:11	1 Corinthians 2:14
Acts 8:20	Acts 28:25	1 Corinthians 2:15
Acts 8:29	Romans 1:4	1 Corinthians 3:16
Acts 8:39	Romans 2:29	1 Corinthians 5:4
Acts 9:17	Romans 5:5	1 Corinthians 6:11
Acts 9:31	Romans 7:6	1 Corinthians 6:19
Acts 10:19	Romans 8:2	1 Corinthians 7:40
Acts 10:38	Romans 8:4	1 Corinthians 12:3
Acts 10:44	Romans 8:5	1 Corinthians 12:4
Acts 10:45	Romans 8:6	1 Corinthians 12:7
Acts 10:47	Romans 8:9	1 Corinthians 12:8
Acts 11:12	Romans 8:10	1 Corinthians 12:9
Acts 11:15	Romans 8:11	1 Corinthians 12:11
Acts 11:16	Romans 8:13	1 Corinthians 12:13
Acts 11:17	Romans 8:14	1 Corinthians 14:2

1 Corinthians 14:16	Ephesians 3:16	1 Peter 1:2
1 Corinthians 14:37	Ephesians 4:3	1 Peter 1:11
2 Corinthians 1:22	Ephesians 4:4	1 Peter 1:12
2 Corinthians 3:3	Ephesians 4:30	1 Peter 3:18
2 Corinthians 3:6	Ephesians 5:18	1 Peter 4:14
2 Corinthians 3:8	Ephesians 5:19	2 Peter 1:21
2 Corinthians 3:17	Ephesians 6:17	1 John 2:20
2 Corinthians 3:18	Ephesians 6:18	1 John 2:27
2 Corinthians 5:5	Philippians 1:19	1 John 3:24
2 Corinthians 6:6	Philippians 2:1	1 John 4:2
2 Corinthians 12:18	Philippians 3:3	1 John 4:6
2 Corinthians 13:14	Colossians 1:8	1 John 4:13
Galatians 3:2	Colossians 1:9	1 John 5:6
Galatians 3:3	Colossians 3:16	1 John 5:7–8
Galatians 3:5	1 Thessalonians 1:5	Jude 1:19
Galatians 3:14	1 Thessalonians 1:6	Jude 1:20
Galatians 4:6	1 Thessalonians 4:8	Revelation 1:10
Galatians 4:29	1 Thessalonians 5:19	Revelation 2:7
Galatians 5:5	2 Thessalonians 2:13	Revelation 2:11
Galatians 5:16	1 Timothy 3:16	Revelation 2:17
Galatians 5:17	1 Timothy 4:1	Revelation 2:29
Galatians 5:18	2 Timothy 1:7	Revelation 3:6
Galatians 5:22–23	2 Timothy 1:14	Revelation 3:13
Galatians 5:25	Titus 3:5	Revelation 3:22
Galatians 6:1	Hebrews 2:4	Revelation 4:2
Galatians 6:8	Hebrews 3:7	Revelation 11:11
Ephesians 1:13	Hebrews 6:4	Revelation 14:13
Ephesians 1:17	Hebrews 9:8	Revelation 17:3
Ephesians 2:18	Hebrews 9:14	Revelation 19:10
Ephesians 2:22	Hebrews 10:15	Revelation 21:10
Ephesians 3:5	Hebrews 10:29	Revelation 22:17

APPENDIX 2

COMMON GREEK TERMS FOR THE HOLY SPIRIT IN THE NEW TESTAMENT

Pneuma

Primary meaning: wind, Spirit

+ This is the most frequently used term for the Holy Spirit.

+ Find it in *Strong's Exhaustive Concordance* at entry #4151.

+ Sample Scriptures: Matthew 3:16; Mark 13:11; Luke 12:12; John 3:6.

Dunamis

Primary meaning: (miraculous) power, might, strength

+ Find it in *Strong's Exhaustive Concordance* at entry #1411.

+ Sample Scriptures: Luke 1:35, 24:49; 1 Corinthians 5:4.

Paraklétos

Primary meaning: called to one's aid

+ Find it in *Strong's Exhaustive Concordance* at entry #3875.

+ Sample Scriptures: John 14:16, 14:26, 15:26, 16:7; 1 John 2:1.

Epaggelia

Primary meaning: a summons, a promise (the Father's promise)

+ Find it in *Strong's Exhaustive Concordance* at entry #1860.

+ Sample Scriptures: Luke 24:49; Acts 1:4; Galatians 3:14.

Dórea

Primary meaning: a gift

- Find it in *Strong's Exhaustive Concordance* at entry #1431.

- Sample Scriptures: Acts 8:20; Acts 10:45; Acts 11:17; Hebrews 6:4.

Chrisma

Primary meaning: an anointing, unction

- Find it in *Strong's Exhaustive Concordance* at entry #5545.

- Sample Scriptures: 1 John 2:20; 1 John 2:27.

ACKNOWLEDGEMENTS

Now's the time to give credit where credit is due. So…

First, I'd like to thank that unnamed pastor who told me over and over, "God can't do everything for you, Mike." You were the one who inspired me to finally dig into the New Testament to discover exactly what the Holy Spirit does, and doesn't, do. The result is this book—so thanks for challenging me. My faith is expanded and empowered because of what you prompted.

Next, a sincere thank-you to Mary Vanden Berg. I wasn't sure anyone would be interested in this book until you looked at my list of ideas and said, "That's the one I want to read." So, in my wisdom (ahem), I tried to talk you into another one, but you said, "No, that's the one I want to read." Without your encouragement, I never would've sat down to write *It Doesn't Have to Be This Hard*. I would've just kept all my Scripture cards (and my thoughts about them) to myself. So, thanks for being the Spirit's voice in my ear at that crucial time.

Chip MacGregor—the man in the gap! Thank you for plucking this off my laptop and being the advocate it needed to become reality. Once again, I'm grateful to you.

Christine Whitaker, Amy Bartlett, and Jonathan Thornton: thank you for believing in this book—and for all your diligent efforts to get it out into the world. I hope that your hopes for it are rewarded with success. (Hope that makes sense—I know I used "hope" a lot in this paragraph!)

Norm and Winnie Wakefield: You insisted I write this book, and spoke to me joy and encouragement about it at every opportunity. What a blessing you two are!

John Sokolowski, my friend. When I told you about this book, you cheered. When I told you I didn't think it'd get published, you refused my disbelief...and cheered me again. When I told you, well, I might write it after all, you took me out to lunch to celebrate—and cheered my soul with your faith. Thank you; I'm honored to be included in your life. Everybody needs at least one cheerleader, right?

Mostly, thank you to the Holy Spirit, who refuses to let me muck around on my own through this Christian life. Truly, I'm most grateful to You for everything.

—Mike Nappa
2025

ABOUT THE AUTHOR

Mike Nappa (M.A.B.T., M.A.E., B.A.C.E.) is an award-winning theologian known for writing "coffee-shop theology" as well as helpful Christian living and devotion books. A best-selling author, his works have been translated into many languages, with millions of copies sold worldwide.

Mike is proud to be a person of color (Arab-American) active in the Christian publishing industry. Learn more about Mikey by Googling his name, looking him up on Amazon, or checking out his website at Bible-Smart.com.

ENDNOTES

1. A. W. Tozer, *How to be Filled with the Holy Spirit* (Mansfield Centre, CT: Martino Publishing, 2010, reprinting Harrison, PA: Christian Publications, Inc., 1952), 9.
2. Bill Johnson, *The Holy Spirit* (New Kensington, PA: Whitaker House, 2024), 179.
3. C. S. Lewis, *Mere Christianity* (San Francisco, CA: HarperSanFrancisco, 1952, 1980), 197.
4. Um, in case you missed it, that was sarcasm. Please don't believe that God watches over us only to punish us! Thanks.
5. Charles R. Swindoll, *Embraced by the Spirit* (Grand Rapids, MI: Zondervan, 2010), 60.
6. Yeah, someday I should write a book about that stuff. But not today. Suffice it to say that our Christian history is pretty messed up...and yet God has managed to make beauty out of it anyway. Go figure.
7. Gregg R. Allison & Andreas J. Köstenberger, *The Holy Spirit* (Nashville, TN: B&H Academic, 2020), 208.
8. Adam Rutherford, *Creation: How Science is Reinventing Life Itself* (New York: Current, 2013), 75.
9. Brian Cox and Andrew Cohen, *Wonders of Life* (New York: HarperDesign, 2013), 103.
10. Lawrence O. Richards, *It Couldn't Just Happen* (Dallas, TX: Word Publishing, 1987, 1989), 67.
11. "Why Does Your Heart Beat?" The Franklin Institute, accessed January 8, 2021, https://www.fi.edu/heart/why-does-your-heart-beat.
12. Lawrence O. Richards, *It Couldn't Just Happen* (Dallas, TX: Word Publishing, 1987, 1989) 26–27.
13. Richards, *It Couldn't Just Happen*, 27–28.
14. Richards, *It Couldn't Just Happen*, 28.
15. Cox and Cohen, *Wonders of Life*, 13.
16. C. S. Lewis, *Surprised by Joy* (San Francisco, CA: HarperOne, 1955, 2017), xi, 279.
17. Louis Berkhof, *Systematic Theology* (Grand Rapids, MI: Wm. B. Eerdmans Publishing Co., 1939, 1941, 1984), 469.
18. From an interview with Greek language scholar, Dustin Scott, conducted by the author on January 12, 2022, at Vintage City Church in Fort Collins, Colorado.
19. Lewis, *Surprised by Joy*, 288.
20. Lewis, *Surprised by Joy*, 290.
21. Yes, I ended up writing a book about the stories people told me. It was titled, *True Stories of Transformed Lives* (Tyndale House Publishers). That book is out of print now, but I think used copies are still available, if you're interested. The stories of Shirley Caesar, Chris Castile, and Eddie Elguera are all from that book.

22. Yeah, I wrote a book about that too. It's called *Hard Way Home* (Harvest House Publishers). At the time of this writing it was still available wherever books are sold.
23. Sharon Ketcham, *Reciprocal Church* (Downers Grove, IL: IVP Books, 2018), 13–14.
24. Henry Clarence Thiessen, *Introductory Lectures in Systematic Theology* (Grand Rapids, MI: Wm. B. Eerdmans Publishing Company, 1949, 1956), 371.
25. Lawrence O. Richards, Ph.D., editor, *The Revell Bible Dictionary* (Old Tappan, NJ: Fleming H. Revell Company, 1990), 491.
26. Alfred H. Ackley, "He Lives," *Worship and Service Hymnal* (Chicago, IL: Hope Publishing Company, 1957, 1965), Hymn #257.
27. Leland Ryken, James C. Wilhoit, Tremper Longman III, General Editors, *Dictionary of Biblical Imagery* (Downers Grover, IL: IVP Academic, 1998), 368–369.
28. Charles M. Schulz. *You Don't Look 35, Charlie Brown* (New York: Holt, Rinehart, and Winston, 1985), 70.
29. Rick Beyer, *The Greatest Stories Never Told* (New York: HarperResource, 2003), 10.
30. George deLucenay Leon, *Explorers of the Americas Before Columbus* (New York: Franklin Watts, 1989), 34–35, 38.
31. J. D. Douglas, Merrill C. Tenney, *The New International Dictionary of the Bible, Pictorial Edition* (Grand Rapids, MI: Regnery Reference Library, 1963, 1964, 1967, 1987), 343.
32. Ryken, Wilhoit, Longman III, *Dictionary of Biblical Imagery*, 14–15.
33. The word "adopt" or a variant of it does show up three times in our NIV translation of the Old Testament, but those are all instances of cultural accommodation for the ears of modern readers rather than physical presence in the original text. The Hebrew word the NIV translates as *"adopted"* in Esther 2:15 actually means "to take." The word translated as *"adopt"* in Job 15:5 is more accurately defined as "to choose." And *"adopted"* in Psalm 106:35 really should be translated as "to learn."
34. John Drane, *The World of the Bible* (Oxford, England: Lion Hudson, 2009), 197.
35. Lesley Adkins and Roy A. Adkins, *Handbook to Life in Ancient Rome* (New York: Oxford University Press, 1994, 1998), 340–341.
36. Charles R. Swindoll, *Swindoll's New Testament Insights: Insights on Romans* (Grand Rapids, MI: Zondervan, 2010), 161–162.
37. Philip Matyszak, *Ancient Rome on Five Denarii a Day* (London, UK: Thames & Hudson Ltd., 2007), 22.
38. Earl Radmacher, Ronald B. Allen, and H. Wayne House, editors, *Nelson's New Illustrated Bible Commentary* (Nashville, TN: Thomas Nelson Publishers, 1999), 1176.
39. Matyszak, *Ancient Rome*, 22.
40. I want to tell you this one last thing, just because I think it's beautiful. Historians report that our early Christian brothers and sisters became imitators of the Holy Spirit's redemptive adoption practice. Christians in that day would often go out of their way to rescue abandoned infants. They'd find a child, bring that child home and raise it as a member of their own family. The Christians became so well known for doing this that it frightened their pagan neighbors who couldn't understand why anyone would want to love and cherish something that had once been *res vacantes*. (from: Justo L. Gonzales, *The Story of Christianity Volume 1, Revised and Updated* (New York: HarperOne, 2010), 60.)
41. Adkins and Adkins, *Handbook to Life*, 339.
42. Merrill C. Tenny, general editor, *The Zondervan Pictorial Encyclopedia of the Bible Volume One A-C* (Grand Rapids, MI: Regency Reference Library, 1975, 1976), 6.
43. D. Stuart Briscoe, *The Communicator's Commentary: Romans* (Waco, TX: Word Books, 1982), 167.

44. Imdb, "Ghostbusters Quotes," accessed August 5, 2025, https://www.imdb.com/title/tt0087332/quotes/?ref_=tt_trv_qu.

45. Editors of Merriam-Webster, *Webster's All-In-One Dictionary & Thesaurus* (Springfield, MA: Federal Street Press, 2008), 281.

46. R. Alan Cole, *Tyndale New Testament Commentaries: Galatians* (Leicester, England: Inter-Varsity Press, 1965, 1983), 16.

47. Hey Ma, lookit me! I finally got to use the word Brobdingnagian in a book!

48. Joseph L. Garnder, editor, *Atlas of the Bible* (Pleasantville, NY: The Reader's Digest Association Inc., 1981), 57.

49. Lawrence O. Richards, *Expository Dictionary of Bible Words* (Grand Rapids, MI: Regency Reference Library, 1985), 195.

50. Richards, *Expository Dictionary*, 130.

51. Ryken, Wilhoit, Longman III, 99.

52. Will Durant, *The Story of Civilization Part III: Caesar and Christ* (New York: Simon and Schuster, 1944), 199.

53. A. J. Langguth, *A Noise of War* (New York: Simon and Schuster, 1994), 327–328, 333–334.

54. Billy Graham, *The Holy Spirit* (Nashville, TN: W Publishing Group, 1978, 1988), 83–85.

55. William Barclay, *The Daily Bible Study Series: The Letters to the Corinthians, Revised Edition* (Philadelphia, PA: The Westminster Press, 1954, 1956, 1975, 1977), 3.

56. Clinton E. Arnold, general editor *Zondervan Illustrated Bible Backgrounds Commentary, Volume 3: Romans to Philemon* (Grand Rapids, MI: Zondervan, 2002), 102.

57. Ben Witherington III, *A Week in the Life of Corinth* (Downers Grove, IL: IVP Academic, 2012), 9.

58. Adkins and Adkins, *Handbook to Life*, 341.

59. Paul J. Achtemeier, general editor, *Harper's Bible Dictionary* (San Francisco, CA: Harper & Row Publishers, 1985), 1021.

60. Reader's Digest, *Jesus and His Times* (Pleasantville, NY: The Reader's Digest Association, Inc.), 131–134.

61. Interestingly, reports from New Testament times indicate that—despite the constant animal sacrifices that occurred daily at the Jerusalem Temple—there were no flies in the building. Also, while birds of prey and scavenger birds were always a problem at pagan altars like those in Egypt and Greece (swooping down to grab and eat butchered meat), those birds didn't interfere with the sacrifices made at this temple. Some people in that time attributed those two things to being miracles of God, while others suggested natural reasons. (See *Jesus and His Times*, page 134.)

62. Richards, *Expository Dictionary*, 54–55.

63. Tenny, *The Zondervan Pictorial Encyclopedia*, 171.

64. Anne Graham Lotz, *Heaven* (Nashville, TN: W Publishing Group, 2001), 37–38.

65. Wayne Grudem, *Systematic Theology, Second Edition* (Grand Rapids, MI: Zondervan Academic, 1994, 2020), 1460.

66. Johnson, *The Holy Spirit*, 55.

67. Abraham Kuyper, *The Work of the Holy Spirit* (Grand Rapids, MI: Christian Classics Ethereal Library, no copyright year given), 390.

68. "Juha and His Donkey" is adapted and retold from: Salma Khadra Jayyusi, editor, *Tales of Juha* (Northampton, MA: Interlink Books, 2007), 48–49.

69. Graham, *The Holy Spirit*, 133.

70. Tozer, *How to be Filled*, 18–19.

71. Mark D. Roberts, *The Story of God Bible Commentary: Ephesians* (Grand Rapids, MI: Zondervan, 2016) 184.

72. Roberts, *The Story of God*, 184.

73. Out of respect for the Christian leader, I've decided not to footnote the source for that person's comments here. I don't want to go around name-calling everyone who may or may not disagree with me on theology, and besides, we agree on more things than we disagree anyway. I did, however, quote that person exactly here.

74. Madeleine L'Engle, *Walking on Water* (Wheaton, IL: Harold Shaw Publishers, 1980, 1998), 12.

75. R. A. Torrey, *The Presence and Work of the Holy Spirit* (New Kensington, PA: Whitaker House, 1996), 81

76. Michael D. Hattem, "The 'War on Christmas' in Early America." *The Junto*, December 23, 2013. https://earlyamericanists.com/2013/12/23/the-early-american-war-on-christmas/.

77. Joukowsky Institute for Archaeology & the Ancient World, "Archaeologies of the Greek Past: Olympic Games," Brown University, https://www.brown.edu/Departments/Joukowsky_Institute/courses/greekpast/4881a.html.

78. *The Princess Bride*, directed by Rob Reiner (1987; Santa Monica, CA: MGM Home Entertainment, 2000) DVD.

79. We don't know exactly when Jesus told His disciples to wait in Jerusalem, but we do know that Pentecost is fifty days after Passover, when Jesus was crucified. (See John 19:14–16). We also know that Jesus stayed among His disciples for forty days after His resurrection. (See Acts 1:3). So, mostly likely, the disciples waited a minimum of ten full days after Jesus ascended into heaven (see Acts 1:9) until the day of Pentecost when the Holy Spirit came in baptizing power.

80. Beth Wenger, "Mikveh," *Jewish Women's Archive*, June 23, 2021, https://jwa.org/encyclopedia/article/mikveh.

81. Achtemeier, *Harper's Bible Dictionary*, 92.

82. Leland Ryken, James C. Wilhoit, Tremper Longman III, General Editors, *Dictionary of Biblical Imagery* (Downers Grover, IL: IVP Academic, 1998), 73.

83. Clinton E. Arnold, editor, *Zondervan Illustrated Bible Backgrounds Commentary, Volume 2: John, Acts*, (Grand Rapids, MI: Zondervan, 2002), 65.

84. Arlin Cuncic, MA, "What Happens to Your Body When Your Brain Is Thinking?" *Verywell Mind*, March 03, 2023, https://www.verywellmind.com/what-happens-when-you-think-4688619#toc-anatomy-of-a-thought.

85. "Rebecca Saxe: The Brain vs. The Mind," TVO Today, July 24, 2012, https://www.youtube.com/watch?v=vLcdKXE4R0s.

86. Michael B. Sweeney, with a Foreword by David Copperfield, *Brain Works* (Washington, DC: National Geographic, 2011), 7.

87. Stephen L. Macknik and Susana Martinez-Conde, with Sandra Blakeslee, *Sleights of Mind* (New York: Picador, 2010), 60–61.

88. If you're not familiar with how the Bible is organized and you'd like a simple way to understand that, check out my book, *Welcome to Bible World* (The Good Book Company, 2022). Yes, it's a kids' book, but so what? You'll learn how to navigate Scripture and have fun at the same time. And, when you're done, you'll know more about the Bible than most Christian adults anyway. Hope that's helpful.

89. Richard Shotton, *The Choice Factory* (Hampshire, Great Britain: Harriman House, 2018), xi, 34.

90. Jennifer Delgado, "Acta non verba, facts or words?," *Psychology Spot*, https://psychology-spot.com/acta-non-verba-meaning-deeds-not-words.

91. Charles R. Swindoll, *Swindoll's Living Insights New Testament Commentary Volume 9: Philippians, Colossians, Philemon* (Carol Stream, IL: Tyndale House Publishers, 2017), 65.

92. Ruth A. Tucker, *Parade of Faith* (Grand Rapids, MI: Zondervan, 2011), 63, 79–82, 192.

93. Stephen M. Miller, *The Jesus of the Bible* (Uhrichsville, OH: Barbour Publishing, 2009), 319.

94. Lawrence O. Richards, *Expository Dictionary of Bible Words* (Grand Rapids, MI: Regency Reference Library, 1985), 553.

95. As quoted by Charles R. Swindoll in *The Tale of the Tardy Ox Cart* (Nashville, TN: Word Publishing, 1998), 513.

96. *The Boys: The Sherman Brothers Story*, directed by Gregory V. Sherman and Jeff Sherman (2009; Burbank, CA: Walt Disney Studios Home Entertainment, 2010) DVD.

97. Costi W. Hinn, *Knowing the Spirit* (Grand Rapids, MI: Zondervan Books, 2023), 108–109.

98. E. E. Cummings, "i thank You God for most this amazing," *100 Selected Poems* (New York: Grove Press, 1923, 1954), 114.

99. Gerald F. Hawthorne and Ralph P. Martin, editors, *Dictionary of Paul and His Letters* (Downers Grover, IL: InterVarsity Press, 1993), 985.

100. Patrick Cavanaugh, *Spiritual Lives of the Great Composers* (Grand Rapids, MI: Zondervan, 1992, 1996), 27, 29–30.

101. Lloyd John Ogilvie, *Conversation with God* (Eugene, OR: Harvest House Publishers, 1993), 16.

102. Ray Summers, *Essentials of New Testament Greek* (Nashville, TN: Broadman Press, 1950), 38.

103. Eugene H. Peterson, *The Contemplative Pastor* (Grand Rapids, MI: William B. Eerdmans Publishing Company, 1989, 1993), 103–104.

104. George Arthur Buttrick, *The Interpreter's Dictionary of the Bible, Volume 3 K-Q* (New York: Abingdon Press, 1962), 867.

105. Jody Brolsma, *Praying to Change Lives* (Grand Rapids, MI: Discovery House, 2019), 57–59.

106. From an interview by the author with Ken Wakefield, 1998.

107. Wayne A. Detzler, *New Testament Words in Today's Language* (Wheaton, IL: Victor Books, 1986), 380.

108. Martin Luther King, Jr., *Strength to Love* (Minneapolis, MN: Fortress Press, 1963, 2010), 37.

109. Anne Graham Lotz, *Jesus in Me* (Colorado Springs, CO: Multnomah, 2019), 211–212.

110. Tremper Longman III, editor, *The Baker Illustrated Bible Dictionary* (Grand Rapids, MI: BakerBooks, 2013), 563.

111. W. E. Vine, *Vine's Complete Expository Dictionary of Old and New Testament Words* (Nashville, TN: Thomas Nelson Publishers, 1984, 1996), 382.

112. Roy F. Baumeister and John Tierney, *Willpower* (New York: The Penguin Press, 2011), 167–171, 179–183.

113. Ron Rhodes, *The Heart of Christianity* (Eugene, OR: Harvest House Publishers, 1996), 115.

114. E. Boyd Barret, SJ, *Strength of Will* (New York: P. J. Kennedy and Sons, 1915), 16.

115. Martin Luther King, Jr., *Stride Toward Freedom* (New York: Harper & Brothers, Publishers, 1958), 134–138.

116. Jean-Pierre Isbouts, *Who's Who in the Bible* (Washington, DC: National Geographic 2013), 277.

117. Ronald Brownrigg, *Who's Who in the New Testament* (New York: Holt, Rinehart and Winston, 1971), 79.

118. Keith Houston, *The Book* (New York: W. W. Norton & Company, 2016), 96.

119. Richard J. Foster, *Celebration of Discipline*, special anniversary edition (New York: HarperOne, 1978, 2018), 1–2.

120. Gary Thomas, *Sacred Pathways*, updated and revised edition (Grand Rapids, MI: Zondervan Books, 1996, 2010, 2020), 8.

121. William Steuart McBirnie, PhD., *The Search for the Twelve Apostles* (Wheaton, IL: Tyndale House Publishers, 1973), 75.

122. Charles R. Swindoll, *Embraced by the Spirit* (Grand Rapids, MI: Zondervan, 2010), 111–114.

123. Houston, *The Book*, 97–100.

124. *The Lost Leonardo*, directed by Andreas Koefoed (2021; Culver City, CA: Sony, 2021) DVD.

125. James Fell, "Testament of a Lapsed Atheist," *jamesfell.com*, September 13, 2019, https://jamesfell.com/testament-of-a-lapsed-atheist/.

126. James Fell, *The Holy Sh!t Moment* (New York: St. Martins Press, 2019), 166–167.

127. Charles R, Swindoll, *Swindoll's Living Insights New Testament Commentary, Volume 14*: 1, 2, & 3 John, Jude (Carol Stream, IL: Tyndale House Publishers, 2018), 123–124.

128. Max Lucado, *Help is Here* (Nashville, TN: Thomas Nelson, 2022), 126.

129. *Chicago*, directed by Rob Marshall (2002; : Miramax, Buena Vista Home Entertainment, 2003) DVD.

130. James Surowiecki, *The Wisdom of the Crowds* (New York: Anchor Books, 2004, 2005), 43.

131. Robert B. Cialdini, *Influence*, Fifth Edition (Boston, MA: Pearson Education, Inc., 2001, 2009), 109.

132. Robert Greene, *The 48 Laws of Power* (New York: Penguin Books, 1998), 45–46.

133. Vine, *Vine's Complete*, 382.

134. C. S. Lewis, *The Joyful Christian* (New York: Touchstone, 1977, 1996), 30.

135. Lawrence O. Richards, *Expository Dictionary of Bible Words* (Grand Rapids, MI: Regency Reference Library, 1985), 479–480.

136. Richards, *Expository Dictionary*, 375–376.

137. Richards, *Expository Dictionary*, 260.

138. Len Woods, *Understanding the Holy Spirit Made Easy* (Carol Stream, IL: Rose Publishing, 2018), 86.

139. Merrill C. Tenney, general editor, *The Zondervan Pictorial Encyclopedia of the Bible, Volume 5 Q-Z* (Grand Rapids, MI: Regency Reference Library, 1975, 1976), 336.

140. Millard J. Erickson, *Christian Theology* (Grand Rapids, MI: Baker Academic, 19836, 1998), 891.

141. Erickson, *Christian Theology*, 891.

142. Craig S. Keener, *Gift & Giver* (Grand Rapids, MI: Baker Academic, 2001, 2020), 131.

143. Linda Carlson Johnson, *Mother Teresa Protector of the Sick* (Woodbridge, CT: Blackbirch Press, Inc., 1991), 55–56.

144. There are those, whom I respect deeply, who disagree with me on the idea that leading, guiding, and pastoring can be grouped together as one. I understand the perspective, but am more intellectually comfortable with the way I've paired them here. Still, I look forward to reading my friends' next books on the topic!

145. That's not to say that *diakonia* was not an official position in the early church—it certainly was. I'm just pointing out that the term was never *limited* only to an official position. People acted as *diakonia* with or without the title. Serving and helping were natural expressions of authentic Christian faith for everyone.

146. Keener, *Gift & Giver* (Grand Rapids, MI: Baker Academic, 2001, 2020), 121–122.

147. It's helpful to note that the Spirit's healing can also include things like emotional, mental, social, and relational recovery, and even demonic exorcism. However, in the context of 1 Corinthians 12:9 and 12:28, Paul is clearly addressing miraculous, physical healing, so that's why I've focused on that here.

148. J. P. Moreland, *A Simple Guide to Experience Miracles* (Grand Rapids, MI: Zondervan Reflective, 2021), 91–92.

149. Saint Augustine, Marcus Dods, translator, *The City of God* (Peabody, MA: Hendrickson Publishers, 2023), 740.

150. "Religious Change in America." Public Religion Research Institute, PRRI, Mar. 2024, page 5, www.prri.org/wp-content/uploads/2024/03/PRRI-March-2024-Religious-Change.pdf.

151. For an excellent documentation of modern, miraculous healings, I'd highly recommend the book, *Miracles Today* by prominent theologian, Craig S. Keener. Also, you may be interested in the intensely readable book by Eric Metaxas, *Miracles*.

152. L'Engle, *Walking on Water*, 11.

153. Achtemeier, *Harper's Bible Dictionary*, 383–384.

154. Keener, *Gift & Giver*, 116.

155. Craig S. Keener, *Miracles Today* (Grand Rapids, MI: Baker Academic, 2021), 3.

156. Don Campbell, Wendell Johnston, John Walvoord, and John Witmer, *The Theological Wordbook* (Nashville, TN: Word Publishing, 2000) 281.

157. Campbell, Johnston, Walvoord, and Witmer, *The Theological Wordbook*, 281.

158. "Religious Change in America." Public Religion Research Institute, PRRI, Mar. 2024, page 6, www.prri.org/wp-content/uploads/2024/03/PRRI-March-2024-Religious-Change.pdf.

159. Public Religion Research Institute, "Religious Change in America," 5.

160. Leslie B. Flynn, *19 Gifts of the Spirit* (Colorado Springs, CO: NexGen, 2004), 204.

161. Dr. Larry Richards, general editor, *The Discovery Study Bible* (Grand Rapids, MI: Zondervan, 2004), 1525

162. Grudem, *Systematic Theology*, 1326.

163. Francis Chan with Danae Yankoski, *Forgotten God* (Colorado Springs, CO: David C. Cook, 2009), 148.

164. Erickson, *Christian Theology*, 892.

165. Torrey, *The Presence and Work*, 86.

166. Mary Karr, *Lit* (New York: Harper Perennial, 2009), 219–220, 330–338.

167. Here's where you can find my article titled, "Do I Really Need to Go to Church?" which is adapted from the email I sent to this reader: https://nappaland.com/articles-bible-smart/do-i-really-need-to-go-to-church/.

168. Rachel Held Evans, *Searching for Sunday* (Nashville, TN: Nelson Books, 2015), 182.

169. US Forest Service, "Pando – (I Spread)," *FS.USDA.Gov*, https://www.fs.usda.gov/detail/fishlake/home/?cid=STELPRDB5393641.

170. Robert Waldinger, MD, and Marc Schulz, PhD, *The Good Life* (New York, Simon & Schuster, 2023), 3, 18.

171. Waldinger, and Schulz, *The Good Life*, 29.

172. Jonah Lehrer, *How We Decide* (Boston, MA: Houghton, Mifflin, Harcourt, 2009), 181–183, 187.

173. Tad Tuleja, *Fabulous Fallacies* (New York: Galahad Books, 1982), 184, 188.

174. Walter C. Kaiser Jr., and Duane A. Garrett, general editors, NIV *Archaeological Study Bible* (Grand Rapids, MI: Zondervan, 2005), 2043.

175. Len Woods, *Spiritual Life Hacks* (Eugene, OR: Harvest House Publishers, 2019), 131–132.

176. Clare Thomson, *Culture Smart! Estonia* (London, UK: Kuperard, 2007, 2008), 29.

177. Emily Anderson and Michael Spilling, *Cultures of the World: Estonia* (New York: Cavendish Square, 2019), 6–7, 27.

178. D. James Kennedy and Jerry Newcombe, *What if Jesus Had Never Been Born?* (Nashville, TN: Thomas Nelson Publishers, 1994), 3–4.

179. Hawthorne and Martin, *Dictionary of Paul*, 732.

180. David J. Williams, *Paul's Metaphors* (Peabody, MA: Hendrickson Publishers, 1999), 13, 26.

181. Graham, *The Holy Spirit*, 158.

182. Allison and Köstenberger, *The Holy Spirit*, 170.

183. Louis Berkof, *Systematic Theology, Fourth Revised and Enlarged Edition* (Grand Rapids, MI: Wm. B. Eerdmans Publishing Co., 1939, 1941), 252–253.

184. Berkof, *Systematic Theology*, 253.

185. Berkof, *Systematic Theology*, 253.

186. Lawrence O. Richards, *The Teacher's Commentary* (Wheaton, IL: Victor Books, 1987), 561.

187. F. F. Bruce, *Hard Sayings of Jesus* (Downers Grove, IL: InterVarsity Press, 1983), 90.

188. Bruce, *Hard Sayings*, 89–90.

www.ingramcontent.com/pod-product-compliance
Lightning Source LLC
Chambersburg PA
CBHW051419090426
42737CB00014B/2744